DATE DUE

LATIN AMERICAN CENTER
UNIVERSITY OF CALIFORNIA
UCLA — LOS ANGELES, 1967

WM. W. WINNIE, JR.

LATIN AMERICAN
DEVELOPMENT

LATIN AMERICAN STUDIES
VOLUME 8

LATIN AMERICAN DEVELOPMENT:
THEORETICAL, SECTORAL, AND OPERATIONAL APPROACHES

by

William W. Winnie, Jr.

Professor of Sociology, Colorado State University

Latin American Center   University of California
Los Angeles   1967

Published under the editorship of
JOHANNES WILBERT

This volume resulted from a project sponsored by the Organization of American States and the Peace Corps through the Chancellor's Committee on International and Comparative Studies of the University of California, Los Angeles. This project was conducted within the framework of the Latin American Center under the direction of William W. Winnie, Jr.

Publication co-sponsored by the

Centro Latinoamericano de México
Guadalajara, Jalisco, México

To the memory of my father

TABLE OF CONTENTS

PREFACE

The need to view development as something more than a strictly economic process has become increasingly apparent during the last few years. Programs and projects which are found to be technically sound and economically well-conceived in the analysis that precedes implementation commonly encounter unforseen difficulties when they are put into the field, or simply fail to produce the expected benefits. Often the shortcomings can be traced to human elements which were not taken into account in time.

In retrospect, it is easy to consider these social, cultural, and political elements which "interfered" with the success of a project to be so obvious that their neglect can only be chalked up to "planning errors." Yet such "errors" still occur so frequently, in spite of the successful use of a more comprehensive approach by a few pioneers, that it is apparent that few of the engineers, economists, and other specialists involved in project preparation and implementation normally forsee problems in these spheres. This is not surprising. There is little in the training of these professionals which would sensitize them to such considerations, and it is as unreasonable to expect them to recognize the possible influence of social factors as to expect the sociologist to appreciate the technical details of bridge design.

This book was prepared as a condensed text for a brief but intensive course aimed at helping specialists in

ix

other subjects to recognize human problems in time to make suitable adjustments in their plans, and at making future field personnel sufficiently aware of such problems to recognize emergent situations before they become so severe as to prejudice the success of an entire project. Similarly, its emphasis on the relationships among different aspects of development should aid the technician in identifying potential by-product benefits that may be attained through minor modifications in project plans at little or no additional cost. There is no intention of equipping the student to deal directly with social and cultural problems himself—this would require professional training at least as prolonged and as intensive as that of the economist or the engineer. On the contrary, the objective is to acquaint him with the socio-cultural aspects of development only to such an extent that he should be able to recognize the need for specialized assistance in these subjects when it arises.

Thus no attempt has been made to assemble a catalog of socio-cultural problems which have been associated with past development efforts, or a "cook book" which might magically give the user the practical benefit of all existing knowledge in the social sciences. Rather, development is viewed as a complex process which impinges upon every aspect of human life. If the economic or technological features of this process seem neglected, it is only because it is assumed that the reader is already well acquainted with those which are most important in his work, or will study them in another course which has been carefully coordinated with this one.

The course for which this book was written emerged from an inter-disciplinary project conducted in the Latin American Center of UCLA from late 1965 to 1967. After selected experts had prepared background papers on a wide variety of subjects related to development, and these had been reviewed by colleagues in other fields, the entire group met for a week of intensive discussions on the course, the manner of presenting it, and the teaching materials for it: this meeting was the Workshop on Development held at UCLA in April, 1966.

When I gave this course in a university summer session in Guadalajara later in 1966, I found that it was necessary to spend so much of the 28 hours of class meetings on basic ideas that practically no time remained for discussion. Yet from the start of the project it had been agreed that discussions drawing upon the backgrounds of the individual trainees would be indispensible. As a solution, it was suggested that the material covered in those lectures be reduced to writing. That suggestion gave rise to the preparation of the present text.

Some mention of the way in which the various sections of the book were written is in order at this point. Each section is intended to give the reader a brief, non-technical introduction to its subject, a short treatment which he can reasonably be expected to read before the topic is discussed in class. The papers prepared by various members of the group for the 1966 Workshop on Development were too long to be suitable for the purpose at hand; moreover, they were prepared as working documents for a meeting of seasoned professionals, most of whom have had long experience in development work in Latin America. Since this book is intended for a different type of group, a different emphasis is called for. Some matters which would have been superfluous for the Workshop because they are well understood by all of the participants need to be introduced here as background for other points; and, conversely, because the scope of the treatment must be severely restricted if the various sections of such a book as this are to be kept to a reasonable length, some matters of great technical importance for purposes of the Workshop must necessarily be omitted here. These are some of the considerations which lay behind the conclusion reached in the Workshop itself that its materials should be regarded as a pool upon which the individual instructor would draw to prepare a course adapted to his particular purpose.

In preparing the individual lectures for the Guadalajara presentation of the course, I drew as much as time permitted upon the small library which I took with me for the purpose, as well as the Workshop materials and my own personal experience. For some topics, the lecture was based almost entirely on the Workshop; for most, I was able to bring in at least a small amount of additional material, usually of types suggested for further work on the subject during review of the original papers in the Workshop. A few points—particularly family institutions and development—had not been dealt with as such in the Workshop, and it was therefore necessary for me to prepare those classes exclusively on the basis of other sources. Chapter 4 is entirely new: by design, the question of implementation of development, referred to here as an operational approach, was not covered in the preparations for the 1966 Workshop, and it was decided at that time that this should be the subject of a later meeting of a similar type.

Since a fully documented and otherwise much more detailed book is to be prepared later, it was decided that documentation in this one should be kept to a minimum. Nevertheless, some is essential to accomplish two purposes. The first is to give credit to my colleagues where I have made use of the materials they prepared for the Workshop, to the authors of published materials from which I have drawn heavily, and to the authors and publishers who generously gave permission to quote passages from their publications. I have attempted to accomplish this by means of footnotes to the relevant subtitles. The second purpose it to guide the reader to additional publications on Latin American development, publications which are both suitable as a next step in reading on the subject, and at the same time are reasonably accessible. This, too, I have attempted to do in part in the footnotes to the various subtitles to direct the reader to additional materials on the same subject. In addittion, the bibliography provides references to selected sources of a more general nature.

I should also like to mention that the original plan for preparing this book—a plan which was later modified—required that it be written in so short a time that it was impossible to consult other members of the working group until after the first three chapters had been completed. Because of the pressure of time associated with that plan and the small difference in cost between setting type in Guadalajara and a special typing for mimeograph in the United States at a time when the available secretarial resources already were overtaxed, the first copy circulated to members of the group was in the form of galley proof. Because its high cost makes typesetting so definitive an operation in the United States, I fear that some members were reluctant to offer as many suggestions as they might otherwise have done. Thus, even though my colleagues have made many valuable suggestions which have resulted in considerable improvement over the original version, I must accept full responsibility for the ideas and interpretations set forth here.

At the same time, I wish to express my gratitude to all of the members of the working group for their efforts in the project and, especially, for all I have learned from them. Their collaboration has been so important that their names are listed on a separate page at the end of this preface—with the customary disclaimer, for the benefit of those who would not wish to be blamed for things I have said. I am especially grateful to those members of the working group who have opinions which differ from my own for broadening my perspectives and for convincing me that, for all of our scientific progress in recent years, development is a process which is understood far from completely.

Special mention should be made of Professor Ralph L. Beals of UCLA and Professor Sam Schluman of Colorado State University, who, in addition to taking an unusually active part in preparing and reviewing documents for the Workshop, served as chairmen of the two subgroups into which the larger working group was divided during the meetings. Mr. Earl Roueche of the Organization of American States followed the project closely from start to finish, and offered many valuable suggestions on substantive as well as administrative matters. Similarly, I should like to thank Mr. Frank Mankiewicz, then of the Peace Corps, for his support.

One sociologist who was not himself a member of the working group made as great an intellectual contribution as any other individual—I refer to Professor T. Lynn Smith, whose *other* former students will recognize in the section on rural development problems a frame of reference they first became acquainted with in his classes, and who will find a number of their old professor's other ideas, now at second hand, scattered throughout the book. Also to my colleagues through the years— now too numerous to mention all of them by name, but who have given freely of their thoughts and stimulated mine— I offer heartfelt thanks.

I am especially grateful to Dr. Johannes Wilbert, Director of the Latin American Center, for providing the setting in which the project was carried out, and for many invigorating discussions on the development process. Finally, the project could never have been undertaken without the generous financial support provided by the Organization of American States, the Peace Corps, and the UCLA Chancellor's Committee on International and Comparative Studies. I wish to thank all of these organizations for their sponsorship and, even more, for the confidence they placed in me personally by supporting the project.

William W. Winnie, Jr.
Los Angeles, California
May, 1967

UCLA WORKING GROUP ON
DEVELOPMENT AS AN INTEGRAL PROCESS
FOR THE 1966 WORKSHOP ON DEVELOPMENT

UCLA Participants:

Ralph L. Beals .... Anthropology
Peter T. Furst .... Latin American Center
Kenneth L. Karst .... Law
Arnold I. Kisch, M. D. .... Public Health
Milton I. Roemer, M. D. .... Public Health
Gordon C. Ruscoe .... Education
Charles L. Senn .... Public Health
William D. Van Vorst .... Engineering
Johannes Wilbert .... Latin American Center
William W. Winnie, Jr. .... Latin American Center
Michael Y. Yoshino ..... Graduate Business Administration

Participants from Other Institutions:

Fernando Cámara B. .... Instituto Nacional de
                                Antropología é Historia (México)
Peter Dorner .... University of Wisconsin
Luigi Einaudi .... Rand Corporation
Rev. Francis X. Grollig, S. J. .... Loyola University
Benjamin Higgins .... University of Texas
Arnold Kent .... Northrop Corporation
Angel Palerm .... Organization of American States
Earl Roueche .... Organization of American States
Sam Schulman .... Colorado State University
Blen D. Stoker .... Organization of American States
George P. Turner .... Organization of American States
Francis Violich .... University of California, Berkeley

This book is based in part on working documents prepared for the Workshop by various members of the group, and on discussions during the Workshop. The present text was written by Dr. Winnie, and the views expressed in it are not necessarily the same as those of any other member of the group.

CHAPTER 1

INTRODUCTION

The closing days of World War II were punctuated by the use of an instrument of mass destruction many times as effective as any previously known. The reaction that mankind had invented a weapon capable of putting an end to the human race itself in the event of another world war was immediate and widespread, and the hope of preventing renewed global conflict became much more important as a human motivation than ever before.

World War II never was so widely touted as a war to end wars as its predecessor a generation before, and the impotence of the League of Nations in preventing it was still fresh in the memory of statesmen and scholars throughout the world and of the public at large in the industrialized countries. Even before the atomic bomb was revealed, a new world forum was being established, and suddenly the importance of its role as a peace-keeping mechanism took on a much more profound meaning.

Moreover, leaders of the major powers of the West, while realizing that the most destructive of past wars had been those between peoples who were very closely akin to one another in the world's family of nations, saw in the great differences in material well-being and general freedom and welfare which existed between the masses in the poor nations and the people of their own the possible seeds of a struggle more bitter than either of the two world wars. They also saw in international communism a force which might deliberately promote such a struggle through its efforts to bring the poorer nations into its fold. For practical as well as for humanitarian reasons, then, elimination or at least reduction of those differences through improvements in the poor nations became a major goal of the Western powers, and one which was incorporated in the purposes of the United Nations from the start.

The United States was the only one of the major powers which emerged from the war with a large capacity to immediately underwrite foreign assistance programs—the others were faced with major domestic reconstruction requirements of their own. For a few years, European and Japanese reconstruction absorbed almost all of the public resources which were available on an international basis. Gradually, however, these needs were satisfied. The once-aided countries themselves began to join the United States as donors of foreign aid, and the attention of all shifted toward the parts of the world which had been less prosperous at the beginning of the war. The Latin American countries, most of which had been strongly in favor of the Allied cause during the war, were among those parts of the world, and few of their spokesmen hesitated to point out that they, too, were among the poorer nations of the world and easy targets for communism if nothing were done to improve their situation. As European commitments were fulfilled, the attention of United States foreign assistance gradually shifted to other parts of the world, including Latin America.

European assistance had been a matter of aiding industrialized countries as they repaired wartime damages. Clearly the situation in Latin America, Africa, and Asia was a very different one from that of these technologically-advanced nations: the requirement here was to bring the benefits of modern technology to peoples who previously had not enjoyed them. Assistance in this case would be technical assistance. It was easy to assume that the desired ends could be attained by merely transplanting the technology which already existed in the advanced countries.

Gradually, however, it became apparent that this was not the case, that more was required than technical know-how. Economics, both in the sense of theoretical knowledge and in the sense of financial assistance, would be required in much larger amounts than previously supposed, and emphasis in assistance programs shifted in that direction. Yet achievements remained disappointing. Probably the majority of those concerned with high-level planning of development assistance throughout the postwar period have believed that much more is involved in lessening the differences between the rich countries and the poor than technological and economic change. Technology and economics, however, were the areas on which conscious efforts had been concentrated in the industrialized nations, where socio-cultural changes to a large extent had been allowed to take care of themselves, and where, in some respects at least, they preceded technological change. The assumption in technical assistance programs was that socio-cultural change would arise from technological and economic changes in the recipient countries, and this assumption was reinforced by the principle of self-determination or non-intervention—a principle which is especially important in Latin America, where memories of past experiences with the United States Marines were not completely dead even before the recent crisis in Santo Domingo. Under this principle any effort on the part of the donor countries to influence the political or social situation would be viewed as meddling in the internal affairs of another country, and therefore taboo.

It did not become apparent until well over a decade after the end of World War II that social, cultural, and political considerations also would have to be taken into account if technical and economic aid were to be truly effective. At the same time, it also became clear that this would not require abandoning the principle of self-determination, but could instead take the form of pointing out alternatives within a framework of domestically-determined policies.

During this same period, the inter-American system began to undergo profound change from what in practice had been little more than an international debating society to a truly effective organism for formulating international policy on a hemispheric basis and assisting the individual member-states in implementing the policies they had taken part in creating.

The changes which are taking place in the inter-American system would be far less significant than is the case if they were limited to modifying the structure and functions of the official agencies involved. Along with the organizational structure which has evolved for inter-American policy-making and action during the last two decades there has also evolved a set of formal goals and objectives of development to which the members of the system officially subscribed in the Charter of Punta del Este. Moreover, in the six years which have gone by since that time, development efforts in Latin America have undergone more or less continuous review and, always within the general framework of the original goals, modifications have been made and positions strengthened in a continuation of the same general set of efforts. Most recently, the Inter-American Economic and Social Council has drafted two new chapters containing the inter-American economic and social goals for incorporation in the Charter of the Organization of American States, and forwarded them to the OAS Council for approval. Agreement on as broad and specific a set of goals as these by more than two nations is in itself an historic occurrence. It reflects above all the anxiety of Latin American leaders to foster the most rapid possible development of their own countries along certain lines through both international and domestic efforts. Before examining the formal goals of development in Latin America, however, it would be well to examine the nature of the general process referred to as development in order to better appreciate the importance of these goals in the context of major world-wide and hemispheric trends.

THE NATURE OF DEVELOPMENT

We are living in a period of especially rapid change in the world, a period which is without precedent in two ways. First, never before has there been such rapid and profound change in ways of life throughout so much of the world. Secondly, conscious efforts to promote such change have become increasingly important during the last 100 years, and especially since the end of World War II. The general process has come to be referred to as "development." How does it differ from other types of change?

First of all, development implies change from existing conditions toward others which are considered more desirable. But there is an important question —more desirable for whom? In any human change, something old is given up, and something new is substituted in its place. When an effort is made to define development in terms of "desirable" change, the point is soon reached at which a series of value judgments must be made, and beyond that point it is difficult to achieve any general agreement and impossible to make decisions on grounds of science alone. In practice, many policy and operating decisions in development are in fact made on the basis of value judgments —sometimes even when other grounds are available.

In seeking to define development, however, it is not necessary to resort to value judgments about which there is little agreement. It would be difficult to dispute that the rise and spread of industrialism and its products constitute a major cultural revolution comparable to the Neolithic Revolution. In this sense, the Industrial Revolution and industrialization refer to technological changes in agriculture and other sectors, not just to the creation of factory industry, and also to changes in ways of life reaching far beyond the production systems.

The Neolithic Revolution involved change from life in small, relatively impermanent groups collecting food, to life in larger, relatively permanent and stable groups producing food—accompanied by enough increase in man's efficiency at the basic job of feeding himself to enable him to devote substantial efforts to other endeavors. Vastly increased population density and altered patterns of social interaction accompanied these technological changes, as did the emergence of urban centers and, with them, important contrasts between rural and urban life. However, production still depended upon human and animal energy, and the mere satisfaction of creature requirements still required the efforts of the vast majority of the people.

The Industrial Revolution, in comparison, is based on change from life in such food-producing groups, which still were comparatively small, to a situation in which a small fraction of the population produces enough food for all, and most people live in very large food-consuming groups whose productive efforts are directed toward supplying further goods to increase productivity, luxuries, the exchange of goods between producers and consumers, and other services. The urban and rural segments of the society remain interdependent, and the contrast between urban and rural life increases in some respects. But the industrialized society is fundamentally an urban society, and the rural component accounts for only a small fraction of the total population.

As in the Neolithic Revolution, it is possible to identify a basic set of technological changes at the heart of the process. In the Neolithic Revolution, human and animal energy, aided by some simple tools, was applied to nature to selectively increase the reproduction and growth of desired plants and animals. In the Industrial Revolution, inanimate energy is replacing human and animal energy, and the effectiveness of all energy inputs is being multiplied many times over by increasingly complex tools and machinery.

Technological changes, however, are only part of the process. Certain economic and social changes are implicit in the technological changes. With the development of elaborate machinery, the need for specialized skills and knowledge vastly increases. The combination of large capital requirements and specialized individual aptitudes to use the capital goods requires great individual specialization by tasks and a considerable mixture of individual specializations at any one production site. Through the increased specialization and efficiency inherent in the new technology, each production unit turns out goods and services of only one or a few kinds, but in much greater volume than could be consumed by its workers. At the same time, the range of goods and services any given production unit turns out becomes too narrow to satisfy all consumption requirements of any individual. Consequently, the amount of trade must increase greatly. There are many other types of economic change, as well as further economic ramifications of these types; however, the points mentioned serve to introduce the idea of an economic "subsystem" which undergoes change in conjunction with a changing technological subsystem.

If any one broad part of the technological component of the Industrial Revolution is examined carefully, it will be found that historically certain other changes always have occurred in association with it, changes which apparently must occur if the technological change is to be operative. Examination of such groups of changes eventually leads to types of change which lie outside both the technological and economic subsystems. The next step in the same line of reasoning already started in connection with economic change leads to the conclusion that much larger social groups are required in industrial than in non-industrial society. These groups, moreover, are bound together more by differences among their members than by similarities. That is, functional interdependence of the various individual members becomes much more important, at the same time that the type of cohesiveness based on similarities among the members becomes much less so.

Another type of change which lies outside the strictly economic and technological spheres involves the preparation of the young for performance of their adult roles in society. Whereas in pre-industrial society the youth is very likely to follow the occupation of the parent of the same sex, and to learn all he needs to know to perform as an adult from playmates and older relatives, the growing specialization which accompanies industrialization makes it highly improbable that his occupation will be the same as his parent's. The educational functions of the family and other local groups are therefore weakened simply because those groups do not possess all of the knowledge that needs to be transmitted to the youth, and broader levels of the society develop mechanisms (including those of the formal educational system) to perform these functions.

As the importance of larger units of the social structure grows, so do conflicts of interest between them and local groups, including the individual family. The rising levels of living which accompany increasing productivity are not equally characteristic of all groups. Almost by definition, the dominant elements in the power structure of the larger units fare well; at the same time, some characteristics of groups which lag behind in the process of change come to constitute threats (e.g., health) or at least eyesores (e.g., housing) in the view of the dominant group. An enclave living, perhaps by choice, under unsanitary conditions and in ill health is a reservoir of infection for the majority who wish to be healthy—even though the enclave may represent the typical condition of some past period. In this way, pressures for further change build up, and efforts are made to deliberately produce certain changes which are considered especially desirable. These efforts may be referred to as *sponsored development* to distinguish them from changes which take place spontaneously.

When the entire process of change associated with the spread of industrialism is examined in broad perspective, it is found that each component influences and is influenced by many others. One can deal with "subsystems of change" in the abstract, but in practice the process is one integral whole made up of numerous interrelated parts. Whether referred to as the spread of industrialism or as development, this process appears inevitable and irreversible. With or without guidance, it ultimately will produce major changes in the life of all mankind. The question is not *whether* changes will occur, but what form they will take; whether they can be accelerated or slowed down; and the extent to which the identification and selection of alternative courses of action can mitigate the social costs of change while securing its benefits. But here again, one begins to approach decision-making based on value judgments, where the social sciences at best can only hope to point out alternatives and their consequences, to assess the "cost" of desired changes in terms of what must be given up to achieve them, and to identify obstacles to change inherent in the value system and other features of the society.

THE TRADITIONAL-TRANSITIONAL CONTINUUM

Up to this point, development has been treated as change from one set of interrelated conditions (under-developed, traditional, etc.) to another (developed, modern, industrialized, etc.) It is easy to think in terms of a dichotomy in which any society is either traditional, and therefore the epitome of stability, or modernized, a situation in which change itself has become institution-alized. The truth of the matter, however, is that all societies are in a constant state of flux. Some change very slowly and others change more rapidly, but a certain amount of change is normal to all. "Develop-ment" involves accelerated change in certain directions. On the societal level, it is extremely rare for components of this process to involve even nominally instantaneous substitution of "a" for "b"—ordinarily, the change is a matter of initial acceptance of a new idea, object, or practice by a few innovators, followed by gradual adoption in other parts of the society.

The mechanization of tortilla-making in Mexico offers a good illustration of this point. Until only recently, all tortillas were made by hand, a time-consuming process which accounted for a major part of the working day of most women. Properly prepared corn is ground on a *metate* to prepare the dough, then the tortillas are patted out individually between the hands. Mechanization has taken place in both steps. Grinding may now be accomplished in inexpensive hand-operated machines which resemble the meat grinder common in the United States, and in many settlements it is done by commercial establishments with larger mills driven by electric or gasoline motors. Two types of simple presses designed for household use are available to form tortillas rapidly and effectively. In addition, tortilla factories have been established even in many small towns throughout the country. In this case, adoption, which still has not been universal, is on a household-by-household basis, and even at the household level the woman may continue to make occasional use of the traditional methods just as a few women in the United States today occasionally make bread at home. The installation of a commercial corn mill in a village where none existed before may produce an almost immediate change from the use of metates to mechanized milling by many households, but even in this case adoption is not a matter of overnight change by the entire village. On a broader level of society, the corn mills have been established one at a time, and the shift from the metate to mechanized milling has been a gradual one which has not yet been completed.

Some innovations, like those involved in the mechanization of tortilla-making in Mexico, encounter relatively little resistance and spread rather rapidly throughout the society; others spread more slowly. On the societal level, change is not a matter of immediate substitution of one system for another, but of gradual adoption and adaptation of new ideas and practices, one or a few at a time. There are "leads" and "lags" in this process, in the sense that some innovations are adopted before others. Early changes may be less than wholly consistent with other features of the system, and in that case they themselves tend to stimulate further change once they have been adopted. Ideally, any socio-cultural system must be a functioning whole in which each part is totally consistent with every other, but in practice the more normal situation is that the system approaches this ideal state, but fails to attain it because normal change processes continually produce new, but ordinarily minor, inconsistencies while eliminating others. Thus, it is more correct to think of a *strain toward consistency,* rather than absolutely perfect internal consistency, as the typical condition in any system at any given time.

The pure concept of traditional society refers to a situation in which the way of life has undergone little if any change related to the Industrial Revolution, a system in which things are done in the ways in which they are simply because that is the way they "always" have been done and is, in fact, the only way in which the particular group in question could conceive of doing them. Change does indeed take place in such a system, but it takes place extremely slowly and is virtually imperceptible to members of the group and outsiders alike. This polar concept of "traditional society" holds true in only rare and unimportant parts of Latin America today. Some change in the direction of industrialism has taken place in all countries and in almost all individual communities of the area. It is clear that Latin American societies are in the throes of a transition from their "traditional" state toward a situation which differs from it in many important respects.

Even though it is clear that the societies of Latin America are societies in transition, it is impossible to indicate the specific characteristics of the "end product" toward which they are moving. None of them is among the advanced countries of the modern world, but all are changing in the direction of becoming more like those countries. At the same time, however, the advanced countries themselves are experiencing change, and in some ways are changing even more rapidly than the underdeveloped countries of the world. It is even more difficult to envision the "end product" toward which these countries are moving. "Modern" society, then, is not a single static model, but the situation existing at a given point in time; the characteristics of this situation depend upon *which* modernized society is under consideration, and what point in time is taken as a base level. "Traditional" and "modern" are convenient abstract concepts representing the opposite poles of a continuum, but the polar traditional condition exists in pure form in few parts of the contemporary world, and the modern pole of the moment is itself but a transitory stage. It is more correct to think of a traditional-transitional continuum, and in present-day Latin America conditions range from situations which are not far removed from the traditional pole, in many rural communities, all the way to others in major metropolitan centers which are similar to those to be found in cities of the most advanced countries of the world.

As more and more characteristics of industrialism are adopted, and departures from the traditional situation increase, the resistance to change characteristic of traditional societies diminishes, and change becomes more rapid. Many traditional characteristics are present throughout the system, but they are intermingled with modern ones in such a way that inconsistencies within the system are more apparent than before and themselves serve to stimulate further change. This is the situation in which all of the Latin American countries find themselves today.

THE CONCEPT OF THE LIMITING FACTOR

There are always some forces at work in a socio-economic system which favor particular changes, and others which serve as restraints. These restraining forces are indispensable for the effective operation of the system, for without them the forces of change would lead to chaos since some changes which they favor would be incompatible with others and with the existing characteristics of the system. In development, some particular restraint always is the immediate obstacle to any specific change, a feature which serves as the immediate limiting factor impeding change in a given desired direction.

Returning once again to the example of the mechanization of tortilla-making in Mexico, the woman of a particular household may want a home tortilla press but finds that she has no money other than that required to buy corn and other food. In this case, the lack of funds is the limiting factor which prevents adoption of the tortilla press by the individual household. However, when funds become available and this limiting factor is thereby removed, another may take its place: her husband may think press-made tortillas do not taste as good as hand-made ones, and exert pressure to avoid purchase of the press or to avoid its use even after it has been bought. When the situation is viewed in terms of all the households of an entire community at a given moment, the poverty of the community may be the factor which limits the further spread of use of tortilla presses. Yet if family incomes increase, say through an expansion of wage labor outside the home community, further adoption of the tortilla press may be far less widespread than would have been predicted because lack of funds was an important impediment to adoption in relatively few households. On the national level, the scarcity of foreign exchange or domestic capital may be the immediate limit which impedes further expansion of factory industry—but relaxation of this limit may produce surprisingly little expansion because the *next* limit, perhaps the scarcity of organizational ability to put factories into operation, lies little beyond the first one.

Many elements may act as limiting factors. When change takes place at one point in the system, it is quite likely that it will remove a limiting factor which has been acting to prevent another change, perhaps an undesired one. It is for this reason that accelerated change in the general direction of modernization becomes self-generating to some extent in the transitional society. The strain toward consistency tends to maintain those limiting factors which prevent change that is not consistent with both the existing situation and that toward which the society is changing, and at the same time to permit removal of obstacles to changes which are consistent with both.

THE OBJECTIVES AND GOALS OF DEVELOPMENT

The identification of some general directions of change which appear to be inevitable components of development does not mean that the whole world ultimately will be like any particular area, for example the Northeastern United States. No firm basis exists for predicting the nature of the end product of development—much evidence in fact suggests that the institutionalization of change itself may be a necessary component of industrialism. Even when some general directions of change are accepted as inevitable components of development, a great latitude for choice remains in deciding both general objectives and specific actions in sponsored development.

The capacity of social science, as such, is limited by its nature to three functions in sponsored development: (1) identification of opportunities for action and obstacles to proposed changes; (2) pointing out available alternative courses of action; and (3) predicting the consequences of various possible actions, including the "social cost" of proposed changes. Development decisions almost always rest ultimately upon value judgments which may or may not be based upon these three elements. This is equally true whether one is setting general objectives of development, selecting among specific programs and projects which compete for available resources, or carrying out those programs and projects which are selected for implementation. The presumption is that decisions which are based in part on what the social sciences have to offer are less likely to involve consequences which in one way or another are unfavorable, than are decisions which do not take these resources into account.

Many different levels of decision-making are involved in development, as well as different types of decision-making at each level. Our concern here is with broad goals and objectives, and the decisions related to these are made on the very highest levels by politically-dominant groups. This type of decision-making might be referred to as "policy-making on the political level."

Most development policy of this sort is made on the national level. However, there is such general agreement on some points of policy that world-wide desiderata may be stated. These include the elimination of hunger; increased per capita income, especially among low-income groups; control of contagious disease; improved housing for low-income groups; and universal education. The agreement at this level is on vague and general goals, *not* on specific details of the end-product or on how change is to be accomplished. On the inter-American level, there is more complete and formal agreement on objectives which are both more specific and more numerous. The major points listed in the Charter of Punta del Este in this respect are as follows:

—An increase of 2.5 per cent per year in per capita income.

—More equitable distribution of income, raising most rapidly the level of living of the neediest groups in the population, at the same time that a larger proportion of the national product is devoted to investment.

—Balanced economic diversification, with decreasing dependence on one or a few export products.

—Accelerated industrialization.

—An increased level of agricultural productivity and improvement of related storage, transportation, and marketing facilities.

—Comprehensive agrarian reform, replacing latifundia and minifundia with more equitable units.

—Elimination of adult illiteracy, and expansion of educational facilities and their use.

—Increasing the expectation of life by at least five years; improving health in general; controlling communicable disease; and providing adequate water supply and sewage disposal facilities for at least 70 per cent of the population.

—Increased construction of low-cost houses for low-income groups.

—Maintaining stable price levels, avoiding both inflation and deflation while maintaining an adequate rate of economic growth.

—Strengthening of existing agreements on inter-American economic integration.

—Development of cooperative programs to stabilize export prices and foreign exchange earnings.

The Alliance for Progress originally was conceived of as a ten-year program. Once the great initial enthusiasm over these objectives had become tempered by sober analysis, it became clear that a much longer period would be involved. Rather than being abandoned as over-ambitious, however, the goals have been reaffirmed on several occasions since 1961, and it is now expected that they eventually will be made a formal part of the Charter of the Organization of American States. The draft amendments to accomplish this list fourteen major objectives, most of which correspond to the major points of the Charter of Punta del Este:

—A substantial and sustained increase in the per capita national product;

—Equitable distribution of national income;

—Adequate and equitable systems of taxation;

—Agrarian reform;

—Accelerated and diversified industrialization;

—Domestic price stability;

—Fair wages;

—Eradication of illiteracy;

—Extension and application of modern medical science;

—Proper nutrition;

—Adequate housing;

—"A healthier and fuller life;"

—Promotion of private initiative and investment; and

—Expansion and diversification of exports.

Mobilization "of their own national human and material resources" by the member states is considered one of the "fundamental conditions for their economic and social progress" in the draft amendments.[1]

Returning once more to the concept of development as an integral process, the inter-American goals are expressed in terms of attaining certain characteristics which have accompanied the Industrial Revolution in the countries which are now highly industrialized. Some of them relate to areas in which direct action may be taken to produce the desired results. Adequate housing is an example of this type. Others, such as domestic price stability and income distribution, concern features which, although they are to some extent subject to governmental action, are nevertheless symptomatic of other characteristics.

Chapter 2 is concerned with a few types of characteristics and changes which are associated with the development process, but which as a rule are not

---

[1] Adapted from *Survey of International Development*, Vol. III, No. 7 (July 15, 1966), p. 4.

the objects of change programs. In Chapter 3, attention is once more focused on some of these inter-American development goals, but there they are viewed in terms of the nature of the characteristics it is desired to change and the types of action which are or may be taken to produce development in these areas. In both cases, however, an effort has been made to view the particular subjects within the general context of development as an integral process.

CHAPTER 2

THEORETICAL APPROACH

Many scholars have written on development theory. Most of them are economists who are concerned specifically with the theory of economic growth; other social scientists for the most part have couched their theoretical presentations in terms of so long a time perspective that there is little hope of finding direct linkages between their work and the practical, everyday problems involved in development. I have no intention of attempting to present here a full-blown theory of development—the fact of the matter is that our theoretical knowledge *of a type which might be applied to guide development decisions* remains woefully inadequate. For one thing, theory based primarily upon economic, or social, or cultural, or political, or psychological considerations probably can never be developed to such an extent that it adequately explains the intricacies of the complex web of relationships characteristic of the total change process, even in terms of one of the component subsystems of change. Until this is achieved, there is little hope that theory can go one step further and attain at least partial success in predicting the outcome of specific proposed efforts to produce particular changes, and in predicting the secondary changes which may take place in other parts of the system as a result of those efforts. Yet both academic and bureaucratic structures are such that it is difficult to attempt to build theory which cuts across the lines of the conventional academic disciplines.

Another reason that existing theory is inadequate for the purposes of development is that, in spite of important advances in the recent past, it remains true that a great deal of social-science theory either is so broad and general that it cannot be applied to anything, or is so highly specific to a particular situation that few other cases can be found in the entire world which meet the conditions on which the generalizations are based.

Even though it would be premature to attempt to offer a comprehensive theory of development in this chapter on the theoretical approach to the development problem, it is nevertheless possible to single out certain socio-cultural features and to examine them in terms of their place in the total change process. Economic features are brought into the treament, and could be dealt with similarly in their own right.

Three aspects have been chosen for separate consideration: value orientations, religious institutions, and family institutions. Three others which might have been considered in about as much detail, but are not because of time and space limitations, are scarcely more than mentioned at the close of the chapter. All of these points, and others as well, are extremely important in planning and implementing sponsored development, for even though none is an area in which direct action usually is taken, all of these characteristics have an important bearing on the success or failure of most action programs, all of them are influenced to a greater or lesser degree by the results of those programs, and all of them do change as development proceeds.

VALUE ORIENTATIONS AND DEVELOPMENT[1]

Values are the rules of the game by which people guide their conduct. Every human group makes distinctions, which are widely accepted among its members, between "good" and "bad," desirable and undesirable, and acceptable and unacceptable conduct. For example, it is "bad" to kill—unless the victim is an enemy of your society, and it has given you the job of killing as many of the enemy as possible under certain circumstances. Similarly, in our own culture, it is "good" to make a high score on an examination—as long as one does not resort to disapproved conduct (cheating) to do so. Both of these examples are specific and concrete. Most values concern less obvious rules which are more abstract and ephemeral.

It is possible to recognize three types or levels of values. First, there is the matter of what people *say* is right and proper. These are the *ideal* values, and they usually have only a very loose relationship to what people actually do. Secondly, there is the matter of what each individual thinks or believes is right and proper. This has a closer relationship to what actually happens, but is still somewhat on the angelic side. Finally, values are expressed in the way people actually behave. Most individual members of any society stay within the framework of what the society as a whole evaluates as desirable or at least acceptable. These are the *real*, as opposed to the ideal, values. They may never be verbalized, but they are the rules everyone knows.

---

[1] A paper on this subject was prepared for the 1966 Workshop on Development by Sam Schulman; the present treatment, particularly the paragraphs on Latin American value orientations and development, is based in part on that paper. For a selection of articles on Latin American values, see Dwight B. Heath and Richard N. Adams (eds.), *Contemporary Cultures and Societies of Latin America* (New York: Random House, 1965), pp. 475-555.

To return once more to the tortilla example, the man of the house may truly believe that his resistance to tortillas made with a home tortilla press or in a factory is a matter of how they taste, that is, the ideal level corresponds with the intermediate one. However, adoption of machine-made tortillas removes a major limit upon change in the status of women. The woman is supposed to spend her time at home preparing food, cleaning, etc. The "good" wife does not and cannot spend much time outside the home under the traditional system, partly because she spends several hours each morning making tortillas. The "mechanization" of tortilla-making frees her time for activities outside the home while still allowing her to meet the material requirements of being a "good wife," and therefore is contrary to the values on the third, or real, level. This third element is probably far more important in creating resistance to the mechanization of tortilla-making than either the taste of the product or the fact, reported to American students in Guadalajara when they began asking questions after listening to a lecture which presented the same content as these paragraphs, that machine-made tortillas sometimes come out so thin that it is difficult to pick up beans with them.

It is sometimes desirable to refer to "cultural" or "social" values, which are widely accepted and characteristic of almost all members of the society or at least some broad segment of it. The cultural values provide the framework within which individuals and minor components of the society may fill out their own individual systems.

It was stated in the preceding paragraph that cultural values are characteristic of at least a broad segment of the society. While the society as a whole sets general guidelines which are accepted by all groups, there is some variation in the remainder of the value system among various components, especially among social classes. Most underdeveloped countries offer good examples of two-class society, in which the great mass of the population belongs to the lower class.

Within that class, variations in income, prestige, educational levels, etc. are rather small. At the same time, a small but very conspicuous percentage of the population makes up the upper class. A true middle class, as sociologists in the United States and Europe define it, may be completely lacking, and the small "middle sectors" may be made up of lower components consisting of people of lower-class origins who have done especially well in terms of income and wealth, educational attainments, and perhaps political power but *not* social origins, and upper components consisting of individuals of upper-class origins who have made out badly. Ideal values may be virtually identical up and down the social scale, but real values differ greatly. For example, manual work is acceptable for members of the lower class, but is considered dirty and demeaning for members of the upper class. A high positive valuation on work is often considered an identifying feature of a true middle class, and its absence from most groups in the middle sectors of Latin American populations—which regardless of origin seek to emulate the upper-class disdain for manual labor—is one reason that social scientists are reluctant to regard them as middle-class groups. Parenthetically, it should be noted in this connection that many middle-sector groups in Latin America—including some in rural areas—are taking on certain middle-class characteristics, and argument over the extent to which a true middle class exists in Latin America today is a favorite pastime among some social scientists in academic circles. [1]

A word should be said about deviations from the cultural values, for some types of deviant individuals are important in the development process as innovators. Every society includes a few individuals who do *not*

---

[1] A much more comprehensive, well documented treatment of class structure and its characteristics throughout Latin America is available in Ralph L. Beals, "Social Stratification in Latin America," in Heath and Adams, *op. cit.*, pp. 342-360.

share its values completely. These are the geniuses, the "idiots," the criminals, and the individuals who are just a little odd in a favorable or unfavorable way—which particular category is applicable depends upon the nature and extent of the deviation. Truly effective innovators probably depart, but only slightly, from the cultural values of their own groups.

Value systems and value orientations. Many specific values are associated with situations which occur over and over again. They refer to a welter of specific points. On a broader level, it is possible to recognize "value clusters" of closely related and sometimes functionally interdependent values; and on a still higher level of generalization, these clusters are related to one another in such a way that collectively they make up a complete system of interdependent parts. Within such a system there are some major items around which many value clusters and specific values focus, and these points are referred to as core values or value orientations.

Values and development. The existing value system of any group evolved over a long period of time as a unified whole. It amounts to a set of rules for fulfilling the biological and psychological needs of members on the basis of what is available within the area in which the group lives. It is a system that demonstrably works, a product of continuous and continuing biological and cultural processes. Among other things, it provides answers as to how to cope with catastrophes and external forces in general—this is one of its major functions, and it therefore is not surprising that the value system ordinarily embodies many features which operate to repel change.

Change in values may be viewed in two ways. In one, values are the part of a culture which is most resistant to change. While relatively little is known about the manner in which values do change, it is clear that, in any society, this is the area which is most resistant to alterations, even though not all values are equally immutable.

The second view is, in effect, only a different expression of the same principles. According to this view, values are the foundations of the whole culture, and unless some changes in values occur, no *significant* change has taken place in the culture. In other words, many features of a culture are mere superficialities, things that are as they are simply because they have to be *some* way if the society is to function, but many of the existing alternatives are equally acceptable. For example, if a concrete laundry-place is built to get the women of a rural Latin American community away from the river bank, there is a very good chance that it will be accepted—*if* it meets local standards of decency and temporary escape from the men of the community, and offers a suitable site for the social interaction which accompanies the activity for which it is intended. If, on the other hand, it is located next to a trail used by men on their way to the fields, it quite likely will be rejected because laundering and associated activities are supposed to be done in a otherwise acceptable place out of view by men. Acceptance in the first instance would require no change in values; acceptance in the second case would require a change in values associated with relations between the sexes, and possibly others as well.

Some particular values and value clusters are closely associated with the types of change involved in the development process. Those related to time and work are particularly important, for however development is defined in detail, a change in production systems always is involved. A particular cluster of values relating to work, thrift, and time emerged in the United States and some other now-industrialized areas at an earlier stage in their development. One of these values holds that work is good for the soul. A sharp distinction is made between work (productive activity) and leisure, but even leisure should be used in productive ways, for example, to do embroidery or to improve the mind.

In contrast to this, most people in any specific age-sex group in Latin America (and probably in underdeveloped areas in general) "always" have done certain things in a certain sequence and in proper relation to natural and supernatural events. They do these things because they must be done, because life "always" has been that way—and they are likely to show surprise that anyone even *asked* about them. The distinction between work and leisure is not so necessary as in industrialized society, and to the extent that such a distinction *is* made, work is likely to be regarded as a *castigo,* a punishment visited upon man, and to have no particular effect, beneficial or otherwise, upon his soul. Note, however, that the individual can fulfill other expectations only through work—for example, feeding his family or sponsoring a fiesta requires the product of labor—and his performance therefore is disvalued if he does not work.

This same cluster of values places a high positive value on thrift. It is "good" to forgo transitory pleasures of the moment (consumption) to avoid suffering hardship later on—this is the idea of saving for a rainy day. It also is "good" to put the savings to work, that is, to invest rather than to hoard. This principle is reflected in a common saying in the United States: sow that ye shall reap. The same saying is available in the same everyday source in Latin America, but it is seldom if ever heard in Spanish, a language which is much more given to sayings than English, and this is a reflection of the fact that the principle is of little importance in Spanish-American values. The Latin American who is reasonably thrifty by Anglo American standards is likely to be considered the worst of tightwads by his compatriots.

In the most common view in the United States, "time is money," or at least it is scarce and valuable. In English, a clock runs—but in Spanish it walks—*el reloj anda.* Such time orientations are closely associated with the values related to work and leisure. If one customarily does only that work which is necessary in order to fulfill the society's expectations of him, then sits and watches the river go by with ample time for the latter activity in most seasons, then he does not have much motivation to treasure time as such. In the agricultural societies of Latin America, the limiting factor in production most commonly is the amount of labor available at some brief period of peak demand during the agricultural cycle—during the rest of the year, time is abundant.

Another feature related to time orientations is that there is little need for coordination when most individuals of the same age and sex perform essentially the same tasks. If someone is late in these circumstances, it usually is a simple matter for the person waiting for him to go right ahead with whatever he was doing. In industrial society, the production system requires a high degree of coordination in terms of time, and in other parts of the society all sorts of values relating to respect are associated with punctuality.

These values associated with work, thrift, and time all bear mainly upon the production side of the economic subsystem. Changes on the consumption side of that subsystem are also required if a more productive system is to be self-sustaining, and in this respect the *ideal of progress* is especially important. This ideal appears to be a universal characteristic of existing industrial societies. Progress is good. If one does not make progress, something is wrong. The ideal of progress emerged in the present industrialized countries sometime during the last century or two, and has since become a major element in their value orientations. It is part of the characteristic institutionalization of change *per se* as a regular feature of the way of life.

In the United States, progress seems the only possible expectation, both on the individual and on the societal levels. It involves both the production and the consumption ends of the economy, and distribution as well. Tangible manifestations of progress include a steady stream of new gadgets which are available to most people; rapidly rising educational levels; spectacular improvements in the highway system; astronauts; more productive machinery; and more efficient markets.

Such expectations of change are limited to an extremely small segment of the population in Latin America. Most people see the world as always the same. Each individual passes through a series of stages in his life cycle, and in each his "world" and his relations to it are much the same as they were for his predecessors and will be for his successors. "Progress" as a positive value has been adopted by only small but influential segments of the population, and even there it is more a wish than a confident expectation.

The discussion of values and development up to this point has focused on features which are characteristic of industrialized society and either are absent or only poorly developed in the transitional societies of Latin America. On the other side of the question, two value orientations which are important throughout Latin America, and which may be common to all underdeveloped countries, act to impede development.

The first of these is an orientation toward the defined and established. If something is not clearly defined, it either does not exist at all or is likely to be dangerous. The external agent of change is automatically suspect for this and other reasons. If he remains in the same community long enough, he may become "defined," and then meet the next limit upon his effectiveness. But initially, any effort he may make toward introducing change is likely to be viewed with distrust simply because he is unknown. By the same token, proposed innovations are likely to be regarded as potentially dangerous because they are ill-defined, or alternatively, they may be considered something from another world and therefore meaningless in this one.

The orientation toward the defined is reflected in religion, education, and law. All have a catechismic approach, and every question has—must have— an answer. In the university curricula, there is a rigidly-specified list of courses for each "career." This orientation also appears in teaching methods and examinations: "This, gentlemen, is how things are." I have spoken, *he dicho,* is a common way to end a lecture. There is little classroom discussion or out-of-class consultation, either of which might be interpreted as questioning the authority of the expert.

A lack of flexibility, a lack of willingness to try untested alternatives and to adapt procedures to operating requirements, all are associated with the orientation toward the clearly defined, and all are obstacles to development. This is one reason that Latin American development proposals often take the form of providing more of some of the same things that already exist in the country, rather than attempting to improve their quality or to introduce new features. This tendency is, of course, true to some degree even in the most dynamic societies—the difference is a matter of degree and of importance in relation to other values.

In one way, the strong orientation toward the defined and established characteristic of Latin American societies favors cataclysmic instead of gradual change. Forces favoring change gradually build up but are resisted until finally the dam breaks as it did in Mexico in 1910. One motive underlying the present interest in development is the hope to control change so that alterations in ways of life which now appear inevitable may take place in an orderly fashion instead of violently.

A value orientation toward the rigidly structured also is important throughout Latin America. All things are thought to have their place in an ascending or descending order, a feature which is reflected in the hierarchical structure of the Church and the family, and in relations with other people in general.

One of the implications of this orientation is that sponsored development activities are likely to be greatly over-organized. An elaborate structure must be created, and so much effort is devoted to determining structures and defining relationships that little remains available for action. The *grandioso proyecto* so typical of many Latin American countries often exists on paper for several years before anything happens in the field, in part because it takes that long to reach agreement on organizational details.

Another way in which the orientation toward the rigidly-structured works to impede development relates to the general attitude of professionals toward work, or more particularly, their concept of what types of work are appropriate for persons in their positions. In their training, if not by birth, they have attained a place in the general social system which is inconsistent with "doing." Some people in the system "do" and others tell them what to do—and the professional's level in the system is such that he belongs to the group which directs the work of others. The engineer of whatever kind characteristically works in an office, and if he needs information from the field or the shop, he sends an assistant to get it; and the agronomist characteristically has studied a great deal about agriculture in books—but his hands may never have touched a plow or a machete.

The present Latin American value systems therefore work to impede development in two respects: first, many of the values which Anglo Americans may consider near-indispensable for development are absent or only of minor importance; secondly, some of the major Latin American value orientations work to prevent changes of some types which are key elements in spontaneous development. In both respects, Latin American values are undergoing change in the direction of becoming more favorable for development, but this change is taking place very slowly. Meanwhile, even though the existing values act to impede changes of the sort required for development, they do not constitute absolute barriers to such change. A major, but often neglected task of development planning is to evaluate proposed actions in terms of their acceptability within the framework of existing values, and their possible impact in promoting changes in values in the direction of overcoming impediments to development in general.

RELIGIOUS BELIEFS AND INSTITUTIONS[1]

Nine-tenths or more of the people of Latin America are at least nominally of the Roman Catholic faith. Therefore there is no need here to devote attention to other major world religions or to theories concerning religion in general. At the same time, three points related to the general nature of Catholicism as it occurs in Latin America are especially important in considering religious beliefs and institutions in relation to development.

First, religion in general is concerned with man's relations with the supernatural, and Catholicism is no exception. Like many other organized faiths, it closely links relations with the supernatural to a moral code in such a way that the two features reinforce one another. The major points of the moral code are too well-known to require mention here, except to emphasize that most features of morals and ethics in Latin America do have a more or less direct religious basis, and to remind the non-Catholic reader that Catholicism in general leaves less to individual interpretation in these respects than do the various Protestant sects. Value orientations toward the defined, the established, and the rigidly-structured are readily apparent in Roman Catholicism.

Nevertheless many individuals, and especially many intellectuals, do not completely accept all of the features related to the Catholic Faith: the second of the three

---

[1] Materials for the 1966 Workshop on Development on religion and development in Latin America were prepared by Fernando Cámara and Rev. Francis X. Grollig. The present treatment of the subject is based partly on these materials, but some of the ideas presented here are from other sources and the organization is totally different from either of them. A selection of articles related to religion and development in Latin America is available in Frederick B. Pike (ed.), *The Conflict Between Church and State in Latin America* (New York: Alfred A. Knopf, Borzoi Books, 1964); most are of an historical nature, and deal specifically with the colonial period or the first century of independence, but those in Chapter III, "The Contemporary Scene,"

general points to bear in mind in considering the relation
of religion to development is that there is considerable
anti-clerical sentiment in some Latin American countries,
but that one can be anti-clerical and yet be a devout
Catholic in all other respects. That is, while opposed
to Church ownership of productive resources, views of
the clergy on political matters and the right of the clergy
to express them, etc., one may still subscribe whole-
heartedly to points bearing on relations with the supernatural and to the world-wide position of the Church on
social and economic matters. Rejecting all this, even,
he may still be a staunch defender of the moral code.

Perhaps the third point is the one of greatest
significance: while so much of the population of Latin
America is of the Catholic Faith, the fact remains that
the Church and its representatives were very flexible
(except on a few points of dogma) in converting the
Indians of Latin America during the colonial period.
The religious beliefs and practices that exist today in
any given place in Latin America are a blend of the
official version of Roman Catholicism, sixteenth century Iberian folk beliefs and practices, and relevant
parts of the culture which already existed in the particular area at the time of contact. A fourth element,
the contribution of African cultures, is also important
wherever Negro slavery was a major factor in the
colonial period. Therefore, within the general framework of the Catholic Church, there is considerable
variety in religious beliefs and practices from place to
place in Latin America.

Variety of "Religious" Positions

Because of these features, it is necessary to distinguish among various types of "religious" views or

---

in most cases bear more or less directly on the subject under
consideration here. Arthur H. Niehoff and Juanita Niehoff,
"The Influence of Religion on Socio-Economic Development,"
International Development Review, Vol. VIII, No. 2 (June 1966),
pp. 6-12 is an analysis of the influence of religious factors in the
execution of a selection of specific projects.

positions in considering the relation of religion to development: the official position of the Church, the attitudes of the clergy, the position of Church-linked political movements, and the actual religious beliefs and practices of the people involved in development may all differ from one another, yet all are involved in the relations between religion and the development process.

The official position of the Church is violently anticommunistic, and strongly in favor of social justice as officially defined. The latter includes income for workers at a level adequate to enable them to support themselves and their families at a reasonably comfortable level. At the same time, the social and economic stratification of society is accepted as right and proper. The Church's well-known position on the population problem may be in the process of softening somewhat, but if such a change indeed is taking place it has not yet become effective.

The clergy in Latin America is heterogeneous in its views, and it is therefore difficult to generalize about its position even on a national level. The idea that the clergy is made up of second sons of the elite who hold highly conservative views is now definitely incorrect. Up to the last century, the Church and the clergy were extremely conservative elements in this sense in most Latin America countries, but this is no longer the case.

The importance of the clergy at the implementation stage of sponsored development cannot be overemphasized. This is especially true in the case of projects carried out in rural areas, but even in large cities the priest, if convinced of the desirability of the activity, usually is able to go far in winning the support of the local people.

The Christian Democratic movement is not the only Church-linked political movement in Latin America, but it is by far the most important one. It is perhaps somewhat left of center, but strongly in favor of development and of growing importance. Its approach is an activist one; instead of promising to improve everything for everyone at once, it seems more inclined to assess the

possibilities and then to undertake action which will
produce tangible results within a reasonable length of
time.

Like the attitudes of the clergy, the religious beliefs
and practices of the individuals involved in development
are far from homogeneous. The elite remain conservative and strongly Catholic in the sense of adhering
to traditional Church positions and more or less rigidly
observing the formal aspects of Catholicism. In the
middle sectors, the formal aspects of Catholicism as a
rule are not nearly as strong—again, there is considerable variety, but the approach of the Christian
Democrats is highly consistent with other values and
aspirations, and that movement draws its strongest
support from these groups. It is in the urban middle
sectors that a shift from formal Catholicism or some
variety of folk belief or, more commonly, a blend with
a neutral or negative influence on most change processes, toward a situation more favorable for change, is
most notable. The lower urban sectors are probably
changing in a similar direction, but to a lesser extent.
The rural population, however, in general remains close
to the traditional pole of the continuum with respect to
religion, whatever its nature in the particular place, and
religious aspects there serve to reinforce others favoring
stability.

Religious Traits Related to Development

Several particular features associated with religion
are very widespread in Latin America, and also are
highly significant for development. Only a few of them
are mentioned here to illustrate the type of characteristics in this general area which should be taken into
account in the "public relations" efforts which should
form part of any development project.

The first of these features is a spirit of fatalism,
which perhaps is not a part of religion in the strictest
interpretation, but at least is closely linked to religious
belief. Things are as they are in Latin America because
God made them that way; they will always be so, unless

God decides to change them, and if He does, they will then change without the help of anyone else. Both catastrophes and day-to-day variable occurrences, as well as static conditions, are determined by Divine will and might as well be accepted. This extreme position always is tempered to a greater or lesser extent by rationalism—a person standing in a roadway ordinarily will move out of the way of an approaching vehicle—but fatalism is nonetheless a strong force in preserving the status quo in Latin America. The religious basis of this attitude goes far in explaining the demonstrably great influence of the priest in promoting local support for development projects: the representative of God says we should cooperate, so God must have decided that this change should be made.

The system of *compadrazgo*, or godparenthood, is a quite different type of feature associated with religion. Referred to in anthropology as a system of ritual kinship, *compadrazgo* in Latin America has a strong religious basis historically, although it is not always a strictly religious matter today. The term *compadre* (or *comadre* if the subject is a woman) literally means co-parent, but it is applied to many types of ritual kinship other than that of godparents at baptism. Whatever the particular relationship involved, it is accompanied by many social and economic obligations, obligations which are important in limiting the individual's choice in expenditure of his theoretically available income. At the same time, *compadre* relationships are an important element in the cohesiveness of the local social system. A common tendency to prefer the most influential members of the community in selecting *compadres* can sometimes prove useful when one is seeking to gain local support for a development project—informal leaders quite often are among the members of the community with the largest number of *compadres*. This system is weakening somewhat in modern Latin America, especially in the cities, but even there it remains a significant force in channeling expenditure into traditional places through the economic obligations which accompany it.

A system of individual responsibilties for organizing and sponsoring religious ceremonials is also widespread. Each of these functions is referred to as a *cargo religioso,* and in many communities there is a long series of such *cargos,* interlocking with a similar series of civil *cargos,* which the individual ideally should perform in proper sequence during his lifetime. In practice, the ideal sequence usually is such that no one person could possibly perform the complete series of *cargos;* individual prestige is closely related to how closely one approximates the ideal.

The extreme example of a *cargo religioso* is sponsorship of the fiesta of the patron saint, the *cargo* which usually marks the culmination of the religious series where one exists. Any *cargo* involves a great expenditure of time and money, and is a heavy economic burden on the individual, his kin, and his *compadres.* Like *compadrazgo,* these ceremonial functions are extremely important cohesive elements in the local groups. They also serve as a levelling mechanism in the distribution of wealth within the community, for those who are selected to perform the most costly *cargos* are always chosen from among the candidates best able to afford them. This may be one element, but a minor one, in the marked avoidance of conspicuous consumption which may be observed in many small Latin American towns and rural communities.

The religious, kinship, and economic systems are all closely intertwined in traditional Latin American life, a feature which is apparent in both the *compadrazgo* and the *cargo* systems. These systems are mutually reinforcing and self-sustaining, in such a way that distinction among them is sometimes much easier in abstract theoretical terms than in actual practice related to social realities. These traditional relationships are now greatly weakened in the larger cities, but they have not yet completely disappeared even there; they are strongest in closely-knit independent rural communities, and somewhat less so on large estates.

Change in Religious Beliefs and Institutions

Religious aspects of Latin American societies are changing along with others as development proceeds. As with most other characteristics, departures from the traditional ways are much greater in the cities than in rural areas.

Two general trends may be identified. First, both the official position of the Church and individual attitudes related to religion are becoming less resistant to change as such than they once were, and more inclined toward acceptance of many features of urban-industrial life which might have been heartily resisted a few decades ago. Secondly, the linkages between religious practices and others are weakening, especially in the cities where the simple matter of the logistics of maintaining them becomes too difficult.

These changes are fully compatible with others which have been mentioned, but one should be very hesitant about ascribing causation, at least beyond permissiveness, in either direction. There is as much reason to suppose that the increasing variety of possible uses for available funds results from the weakening economic features of *compadrazgo* relationships and the *cargo* system, as to believe that the opposite relationship prevails. Both changes form part of a system of change and, besides being related to one another, they are related to many other changes as well.

It is sometimes asserted that the Protestant influence in Latin America, although statistically at a very low level, has been important in altering official Church attitudes and those of the clergy and many of the faithful. Again, however, the situation is one of multiple causation. Even if it were not, one would be extremely ill-advised to recommend to a Latin American government that it bring in more Protestant missionaries because their efforts would result in lowering some of the barriers to development.

FAMILY INSTITUTIONS AND DEVELOPMENT[1]

Family institutions are much more important in all aspects of life in Latin America than in the United States. Moreover, "family" in Latin America includes a much wider range of relationships than in the modern United States, where it usually refers only to the unit made up of the man, his wife, and their children. This unit is referred to in the social sciences as the nuclear family. The normal individual in the course of his life-time is a member of two nuclear families: that in which he is raised as a child, or his nuclear family of orientation, and that in which he is an adult member in the roles of spouse and parent, or his nuclear family of procreation. The most common concept of "family" in the United States today refers to the nuclear family with which one is residing; the broadest common meaning reaches out only so far as to include the other nuclear families of which the various members of the first are also members. Thus, when an Anglo American man of fifty refers to his family, he most commonly is making reference only to himself, his wife, and their children, whether the latter are still living at home or not. In the broadest sense, he means to include the following individuals, and no others:

Himself
His wife
Their children

------

[1] Family institutions were not dealt with separately in the 1966 Workshop on Development. The discussion of world-wide trends in family patterns included in this section is based to a considerable extent on William J. Goode, *World Revolution and Family Patterns* (Glencoe: The Free Press, 1963). The literature on family institutions in Latin America is extensive but rather dispersed, and relatively little of it deals directly with family institutions in relation to development. Relevant parts of the sociological studies of Latin American countries and of the anthropological studies of Latin American communities listed in the bibliography of Heath and Adams (*op. cit.*) include a wealth of material suitable for further reading on this subject.

The spouses and children of their own children
His parents
His wife's parents
His brothers and sisters
His wife's brothers and sisters

Today, the concept of family seldom if ever goes so far as to include cousins in the United States. Economic, religious, and other bonds are strongest within the "immediate" family. As a rule they extend outward from it only between parents and offspring, and occasionally between siblings, but these extensions ordinarily are quite weak. This type of family relationships has been described as the "conjugal family pattern."

This conjugal family pattern seems the only logical possibility to the average Anglo American; even the types of family relationships which were common in the country's own recent rural past seem somewhat strange to the modern city dweller. To most of the world's peoples, however, the conjugal family pattern would represent a severe reduction in relationships among kin. Not only are the bonds with individuals who are included in the broadest concept of family in the United States much stronger in most other societies of the world; such bonds also reach out farther in the kinship system to include uncles, cousins, and often more distant relatives as well. When a Latin American says "family" he makes reference to a much more extensive network of relationships than does the Anglo American, and most of those relationships involve many important social and economic bonds in addition to mere kinship.

World-Wide Trends in Family Patterns

Throughout the world, there is a trend toward the conjugal family pattern. The causal connections between changes in the family on the one hand, and urbanization and industrialization, on the other, are not clear; to some extent, all of these trends are probably responses to others. Cause and effect are intricately interwoven, and to a certain degree it is probably correct to think in terms of mutual causation in the sense that family changes are among the causes of urbanization at the same time that urbanization is among the causes of change in family patterns. Whatever the causal relationships, there is a close, but imperfect, fit between the conjugal family pattern and the other social and economic features of urban-industrial society as we know it today, and the trend in family patterns is present in the West and in all other major parts of the world. Its details vary from place to place, and in some special situations changes associated with development may even act to reinforce, rather than to weaken, extended family patterns at least during a transitional phase.

The general trend, however, is toward family patterns resembling the present ones of the United States, that is, it is in the direction of a type of organization in which the individual nuclear family is of much greater relative importance in the total family and kinship structure than it was anywhere in the world on the eve of the Industrial Revolution. However, it is *not* a trend leading to a family system in which the nuclear family is a totally free-floating unit devoid of family relationships with other units of the kinship system, even though it is becoming less subject to the influences of kin, and the bonds between it and other nuclear families are becoming fewer and weaker.

Within the general trend, the various sorts of extended-family relationships which bind individual nuclear families together into larger units are of diminishing importance, whether these relationships initially involve joint residence or not. In situations of traditional types, parents have a strong influence on both the choice of spouse and the time of marriage. This influence can be enforced and maintained because the parents have control over the economic base. In rural areas, the new couple must have access to land in one way or another. Situations in which land is available to them for the taking, such as the expanding frontier in the United States and the period of potato introduction in Ireland, have been quite rare; land usually is not so easy to come by, and the new rural couple ordinarily must either share land with the older generation or receive its land from them.

Traditional societies, including those of Latin America, are characterized by strong economic ties among kin during the entire life cycle of the individual. Such bonds are important even in pre-industrial urban society where the economic base, instead of land, is most commonly a kin-based trade or artisan unit. These stronger relations among kin in traditional societies are necesary for both its social and economic subsystems to function.

With modernization, the economic base of the family unit changes. More and more, the individual takes his place in the production system on the basis of his own achievement rather than on the basis of his ancestry. Education and work experience in non-family units replace the inheritance of land, a trade, or a business as the basis of earnings and the economic dependence of the individual upon his kin decreases, especially at the beginning of the productive ages.

Occupational mobility increases as labor market conditions become more effective in placing the individual in the part of the production system where he is capable of making the greatest contribution and receiving the maximum return for it. This is an important element in the growth of greater vertical social mobility both on an individual and on a generation-to-generation basis, with the general effect of increasing class differences among kin and thereby providing a disincentive to interaction among them. Similarly, greater occupational mobility is accompanied by increasing geographical mobility, which also has the effect of reducing the importance of extended family relationships by increasing the distance between the various nuclear families involved in them.

These are forces which act to weaken bonds beyond the limits of the immediate nuclear family as development proceeds. Some unifying forces also continue to operate, and because of them, it is unlikely that a system based on truly and completely independent nuclear families will ever emerge. Throughout child-hood, the individual's strongest bonds of affection lie within the limits of his nuclear family of orientation, that is, for a period of perhaps twenty years his most important relationships are those with his parents and siblings. Those relationships normally are not terminat-ed when he leaves his original home and either im-mediately or after a period of separate residence forms a new nuclear family, his family of procreation. Rather, they continue as long as the participants live, even though they may become quite weak later on. Since one's spouse and children normally take part in his relationships with members of his nuclear family of orientation, continuation of his contacts with his parents and his siblings automatically produces continuation of grandparent, uncle, and cousin types of relationships. Experience in the industrialized countries to date sug-gests that, no matter how far development proceeds, these broader family relationships continue to exist and to be more or less important features of the social struc-ture, even though they may be expected to lose many of their earlier social and economic functions.

Latin American Family Patterns

What has been said up to this point about the general nature of family patterns in traditional societies and the direction of change in family patterns as development proceeds is as true for Latin American as for any other societies. When Latin American family patterns are viewed in more detail, however, there are marked differences in actual practices between the rural the urban segments of society, and among social classes. Most of the available, highly-generalized statements on the family in Latin America refer to one or the other of two situations: the traditional patriarchal upper-class family system, or the rural "mother-family" common in the Caribbean in which there is a rapid turnover of "husbands" in a unit with a stable core consisting of a woman and her children by a series of different men. These are not the only common types of family situation in Latin America, and numerically they probably are not even the most important ones. Other common types include rural and urban lower-class families in which the same man and wife remain together throughout their adult lives, often without benefit of any ceremony, meanwhile raising as many children as can be born and survive. Within the limitations imposed by the instability of the husband-wife relationship in some situations, all variants of the Latin American family characteristically have strong ties extending outward from the individual nuclear family along both maternal and paternal lines. These bonds are strongest in the rural population and in the upper class; they are probably weakest in the lower-middle sector of the urban population.

The *ideal* of the conjugal family system has been introduced in all Latin American countries. It is appealing to women and youngsters, because it offers them hope of a great increase in independence of action, and to the economically disadvantaged in general, because it offers them hope of upward economic and social mobility. The introduction of the ideal of the conjugal family does not mean that it has displaced earlier family values, however. Initially it draws a few spokesmen and is accepted, if only temporarily, by some of those at the "rebellious ages," but the old values remain and the new ideal is more a source of conversation than of action at the time of its introduction. This new ideal has had an important influence on the family system in the urban population of Latin America outside of the upper classes, probably to a somewhat greater extent in the middle than in the lower sectors. In the rural population and in the upper class, the traditional family ideals remain very strong, even though there probably has been some change in the direction of the ideal of the conjugal family even in these segments of society in all of the Latin American countries.

The older family ideals until very recently were probably relatively uniform throughout all segments of the Latin American social systems, even though in many respects they may never have been closely approximated in practice except among the elite. There was and is some variation from country to country in these ideal patterns, but their basic configurations are similar throughout Latin America.

In the traditional Latin American family ideals, parents exercise considerable control over their children's choice of spouse. This is accomplished as much by control over exposure to potential marriage partners as through actual coercion, however. This ideal corresponds closely to actual practice in the upper class, but in have-not groups, both rural and urban, there is little hope of arranging an especially advantageous marriage and probably there never has been much conscious effort to control exposure. In those groups the choice of spouse may be less subject to parental control in actual practice, but parents nonetheless do possess a definite veto power, in part through their control over the same features which reinforce their influence on time of marriage.

Parents ideally have more or less absolute control over when a son can marry because it is through them that he obtains access to the productive resources required to support himself and his new wife. In the traditional setting, this ideal closely approximates actual practice in most sectors of society. The increasing separation of the labor function from the control of productive resources and the increasing dependence of potential income on the individual's independent placement in the labor market which accompany modernization weaken the coercive power behind this type of parental control. Moreover, these changes not only weaken parental control over age at marriage, but they also make earlier marriage possible because the young no longer have to wait their turn at family resources which are still in use by their elders. Whatever the nature of the causal relationships—both of these points are merely of a permissive nature—earlier marriage is associated with development in the world at large, and this trend probably is operative in Latin America. Yet the ideal pattern remains strong in the upper levels of Latin American society, where the parents' control over the ultimate distribution of family capital can go far in influencing the decisons even of a rebellious youth—who may find it wise to consider as well that his occupational position at the level of society to which he is accustomed depends upon a family enterprise. These considerations are not operative at the middle and lower levels of urban society, where there is little family capital to be distributed and where occupational placement is influenced but little if at all by family relationships. The absence of these constraints is clearly one of the elements underlying the greater departure from traditional ideals to be observed among these groups. In rural society, as in the upper classes, the traditional forces remain strongest. Nothing has occurred in most rural communities to weaken parental control over age at marriage, and the growing pressure of population on the local land base may even have had some influence in the direction of raising the age at marriage in many rural Latin American communities.

Family relationships constitute a very important part of the total way of life, both socially and economically, in the traditional ideals and in actual practice. Among the elite, "everyone" is related to "everyone" else either by birth or by marriage—and if by chance the network of relationships turns out to be incomplete, it can be filled out through ritual kinship connections of the *compadrazgo* system. Family relationships thus form the warp and woof of the entire socio-economic structure, and have an important influence upon all sorts of business decisions, quite often even in corporate enterprise. While the magnitude of the economic decisions which may be influenced by family considerations is much smaller, and the network of relationships is based on locality rather than social class, this blending of family with other social and economic features is equal-

ly characteristic of the independent rural communities
of Latin America. It is less pronounced on large rural
estates, and weakest of all in the urban middle sectors,
but even there, family ties both within and beyond the
limits of the nuclear family exert a much stronger influence on every aspect of life than is the case in most
industrialized countries.

Focus of Other Features on Family Ties

Strong—and reciprocal—linkages between family
relationships and most other social and economic
features are characteristic throughout Latin American
societies. These linkages are most important in terms of
the nuclear family, but are also quite strong throughout
extended family units consisting of the parents and un-
married children of the nuclear family, the married sons,
the sons' wives, and the sons' children. Strictly speaking, an extended family often is defined as a joint-
residence unit. But common residence probably is among
the first of the bonds uniting the extended family
to disappear in the development process, and even in the
most traditional systems there is a continual "branching
off" of individual nuclear families from extended families
to form new residential units. Joint residence of the
new couple in the husband's father's household for a
short period after marriage occurs in Latin America,
but as a lasting arrangement the residence of the entire
extended family in a single household is unusual even
in rural areas, although the tendency for sons' houses
to be located near their father's may be important.

Whatever the residential arrangements, the extended family is widespread and important in Latin
America in other respects. Only three of these sets of
relationships are examined here: economic features,
educational functions, and the role of the family in
protection and the care of the aged and infirm.

Economic features. The extended family is characterized by well-defined mutual economic responsibilities
among its own members and, to a greater or lesser
extent, by a pooling of economic resources in its deal-

ings with the remainder of society. In the extreme case, this latter feature takes the form of a common budget for the entire unit. This type of arrangement does occur, although only rarely, in contemporary Latin America, but even in its absence, mutual economic obligations within the extended family are quite strong. These obligations apply to the requirements of day-to-day living, and are even stronger in terms of major expenditures such as those involved in performing civil and religious *cargos*, where they may even reach out to other extended families of the same lineage. These ties operate to maintain social and economic stability and to restrain desire for change, which would be new and strange and contrary to established custom. On an individual basis, they limit the economic incentive to attempt to increase production or income, because the fruits are spread out among so many people that even in terms of the common good the impact of any increase can be substantial only in rare instances.

As a rule these traditional economic obligations based on kinship do not operate on a strict accounting basis. They are mutual responsibilities, whether on the production or the consumption side of the economy, but the principle of reciprocity inherent in them does not go so far as to require a precise balancing of give and take. Cash borrowing relationships emphasize this tendency: when the loan is not made on a crisis basis or to perform a *cargo*, it is much more likely to be made between *compadres*, where there is a definite and clearly recognized obligation to repay, than among true kin, where the obligation to repay is not so strong and is more on the basis of "pay me back when you can."

Education. In the traditional situation, education outside of the upper class is largely or completely of the non-school variety. That is, the function of preparing the child to perform his adult role is concentrated in kinship and play groups. As occupational specialization increases, the cases in which these groups are unable to perform the vocational part of the educational function become more numerous, and the need grows for a specialized institution, the school. Formal educational institutions, however, are instruments of the broader society, and they almost invariably give most emphasis to the non-vocational part of education. This characteristic, too, can be explained on a functional basis—the traditional informal educational processes prepare the child for traditional life in the local community, *not* for participation in the broader levels of society, and extension of the school system (which already exists in cities, at least for members of the upper class) to the lower segments of society probably is at least as much a response to this requirement as to the need for vocational placement. To the extent that the educational function remains in the family in the transitional situation, it acts to maintain the existing class structure; even formal education may tend more toward a stabilizing than an innovative role, as discussed in a later section.

Protection and care of the aged and infirm. Care of the aged and infirm is a major function of the traditional family system at all levels of society, and accounts for a significant part of the economic responsibilities to which reference has been made. These functions are so consistently transferred to broader levels of society in the process of urbanization, and this change is of such great social significance, that they deserve separate mention. Leaving Granny to her own devices or placing her in an institution for the aged not only reduces the cost of operating her son's household, but also weakens her influence upon all of its members. Similarly, the creation of modern institutions for medical care acts to reduce the importance of one of the earlier functions of the family, as well as to provide better health services for the population at large.

Rural-Urban Differences

Family characteristics differ at least as much as any others between the rural and urban components of Latin American society, and these differences increase as development proceeds. The modern urban economic systems, with overt and highly monetized cost-of-living components, make complete retention of the economic features associated with the traditional extended family system virtually impossible. Moreover, the urban housing situation is such that it is highly improbable that a dwelling unit will be available near the father's home at the precise time the son establishes a new household of his own. Territorial separation among the nuclear families which comprise a given extended family is therefore likely to be greater in the city than in rural communities even when separation related to rural-urban migration is not involved; this, too, works to diminish the importance of extended family relationships and becomes an increasingly important force as the urban centers become larger and more complex. The condominium apartment house may in some circumstances provide a means for reducing such dispersion, but over any considerable span of time it becomes difficult for the newly-formed city couple to find a suitable vacant unit near the home of either set of parents at the time it is needed.

Rural occupations are overwhelmingly agricultural and are among the most resistant to change, a feature which facilitates retention of the educational function within the family in the rural population. When considering new requirements for education either in vocational terms or in the sense of preparing the child for participation in the broader levels of society, one is really dealing with requirements of the urban, not the rural, sectors.

Similarly, specialized institutions for protection and social welfare indeed do emerge as formal functions of broader levels of the society—in the cities. The agencies performing these functions in most Latin American countries have difficulty in meeting urban requirements, and are simply unable because of financial and personnel limitations to establish facilities in rural communities. Most rural people live too far from the nearest facilities to make use of them even if they wish to do so and are

entitled to their services; in addition, rural economic
institutions make possible the continuation of the
traditional—and preferred—practices which are rapidly becoming economically impossible for many city
dwellers.

OTHER SELECTED THEORETICAL ASPECTS

A large number of other features would have to be
considered in any reasonably complete theoretical
treatment of the development process. The three which
have been dealt with up to this point were selected for
discussion in part because of their great importance in
the development process in Latin America, in part
because a more or less adequate start has been made in
preparing materials on these subjects, and in part to
emphasize types of features which are sometimes overlooked in development planning and action or, at best,
are passed off as imponderables because they cannot
be adequately dealt with in conventional economic
analysis. Two other topics (locality group structure
and development, and political, governmental, and
legal institutions in the development process) might
have been presented in similar detail, but are discussed
only briefly here because of time and space limitations.
A third, which is treated, but only in summary fashion,
in its appropriate place at the close of this chapter, is
especially important; it deals with the linkages among
social relationships, production systems, and change
mechanisms, and is not discussed in more detail in this
book only because work on it is not yet sufficiently
advanced for this purpose. No effort has been made to
treat change in the various economic features as such
at this time. Conventional approaches of economic
theory to the development problem in Latin America
are abundant, and I am especially anxious to avoid
premature attempts to deal with this important set of
topics on the basis of a new cross-disciplinary approach.

Locality Group Structure and Development.[1]

Reference is sometimes made to social groups as the "building blocks" which make up society. This is not really a good analogy, for they are not discrete units, but overlap one another to an important extent in that each individual member of every social group is also a member of several others. There are many different kinds of social groups, but all share three characteristics: (1) each group involves more than one person; (2) the various members are in interaction with one another, although this may be indirect in the sense that it takes place through intermediaries, the written word, or mass media of communications; and (3) there is an element of social solidarity or "we feeling" through which the various members identify themselves with the group as a whole. Examples of various types of social groups include the family, a church congregation, and the citizens of an entire nation.

Locality groups are social groups in this sense; in addition, their members have a common area of residence, whether the house-and-lot of an individual family, or the entire territory of a nation. There is some territorial structuring of locality groups in any society: that is, various levels of social integration exist on a territorial basis. The structure is not identical from one

---

[1]This section draws to some extent on rough notes prepared by Fernando Cámara prior to the 1966 Workshop on Development, and on individual discussions of the subject with him and with Sam Schulman. Frank W. Young's "Location and Reputation in a Mexican Intervillage Network," *Human Organization, Vol. 23, No.* 1 (Spring 1964), pp. 36-41, and his earlier work cited there, bear directly on the question of levels in the locality group structure intermediate between the local community and the nation. ECLA, "Rural Settlement Patterns and Social Change in Latin America: Notes for a Strategy of Rural Development," *Economic Bulletin for Latin America,* Vol. X, No. 1 (March 1965), pp. 1-21 provides an excellent synthesis on lower levels of the locality group structure throughout Latin America, and also deals with existing and possible change programs in relation to various levels.

society to another, although some levels—the nuclear
family where it is an independent residential unit, the
local community, and the nation-state—appear to be
approximately comparable from one society to another
even though they differ greatly in relative importance
in the total social structure.

The nuclear family is ordinarily the smallest unit
in the locality group structure except in places where it
is completely immersed in some larger unit of family
structure. The individual nuclear family does not exist
as an isolated unit, however, nor are all of its contacts
with other nuclear families based on kinship. Families
who live near one another often are bound together by
patterns of visiting and mutual assistance in locality
groups intermediate between the family and the local
community which are commonly referred to as neighborhoods. This level may be either weak or strong; sometimes it is totally lacking.

The term *community* is used in a variety of ways
in the social sciences. Here it is used to refer to a
particular level in the locality group structure which,
for the sake of clarity, may be identified as the local
community. This is the smallest type of unit in the
structure which is sufficiently differentiated to meet all
of the day-to-day social and material necessities of the
members. Even within a given region, the area occupied
by a community and the number of its inhabitants can
vary over a considerable range, but it is large enough to
meet the common everyday needs of all who live there,
and yet small enough so that all members may go daily
to a central place within it. One element which is closely related to the size of the community is the complexity
of the society—in a more complex society, a larger
number of people is required to attain this degree of
independence. Another element is the ease of internal
transportation and communication, for where these
facilities are well-developed, people from a larger area
can reach the central place with the required frequency.
In all cases, however, the units of this level of the locality
group structure are too large for each member to be in

close contact with all others; intermediaries, which are absent or functionally insignificant at lower levels, are important even though they may be few in number.

The local community is especially important in development action, for it is at this level that contact between official activities and the general public most commonly occurs, and the project is either supported or rejected by the populace. Successful community development activities, whether by design or by accident, as a rule have been carried out on the basis of such territorial units. Operating units in programs of this type which include something less than the entire community fail to take full advantage of potential demonstration and multiplier effects; those which include part or all of two or more local communities simply invite difficulties, for there commonly is some degree of rivalry, friendly or otherwise, between neighboring communities in Latin America. Local leadership patterns are most strongly developed at this level in Latin America, and ideally any development project should include steps to identify and win the support of these leaders in the area in which it is to be carried out.

Local communities themselves are not free-floating entities in the social structure, yet few of them are linked directly to the central place of the nation. Even in the smaller countries of Latin America there are one or more levels of territorial integration between the local community and the nation as a whole. These levels may or may not correspond with units of the national administrative structure—one's first impression is that they most commonly do not—but they are functionally important in both the social and the economic structure. This level has not been adequately studied in Latin America, and as a rule it is ignored in development planning and action, in part because few people engaged in such activities are even aware of the existence of this type of unit in the socio-economic structure and in part because identification and delimitation of these units would in itself be a substantial research undertaking in any country. However, recognition of this level appears

to hold considerable potential for increasing the effectiveness of development action, first in terms of identifying and making use of "natural" societal channels of
communication, and secondly by making it possible to
increase the effectiveness of regional development
programs by designing them in terms of functional units
in the socio-economic structure instead of the natural
or political boundaries on which most such programs
have been based in the past.

Political, Governmental, and Legal Institutions[1]

The North American stereotype of "political
instability" in Latin America falls little short of being
a caricature. Yet there is some basis in fact for this
stereotype, for there is a rapid turnover of personnel in
the highest positions of political leadership in many,
but not all, Latin American countries. Three features
are characteristic of this type of instability in the
countries in which it occurs. First, change in the personnel occupying the executive quarters chronically takes
place outside of the framework of duly established
electoral procedures. Secondly, such changes result
from revolts which usually can best be characterized as
"barracks uprisings" — that is, they are accompanied
by but limited violence. Thirdly, the change in personnel normally produces no basic shift either in economic,
social, and political policies, or in the domestic power
structure.

Generally, political leadership in Latin America is
much more personalistic than in the United States.
However, the Latin American leader, whether at the
pinnacle of the political hierarchy or at some lower level,
derives his power from the support of influential groups
to a far greater extent than from his personal appeal to

---

[1] Modernizatión is among the major areas of concentration
in political science today, and political features related to development receive great and increasing attention in most fields of study.
Recent items in the literature include S. N. Eisenstadt, *Moder-*

the general public. The traditional seats of political power in Latin America lie in the landed aristocracy, in the groups that control mineral resources, and in the military and bureaucratic organizations themselves. In many of the countries, these latter organizations offer a unique base of economic power through possibilities for graft and the concession of preferential treatment; the resulting severe competition for the most important positions is one element which contributes to the rapid turnover of high-level personnel in public office.

Several newer elements, in addition to these traditional ones, are now important in the power structure of most Latin American countries. The leadership of modernized financial, commercial, and industrial enterprises exerts considerable influence in many Latin American countries, and even to the extent that the individuals involved have emerged from the landed aristocracy—and far from all of them have— the special interests of this group are quite different from those of the traditional seats of power. This group has a great deal to gain economically from further commercialization of the economy, increasing displacement of home-

---

nization: Protest and Change (Englewood Cliffs: Prentice-Hall, Modernization of Traditional Societies Series, 1966); David E. Apter. *The Politics of Modernization* (Chicago: The University of Chicago Press, 1965); and Norman A. Bailey (ed.), *Latin America: Politics, Economics, and Hemispheric Security* (New York: Frederick A. Praeger, 1965). John J. Johnson, "Political Change in Latin America," in Otto Feinstein (ed.), *Two Worlds of Change: Readings in Economic Development* (New York: Doubleday & Co., Anchor Books, 1964), pp. 204-232, presents a brief but comprehensive summary on the subject, and Anthony Leeds, "Brazilian Careers and Social Structure: A Case History and Model," in Heath and Adams, *op.cit.,* pp. 379-404 provides unusual insight on some informal aspects of the operation of a Latin American political system. A preliminary draft on political and governmental institutions in relation to stability and change was prepared for the 1966 Workshop on Development by Luigi Einaudi, who unfortunataly was unable to attend the meetings.

made and artisan products by goods produced in factories, and other economic changes associated with development; if its members are not among the strongest supporters of development in general, it is only because they already are well-off economically and attach greater importance to other values.

Organized labor is also important among the newer seats of power, and its influence is growing throughout the hemisphere; it is no longer a politically insignificant element in any Latin American country. Development promises economic gain for this group as well, and in this case both the leaders and the membership at large are highly responsive to economic motivations, although in practice they are likely to emphasize short-term advantages even at the expense of long-term gains.

A third group which at least potentially constitutes a new and important seat of political power throughout Latin America consists of the urban middle sectors and deviant upper-class intellectuals. This group is neither homogeneous, nor organized as a single unit. Its influence up to the present time probably has been truly effective only through organizations, including trade unions, which represent relatively small segments of it.

A few Latin American countries are organized on a federal basis, that is, the state level of government is relatively strong at least in theory. Generally, however, the political function is very highly centralized in the national government. Offices at lower levels are often appointive in practice if not in theory, and the capacity of those levels is poorly developed for anything more than the collection of taxes and statistics. Consideration of the role of existing political and governmental institutions in the development process in most Latin American countries in practice therefore refers almost exclusively to the national level.

The formulation of development policy is basically a political rather than a technical function, even though ideally it should have a strong technical basis. In Latin America, the short-run interests of the various power groups as a rule are much more influential in determining policy than are technical considerations aimed at maximizing long-term benefits. Direct action by Latin American governments usually is limited to those activities in which private investors have little interest or which are considered public services; indirectly, the same types of incentives and disincentives as used in the United States are employed to stimulate, discourage, or alter private sector activities.

The administrative capacity of Latin American governments for implementing development programs and projects has proven defective in many respects, and its weaknesses have not yet been overcome in spite of the considerable amount of effort which has been devoted to improving public administration in most of the countries during the last few years.

Legal institutions.[1] In one sense, law is the embodiment of tradition and the protector of the status quo. Many legal institutions therefore act as barriers to development. At the same time, the law also works to create and perfect institutions to reward, guide, and facilitate favored conduct, and in this sense it can act to stimulate development. Inequalities in actual application of the law are characteristic of the legal institutions of the Latin American countries. The individual in the lower strata is more likely to see the law as a weapon pointed at him than as his protector—and if he believes there will be no effective protection for him if he does improve his situation, he is much less likely to attempt to improve it.

Social Relationships, Production Systems, and Change Mechanisms[2]

Traditional Latin American socio-economic systems embody many features which act to resist change. Much of the rural population lies in a subsistence sector engaged primarily in producing its own food, and most of the

---

[1] This subject is explored in: Kenneth L. Karst, "Law in Developing Countries," *Law Library Journal*, 1967, in press.

[2] The formal documents and less formal memoranda pre-

rest is made up of landless agricultural laborers on the plantations of the rural export sector. The economic capacity to innovate is extremely limited because of low incomes in both groups, exposure to potential innovations is restricted, and many features of the social system operate to retain the traditional ways. All of these restraints are weaker, but nonetheless present, in the traditional urban sectors. Throughout the society, tendencies toward highly personalized relationships governed by traditional rules, economic bonds which are weak when compared with those based on kinship and other social features, and customs which work to channel expenditures into traditional outlets are characteristic of the economic organization as well as of non-economic relationships.

Although some traditional features remain evident in Latin American urban society even today, the restraints upon change have never been as strong there as in the rural sectors, and some change mechanisms which were both present and operative in even the most traditional of urban situations have become much stronger. The upper and middle levels of urban society always have had greater exposure to potential innovations than any other groups, as well as an important amount of economic capacity to innovate. Actual adoptions in these urban sectors work to increase foreign exchange requirements, the size of the urban production system, or both, and such changes in turn increase economic demand in the rural sectors for either food and raw materials to satisfy the requirements of the cities, or for export goods to provide foreign exchange.

---

pared by Ralph L. Beals in connection with the 1966 Workshop on Development all bear on this subject, although none of them focuses upon it for separate treatment. John H. Kunkel. "Economic Autonomy and Social Change in Mexican Villages," in Heath and Adams, *op cit.*, pp. 438-453 treats the subject in much greater detail with an orientation similar to that presented in these paragraphs. Everett M. Rogers, *Diffusion of Innovations* (New York: The Free Press, 1962) is a recent synthesis of this mainstream of sociological research related to development.

In this fashion the urban sector provides some external economic stimulus for change in rural areas even in the traditional system, a stimulus which works to increase both rural production for city or foreign markets *and* consumption in rural communities of goods produced outside their limits. These changes in turn work to reduce the degree of independence of the rural community; to increase the monetization of its economy; to promote a shift toward a more impersonal and con-tractualized system of interpersonal relationships; and to increase exposure to potential innovations through increasing contacts with the outside world. Increasing population pressure on the land base of the rural community has similar effects on both the economic capacity to innovate and on exposure to potential in-novations once it reaches the point at which further population growth requires an increase in the amount of seasonal wage work outside the home community or permanent migration away from it.

At the same time, economic forces favor larger-scale production and marketing units in the urban centers. Whether or not the impersonal type of organization characteristic of such institutions in the industrialized countries is necessary in order for them to function effectively may be uncertain; however, this is the type of organization which serves as a model for similar institutions as they are created in the Latin American countries, and consequently the increasing percentage of production and marketing which takes place through large-scale organizations is accompanied by a propor-tional weakening of personalism in urban Latin America.

Traditional Latin American societies in their closest approximation of the polar concept of "traditional" never have been true equilibrium situations. Ever since the Conquest their urban components have responded to some external stimuli for change, and these responses have in turn stimulated some change in rural areas. The rate of acceptance of innovations has increased in both urban and rural areas in the modern period of develop-

ment. Economic and social change processes have
both stimulated and responded to one another in
such a way that it appears possible that the total process
of change which is now under way may even be a self-
generating one to some extent.

CHAPTER 3

SECTORAL APPROACH

The general nature of the development process, and some of the institutions and processes involved in it, have been considered in the preceding chapters largely in terms of the question, what happens in development? In Chapter 3, the focus changes. Now we wish to ask instead, what is done about development to make desired changes take place?

Private activities motivated by profit often make important contributions to development. However, these contributions are by-products of commercial activity and their benefit to society at large is incidental to their primary purpose. In dealing with the question of what is done about development, then, we are concerned principally with activities conducted by governments. In Latin America, where sub-national levels are poorly developed and have little authority or capacity to act in most of the countries, this means that most development activities at the present time are either carried out directly by the central governments or at least sponsored and to some extent directed by them.

National governments characteristically are organized into ministries, each with more or less specific areas of operation in a topical sense. There is some degree of uniformity in the list of ministries from one Latin American country to another: most have ministries of finance, education, and health, to mention only three examples. Moreover, even in those cases in which the division of governmental labor among ministries is dissimilar from one country to another, closer examination is quite likely to reveal that the more specific operating units into which ministries are divided are approximately the same in terms of topical specializations, even though the same type of unit may not be assigned to the same ministry in every country.

Each development project normally is carried out within some specific ministry. While technical reasons do not always require that it be so, in practice there is a great concentration of projects which are organized in terms of the fields of responsibility of common units in administrative structure. These fields have come to be called "sectors."

If we wish to examine what is done about development, then, it is necessary to examine some of these sectors. Thus, Chapter 3 represents a "sectoral approach" to development, in the same sense that Chapter 2 is a theoretical approach and Chapter 4 an operational approach. Some sectors are not action areas in the sense that they involve specific development projects and programs; and some areas which are now referred to as sectors cannot even be identified in terms of separate operating units in governmental structure. The first three subjects considered in this chapter— human resources, science and technology, and planning and programming—are of this sort, but the remainder fit the conventional pattern more closely.

HUMAN RESOURCES, SCIENCE AND TECHNOLOGY, AND PLANNING AND PROGRAMMING IN DEVELOPMENT

In a sense, this group of topics may be thought of as establishing the framework within which development action in other sectors is carried out. However, it would be an unacceptable oversimplification to say that human resources are important because betterment in this area is what is to be accomplished in development; that science and technology are important because they provide the set of tools with which to do it; and that planning and programming show how these tools are to be used. This is true in considerable measure, but it is not the whole story. The departure from this simplified view is greatest in the area of human resource development.

Development of Human Resources

There is no generally accepted definition of human resources. To some, human resource development means improving educational levels; to others, it means better health; some would concentrate attention on these two areas together; and still others would define the subject in terms of improving occupational skills and increasing the productivity of labor, with or without better health and educational levels. It is not even necessary to accept betterment of human life and living conditions, however defined, as the ultimate objective of human resource development or of development in general—it is perfectly conceivable that a totalitarian state might wish to improve human resources only in the sense of making them more productive in order to better serve the ends of a small group at the pinnacle of the power structure.

Here, however, the view is adopted that widely accepted goals of development are indeed aimed at making life more pleasant or less unpleasant for those undergoing development, and that those recognized goals which do not appear to do so directly have been accepted because it is widely believed that they contribute indirectly to this end. That is, we choose to beg the question of what constitutes "human happiness" and to assume that stated goals of development at whatever level have been reached for the purpose of ultimately achieving it. When considered in these terms, the matter of human resource development may be resolved into four questions.

First, what kinds of human resources are required, and in what amounts, and when, in order to accomplish the stated goals? This question involves much more than the usual field of manpower planning and development, which attempts to project the number of workers with each type of occupational skills required at various future dates, and the training facilities required to insure that such a supply exists. It does involve manpower planning in this sense, and much more as well. The remainder of the question is more concerned with qualitative aspects than is manpower planning, which, in practice, is largely quantitative.

In the area of education, for example, one view holds that the function of the school is twofold: to instill new desires, *and* to provide the knowledge and skills required to fulfill them. A goal to raise material levels of living depends as much upon the first of these functions as upon increased income, the latter merely being an expression of the second function. Health improvements may not be at issue in formal manpower planning, but unquestionably they are in human resource development, not only because they are universally accepted among the objectives of development, but also because there are some demonstrable connections between health and the productivity of labor.

The alleviation of underemployment itself may be among the stated goals of development; if not, it is at least a derivative goal related to per capita income, and, in addition, it is potentially the largest single short-run source of additional unskilled manpower in most Latin American countries. For example, because of season-to-season variations in labor requirements in agriculture, a great deal of labor is potentially available in rural areas without reducing agricultural production. The problem in this case is to find ways to mobilize and utilize this labor—ways which do not require much skill, but which do contribute to development. This, too, is a human resource problem.

These points do not exhaust the list, but simply illustrate the breadth of the first question, the identification of human resources required to fulfill development goals. The second question is one in which human resource development overlaps even more with development planning and programming: what should be done to fulfill the requirements that have been identified and, given competing needs, how much of it *can* be done?

The development of the human resources required to accomplish development goals is almost certain to bring about other changes as well. The third question is: once the measures needed to fulfill the human resource requirements for achieving development goals have been carried out, what qualitative and quantitative changes have taken place in the population? And finally, in what way do these changes contribute to achieving objectives, especially non-economic ones, which were not among the original manpower requirements?

When viewed in this way, human resource development becomes a component of each and every action area in development. It may appear in the "input" side in terms of manpower requirements, or in the "product" side in terms of attaining the human objectives of development. Most often, it appears in both.

Science and Technology in Development

The two most fundamental types of technological change involved in development were mentioned in Chapter 1. These are: (1) the replacement of animate, and particularly human, energy with inanimate energy in the productive process; and (2) the development of tools, including complex machinery, to multiply the effectiveness of energy inputs whatever their nature.

In the industrialized countries, modern technology developed gradually over a long period; today, it even includes automation, or the replacement of certain lower-level human mental functions by machines. Most of the existing gadgetry of industrialism started as some crude form, which gradually was improved over a period of several decades before reaching the present level of efficiency.

It is true, for example, that the electronic computer did in fact involve a technological breakthrough and a new approach to handling data by means of the presence or absence of electrical impulses. However, it was preceded by a long evolution of punch-card methods for handling many of the same jobs, and in a very real sense the highly refined punch-card technology which already existed, in combination with strong demand for even more rapid methods for processing mass data, was a necessary antecedent for development of the computer. Thus the computer and computer technology suddenly burst upon us in a decade only in a very restricted sense; in a more real sense, they are the product of about half a century or more of evolution of data-processing technology.

Any item of modern machinery can be viewed in about the same way; and when all the items are put together, we have the hardware of the technological component of industrial society. But there is more to technology than an assemblage of hardware—the human component is at least as important.

In the industrialized countries, part of the human component of technology developed even before the hardware; these were the inventors, the Whitneys, the McCormicks, the Edisons, the Fords. Most human adaptations to industrial society in these countries accompanied or followed shortly behind the mechanical innovations. Both were part of the same very gradual process of evolution, and specific momentary changes in either component almost always were small. The entire process extended over several decades, and was gradual enough so that human adaptations occurred to a very large extent on a generation-to-generation basis. There was considerable truth in the saying once popular in the United States that you can take the boy out of the country, but you can't take the country out of the boy. The individual adult was not often forced to make radical changes in his own established ways, and his son grew up in a new system, a system in which educational institutions were geared in part to bridging the gap of cultural change which was taking place from one generation to the next, and to helping the young find their places in a world vastly different from that in which their fathers grew up.

The situation is not at all comparable in the present "developing" countries. Technological innovation unquestionably is a major component of development, however it is defined—for one thing, per capita productivity now is low mainly because of the nature of the present technology. However, no one would suggest repeating the trial-and-error approach of gradual technological evolution which occurred historically in industrialized lands. Modern technology is imported in pieces, and in this sense technological improvement in the developing countries *is* gradual. Nevertheless, these pieces are "finished" pieces, in the sense that they already are the product of a long evolution. These finished pieces are no more compatible with the traditional social system of the importing country than they would have been half a century ago with the then existing social system of the countries in which they were developed.

With the adoption of modern technology, underdeveloped countries are faced with the problem of making much more rapid social adaptations than occurred in the industrialized countries. This may take the form of some compromise between the existing social system and the imported technology, with a certain amount of change in each, but inevitably it involves large adaptations in the social system.

Unless a country is willing to proceed with development at a very slow rate—and this is not the case anywhere in Latin America—the adaptations must occur too rapidly to be limited to generation-to-generation changes of the sort which occurred in the industrialized countries. Many *individuals* must make radical changes in their own already-established ways. On an individual level this results in psychological stress; on the societal level, it is manifested in social tensions and disorganization, and by the disappearance of old norms before new ones emerge.

One truth, a painful one for the leaders of developing countries, is that while this process goes on, the technological advance of the industrialized countries continues at an ever-more-rapid rate. It is widely recognized that the development of new techonology results from the application of scientific theory in the solution of technological problems. Herein lies the basis of one of the dilemmas faced by the developing countries: should some of the scarce resources available to them for development be directed into basic scientific research and teaching on the grounds that scientific capacity must be developed internally if the country is not always to remain behind, or should they be devoted to those areas where their impact on development will be more immediate? This is a question of resource allocation involving a balance between long-range and short-range objectives, as well as other high-level policy questions, and these matters are more the concern of planning and programming than of science and technology.

Development Planning and Programming

The Charter of Punta del Este, in the section dealing with measures aimed at accomplishing the goals of the Alliance for Progress, places great emphasis on the development of adequate national planning and programming mechanisms. This section would not have been included in the Charter if it had not been widely supported. However, it appears likely that "planning" meant different things to different delegates. There are at least three alternative views or concepts of planning, and each supporter of these provisions probably had in mind the one which was most appealing to him personally. The idea of planning for development at all was not universally accepted in Latin America in 1961—it was not even universally appealing. After all, the United States never had had a national development plan, yet its progress did not appear at all inadequate.

Nevertheless, the planning provision was included in the Charter of Punta del Este. Probably at least a few of the individual delegates believed they were supporting planning in each of the following three senses:

1. Long-range macro-economic planning;
2. Project evaluation, selection, and implementation; and
3. "Process planning," that is, planning and programming of the types commonly applied in industrial production processes.

Each of these three types of planning is, in its own way, capable of making valuable contributions to development in Latin America.

Long-range macro-economic planning. Policy-making on the political level provides broad objectives for development rather than precise targets, and general guidelines for attaining the objectives rather than a set of specific measures. In this approach, the planning agency sets particular goals for various economic sectors, both public and private, on the basis of mathematical projections of many international and domestic elements, the framework of high-level development policy, and the allocation of public resources among the public-sector activities during a fairly long future period, say from five to ten years. In practice, this type of planning raises many questions of policy which were not previously apparent, and thereby feeds back into policy-making and goal definition. Thus, even if a macro-economic plan is never carried to the action level, its preparation is far from being an idle exercise since it calls attention to many details which should be taken into account in short-range action programs.

Project approach to planning. The second concept of planning is quite different from the first. Initially, at least, it involves a survey of project proposals which already exist in the various public agencies. Characteristically, several such proposals in various stages of

elaboration exist in any Latin American action agency;
just as characteristically, until this type of planning is
adopted, there is no systematic inventory of them even
at the ministerial level, and no one national agency has
authority to assemble information on the proposals
existing in all others. The first step in the project
approach to planning is to prepare an inventory of these
projects where none yet exists; the second is to identify those projects which appear to offer worthwhile
returns in relation to their costs and the objectives of
development, and at the same time are sufficiently well-
developed to be put into operation in the near future.

In general, experience in the few Latin American
countries where this has been done on a systematic
basis has revealed that once such a screening has been
completed, there are not enough viable projects to
absorb available funding. Therefore, one major criterion
for selection among obviously-useful projects has been
their readiness for implementation.

"Process-planning" approach. The type of planning and programming commonly applied to industrial
production processes is not comparable to either of the
other two types. Ideally, it should be the basis of each
of them to some extent, as well as the basis for laying
out specific actions for the implementation phase.

This approach has been given little or no
attention in discussions of development planning in
Latin America. It is mentioned here because it may be
what some delegates had in mind in Punta del Este and,
more importantly, because if rigorously and systemati-
cally applied, it is capable of substantially increasing
operating efficiency and reducing the costs of development. Some of the major points involved in it are:

—Attempting to forsee all requirements for and
consequences of all phases of proposed action
before it is undertaken.

—Making suitable adjustments in proposals to
make them, their requirements, and their con-

sequences compatible with one another and with other objectives and requirements of development.

—Once the necessary adjustments have been made and the proposal has been re-analyzed in the same fashion and has been put into final form, making the arrangements required to assure that the necessary inputs—all of them—will be available in the proper quantity, at the proper place, and at the proper time. As much as anything else, this is in effect a coordinating job. An obvious illustration of the *type* of task involved is dove-tailing transportation requirements to get all materials on site no later than the time they will be used, and at a minimum cost, preferably taking into account the transportation requirements of all projects going on during a given period. This particular point clearly bears upon the total number of trucks of each type which must be acquired, for example.

—Finally in terms of logic, but as a component throughout the planning process chronologically, making provision to handle planning and execution errors rapidly and effectively as soon as they become apparent in order to minimize expensive work stoppages. Expressed in another way, this point amounts to building effective trouble-shooting mechanisms into each stage of the operation.

This type of planning is much less glamorous than either of the others, for it results in numerous small increases in operating efficiency rather than single large contributions to development. Nevertheless, its effective and consistent application in development administration can yield results which are just as impressive as those of any small number of more spectacular undertakings.

Planning and its effectiveness in Latin America.[1]
No Latin American country is well-known for effective
planning of development or any other kind of action at
any level. Planning, which in practice involves dull
plodding through great amounts of detail to arrive at a
product which is far from spectacular in appearance, is
not the type of effort that is appealing to most Latin
Americans who are qualified to undertake it. None of the
basic values strongly favors this type of meticulous effort
—and planning capacity is scarce for the same reasons
that law is much more popular than engineering in the
traditional pattern of higher education.

The United Nations Economic Commission for
Latin America (ECLA), however, has placed great
emphasis on planning *of the first type* for more than a
decade, and most Latin American economists who are
now professionally active have either studied or worked
in ECLA programs. It is not surprising, therefore,
that long-range macro-economic planning is the most
common type in Latin America. Two other reasons
reinforce the matter of exposure to planning ideas in producing this result. First, this is the type of planning
which offers the greatest opportunities for structuring
and defining, both of which are highly valued, and that
requires the least contact with field operations, which is
not. Secondly, it lends itself well to mechanical application of "modern techniques"—which are appealing
to young professionals and junior professionals for other
reasons—without requiring either considerable development of professional skills and administrative aptitudes,
or work away from the capital city and a desk located
there.

Little by little, the other types of planning are being
applied in Latin American development, usually without
much fanfare and sometimes even without awareness

---
[1] National planning is also considered in Chapter 4 under
"National-Level Programs and National Planning." A comprehensive treatment of the subject on a world-wide scale is
available in Albert Waterston, *Development Planning: Lessons
of Experience* (Baltimore: The Johns Hopkins Press, 1965).

that a variety of planning is involved. International financing agencies, through their formal requirements for project evaluation before granting loans, and for operations control after loans have been granted, have had an especially important influence in this respect. Nevertheless, it is not possible to assert, even after the great expansion of planning efforts that has taken place in the last five years, that planning is the major guiding force it could be in Latin American development today.

INFRASTRUCTURE[1]

Some types of basic facilities are required for effective industrial production and marketing, and yet are of such a nature that their creation usually is not attractive to private investors. The concept of infrastructure, in its original form, referred to such facilities and installations. The major types in this sense are transportation of all sorts, communications networks, and large-scale power installations. The original concept was later expanded to include matters which are sometimes referred to as social fields—health, education, housing, etc.—on the grounds that these, too, are areas in which improvements must take place in the course of development, and in which public investment is required because of disinterest on the part of private investors. These social infrastructure areas, however, do not provide basic services which are essential to, or at least greatly facilitate, the conduct of a wide variety of productive activities by potentially numerous firms, and the concept

[1] Infrastructure conventionally is treated as one or a set of economic or technological fields. An analysis of the reciprocal relationships between infrastructure projects of various types and various social and cultural features would be especially valuable, but is not available. The present summary is intended only to introduce the concept of infrastructure to the reader who is not yet familiar with it, and to point out that more than economics and technology are involved, without adequately developing that subject. Therefore, it does not attempt to incorporate the material prepared by Michael Y. Yoshino for the 1966 Workshop on Development, which is primarily economic in nature.

as it is discussed here is limited to its original scope.

The shortage of infrastructure in this sense is among the more notable economic characteristics of the under-developed countries, and those in Latin America offer no exceptions to this generalization. The existing transportation, communications, and electric power systems of the industrialized countries emerged gradual-ly over a period of several decades, in part through gradual improvement of less efficient installations which would now be obsolete in any part of the world. If the Latin American countries are to meet their goals regard-ing other aspects of the Industrial Revolution, they cannot afford to wait for infrastructure development to take place in a gradual fashion.

Apart from the question of the absolute quantity of infrastructure facilities of various types available in Latin America, there is the matter of their distribution. Existing facilities are highly concentrated around the capital and other major cities. The development of outlying regions and smaller cities is impeded not only by the absolute distance which separates them from the national centers of commercial activity, but also by the lack of facilities which private investors consider in-dispensable for many lines of modern commercial and industrial activity.

While no one would deny that infrastructure fields are primarily of an economic and technical nature, they nevertheless do have important non-economic implica-tions. Poor transportation facilities, for example, are a major element impeding social as well as economic change in outlying areas in Latin America, not only because they impede the expansion of exposure of the local people to potential innovations, but because the degree of isolation associated with them is important in maintaining the monopolies of local merchants, whose power over the local people often extends well beyond the limits of the economic sphere. The results of the construction of a new road in both of these respects commonly are both spectacular and rapid. In brief, infrastructure development, far from being the exclusive concern of economics, cuts across the entire development process. The connections are reciprocal; the local human setting is important in carrying out infrastructure projects, just as the services made available by those projects exert an important influence on the local human setting.

INDUSTRY AND INDUSTRIALIZATION[1]

The growth of manufacturing in specialized establishments in which the amount of capital per worker is very high when compared with any situation in the traditional setting is one of the economic changes at the very core of the development process. If levels of living in the underdeveloped countries are to be raised substantially, sooner or later the amount of factory industry must increase greatly. When viewed in broadest terms, average per capita income is merely another way of expressing average per capita production: traditional production systems are characterized by notoriously low productivity per worker, and the very existence of modernized and highly productive agriculture depends upon the existence of urban markets for its products. To be sure, those urban markets may be located in other countries, that is, a certain amount of modernized agriculture may exist on the basis of export markets— but overseas markets for Latin American agricultural products already are beset by many problems. In one sense those problems may be considered to have arisen as a result of the modernization of agriculture to an extent greater than that commensurate with the amount of technological modernization which has taken

---

[1] This subject is treated only in summary fashion here, although an excellent working paper on it was prepared by Michael Y. Yoshino for the 1966 Workshop on Development. A sociological treatment of the subject, which includes references to the recent economic literature on it as well, is available in Wilbert E. Moore, *The Impact of Industry* (Englewood Cliffs: Prentice-Hall, 1965).

place in the rest of the economy in the exporting countries in Latin America and elsewhere in the world.

The line of reasoning which holds that development efforts should be concentrated upon the creation of factory industry and the infrastructure necessary to support it is based partly on this consideration and partly on the idea that this is the most rapid possible way to raise per capita income. For a number of reasons, such emphasis is much less popular today than it was a few years ago. One of these reasons is that, just as modernized agriculture depends upon urban markets, factory industry is so productive that *it* can exist only if its products are consumed by a much larger population than that made up of its own workers and their dependents. Yet the social organization of the *modernized* agricultural sector is such that most people dependent upon that sector receive scarcely enough income to provide for their bare subsistence needs, while the bulk of the fruits of its greater productivity accrue to a very small group of owners and managers who collectively are so few in number that they do not constitute a substantial market for the products of any one new industry. Therefore, the more common view today is that, while the creation of new factory industry is an extremely important part of the total development process, the modernization of the *traditional* agricultural sector is also indispensable, if for no other reason than because of its roles in feeding the cities and in creating the expanded market required to absorb the products of the new factories.

Earlier in the history of sponsored development activities on an international scale it was widely believed that the scarcity of capital goods—that is, of the equipment required to establish factories—and the domestic capital and foreign exchange required to purchase that equipment were the factors which limited the rate of expansion of factory industry in Latin America. The development of international financing mechanisms and the mobilization of domestic resources during the last few years have gone far in overcoming these obstacles.

Yet the rate of expansion of manufacturing remains disappointing. The principal obstacles at the present time are widely considered to be (1) the scarcity of the entrepreneurial component, that is, management personnel with well-developed characteristics of initiative, responsibilty, and foresightedness, (2) the fact that the type of laborer that is super-abundant in Latin America never has been inside a factory and is neither technically nor socially prepared to perform the role of factory worker; and (3) the small size of the domestic market in many Latin American countries. Experience to date suggests that the first of these problems is the most important one, for it appears possible that the adaptation of workers with non-mechanical backgrounds to factory occupations may not be as difficult as in commonly supposed. At the same time, this experience has raised serious questions concerning the possibility of creating new managerial personnel through relatively short training programs.

Almost all types of manufacturing are considered primarily private sector activities in all of the Latin American countries except Cuba. Therefore, development policy related to industrialization has its direct expression in infrastructure and human resources development, and in the provision of tax and other economic incentives intended to influence the amount, the type, and the location of new industries. Such policies in general tend in the direction of favoring the creation of as much new industry of types which either replace imports or provide products which become the raw materials for other industry as is possible. The question of location is another matter: existing infrastructure facilities, skilled labor supplies, and markets all act to encourage those who establish new factories to locate them in and around the major cities which already have the greatest amount of factory industry. These are the very centers which already are plagued by the most severe problems of rapid urban growth, however, and both for this reason, and because industrial development in outlying centers would provide an important stimulus for other changes in the regions in which they are located, many feel that official policies should provide much stronger incentives than is now the case in most Latin American countries to promote industrial decentralization.

The concomitants of industrialization reach out through the entire socio-cultural system. When considering changes in the nature of the production systems one is in reality referring to the increasing importance of factory-type production units and modern commercial establishments which are not dissimilar to factories in some respects. Urbanization itself invariably has accompanied industrialization everywhere in the world to date, and this association may be of a necessary nature: and changes in educational systems, family structure, various practices associated with religion, and other features which are not primarily economic in nature are closely bound up with the urbanization process. Thus industrialization, while it is usually considered a primarily economic and technical field, at the same time is a field which involves important social change in its own right, and is closely related to many of the other changes which occur as development proceeds, but which are not of a primarily economic nature.

EDUCATION AND DEVELOPMENT[1]

Most people ordinarily think of education only in terms of formal school systems; this is true of many social scientists, even when they are performing as such. For some purposes, however, it is preferable to "back off" from the sets of institutions to which we are

---

[1] Two papers on education and development in Latin America prepared for the 1966 Workshop on Development by Gordon C. Ruscoe greatly increased my own knowledge of the subject, and I have drawn upon their content in preparing this section. However, the interpretations presented here differ in important respects from Dr. Ruscoe's and those of most other specialists on the subject. More conventional treatments are

accustomed, and to consider human society in terms of functions which must be performed if the society is to survive as such and the ways in which those functions can be and are in fact performed.

When this is done, some of the resulting obser- vations coincide with our everyday notions, and others do not. If one studies how people act and react in enough different societies which are not closely related to one another, he eventually will come to the conclusion that "human nature" is largely a matter of *acquired* behavior. People behave toward one another as they do, and go about making a living or making love in the ways they do, simply because those are the established and customary ways in the society in which they live and were raised, and anything else would seem strange, foreign, and improper to them. Anglo Americans find that their ideas of "human nature" work out better in practice in Brazil than they do in India because the historical connections between Brazil and the United States have been closer than those between India and the United States; such similarities in patterns of behavior as can be observed in most cases are the result of points of common heritage, not the result of "common blood." In all societies, the newborn infant is pretty much a blank except for crying in

available in C. Arnold Anderson and Mary Jean Bowman (eds.), *Education and Economic Development* (Chicago: Aldine Pub- lishing Company, 1965), and in Óscar Vera. "The Educational Situation and Requirements in Latin America" and J. Roberto Moreira, "Education and Development in Latin America," both in Egbert de Vries and José Medina Echevarría (eds.), *Social Aspects of Economic Development in Latin America* (Paris: UNESCO, 1963), Vol. I, pp. 279-307 and 308-344, respectively. Some points related to the role of Latin American educational institutions as stabilizing mechanisms were suggested to me from the work of Anthony Leeds, through conversations with him and with Ralph L. Beals. Oliver Popenoe, "The Importance of Edu- cation in National Development," *International Development Review*, Vol. VIII, No. 4 (December 1966), pp. 8-14, also treats dysfunctional, as well as functional, aspects of traditional educa- tional institutions in development.

response to pain; he even has to learn how to obtain nourishment from his mother, one of the first things he does learn.

In this sense, education starts almost at birth—not at the age at which the particular human group starts sending its children to school, if in fact it sends them to school at all. Some societies do not even have such an institution, yet their infants learn, while they are growing into adults, all they need to know to perform all the functions and roles expected of them as adult members of the society. They learn how to behave in relation to others in all different positions in the society—and how to recognize the position of any member they have not met so that they will know how to behave toward him. They learn which ways are acceptable—and which are unacceptable—for doing all sorts of things, among them making a living. This whole process is referred to as "socialization," which is approximately the same as education in the broadest sense. Here our concern is mainly with formal educational systems, but always in the context of the broader process.

Education in the Transitional Society

Traditional society by definition is relatively simple. The number of roles the individual in the rural community may perform as an adult is limited, and all of them are present in his home community. Behavior patterns may be complex, and specific rules applying to relations with particular people may be numerous—but the child has ample time to learn "informally" all that he will need to know as an adult—mostly from the example of his elders.

Even in the urban sector of traditional society, life is more complex, and with development it becomes increasingly so throughout the social system. With increasing social and territorial mobility, the chances that all roles the children will later perform as adults exist in the local setting in which they grow up become much smaller; they need to learn not only how to get along with established and familiar ways and things, but also how to adapt to the new and different. A certain amount of learning goes on throughout life in any society, but the needs for the adult to learn new things become much greater as development proceeds. Moreover, it becomes necessary for more and more adults to communicate with others in the absence of direct personal contact. Both this and the need for continued learning make the widespread ability to read, write, and calculate increasingly desirable.

With development, the conventional knowledge of parents and neighbors becomes less and less adequate for performing the total socialization function, and the need grows for a specialized institution, the school, to do more and more of it, especially with respect to those parts of the process concerned with the relationship of the individual to broader levels of society. The school, then, is a specialized institution to perform part of the general process of socialization—it is not intended primarily to prepare the student for a specific occupation, because while he is in school, there is no way to know what his specific occupation will be. This is true even in rural communities in the transitional society, because initially at least there is no way to tell which students will remain in the rural community, and which will migrate to the city.

Even where the school system is a matter of local responsibility—and it is not to any important extent anywhere in Latin America—functionally it is an instrument of a broader level of society, usually the whole country. In Latin America, the educational responsibility always has been highly centralized. This is true of Church schools, which are much more important than in the United States, as well as of the public school system. When stripped of superficial differences which are more apparent than real as far as the educational function is concerned, these two systems are very similar both to one another, and from country to country throughout Latin America. All are part and product of the same set of very similar cultures.

Qualitative Characteristics of Latin
American Educational Systems

Nothing is to be gained here by entering into great
detail about what the various levels in educational
systems are called in the Latin American countries—they
are not comparable from one country to another, and the
details would serve more to confuse issues than to clarify
broad similarities. Although operated by different
agencies at the university level, the entire educational
system, from the day the child enters school to the
completion of a university degree, tends to be treated as
one continuous sequence. That is, primary school is
designed to prepare the pupil for secondary school; and
secondary school is designed to prepare him for the
university, and the university in turn in designed to
complete his preparation to become an adult member of
the upper levels of the society, complete with an acceptable profession, such as law or medicine.

These are characteristics of the traditional educational system in *all* Latin American countries. Although
there have been some efforts toward change in the last
few decades, so that this now involves some over-
generalization, in principle it is still true. It should be
noted especially that the traditional system makes no
provision for "terminal" primary or secondary education
that will provide an educational base which is suitable,
both from the viewpoint of the individual and that of
the society at large, for broad masses of the population.

Latin American educational systems are such that
each level is designed primarily to prepare *all* of its
students for the next level and finally for membership
in the upper levels of society. This arrangement does
have a social function, that of sorting. The son of an
elite family quite likely will end up high on the scale
even if he does not complete a university education; he
learns a lot of rules of elite behavior at home. Others
are very unlikely to make it all the way through the
university level—or even to it—unless they learn "proper behavior"—and in this sense, the educational system

plays a major part as a "sorting institution" in vertical social mobility.

The educational system and development. The educational system's contribution to development can be evaluated in several ways. First, consider its role in selecting and preparing middle- and upper-level manpower, the people who later in their lives will perform the leadership functions in the development process. The qualities which will be required in these future leaders include initiative, responsibility, and organizational ability. A Latin American would be likely to add persuasiveness, which many Anglo Americans would put well down in a longer list.

If the educational system, in addition to working efficiently as a mechanism for social sorting, also identifies and selects individuals with potential aptitudes and personality traits required for development in this sense, and develops those potentials, and ultimately is instrumental in placing those individuals in positions of responsibilty in development, then it can be said to be performing a function strongly favoring development. A corollary to all of these "if's" is, of course, that the system also works effectively to eliminate those who cannot or do not develop these qualities for such positions. That is, if the educational system performs this function effectively, it will take the very best raw material from all levels of society, and develop these characteristics in it, while diverting other individuals to other positions in the social system. On the other hand, if the social sorting process is unrelated to these characteristics, or if the system works to discourage their development, it functions *against* development, or at best is a neutral factor.

All levels of Latin American educational systems tend toward a catechismic approach. The most successful student is the one who is most successful at memorizing what the teacher said, and returning it approximately verbatim in recitation (if any) and on examinations. At lower levels, where there is some recitation, it often

takes the form of the entire class standing and repeating, parrot-fashion, the day's "lesson."

At any level, the student who questions the teacher
is likely to have his examination graded more rigorously
than others—and perhaps even to be informed directly
that his questions are not welcome. After all, he is here
to learn what the recognized expert has to say, and he
had best let him say it—without questioning his
authority. Anglo-Americans who have gone to Latin
America to teach almost always claim that their classes
are unresponsive—and they are, because they have
learned that it is wise to be. That is, initiative is not
welcomed.

The examination system—to take just one
element—does nothing to encourage responsibility. As
a rule, the student has more than one chance. If he fails
the "ordinary" examination, there is an "extraordinary"
examination later on by which he may also complete
the course.

By and large, then, the characteristics of the
educational system act to discourage qualities that are
very important for development leadership, whether in
the public or the private sector, and to reinforce the
status quo. Those who do *not* possess the qualities
mentioned are selected as often as those who do.

The traditional, and still the usual, Latin American
school systems also operate to maintain the status quo
in some respects in terms of lower levels of future manpower. While educational institutions generally are not
expected to prepare the student for a specific vocation,
a major argument for increased schooling as a part of
development is that they better prepare the student in a
general way for vocations which become more common
as development proceeds. In particular, future production workers in industry are important in this sense.

Present Latin American educational institutions
fail to make this type of positive contribution to development in two respects. First, they reinforce values contrary to work with the hands—and instill such values in
the successful student who had not previously acquired

them at home. Secondly, they are designed to lead to positions in the upper reaches of urban society, and one who goes to school more than a year or so normally is motivated to do so by aspirations to a desk job, not a production job of any sort.

The conclusion seems inescapable: the educational system as it exists today in any Latin American country reinforces traditional values and the existing order of society. It does not make a substantial contribution to development either by selecting and preparing those with the most suitable leadership potentials for the purpose, or by providing instruction which will better prepare those who later work in new or expanding vocations for their future occupational roles. Its contribution to development is more generalized, in the direction of preparing the student for life in a more complex society by instilling literacy and arithmetical skills and knowledge of affairs at broader levels of social organization in his own country and abroad.

In this sense, Latin American education is designed to prepare the student for urban life. It provides him with the basic skills and knowledge required for participation in the middle and upper reaches of city life. In some respects, for example political awareness and persuasiveness through the spoken word, it seems more effective than educational institutions in the United States in doing so.

However, the bulk of the Latin American population is rural, not urban, and is likely to remain so for some time to come; even in the cities the middle and upper social strata represent the minority of the population. Rural schools in Latin America are almost always direct transplants of institutions originally developed to serve the needs of traditional upper and middle-class urban society. In contrast to the United States, where until not long ago education was strongly rural-oriented and even introductory college economics classes drew most of their examples from agricultural situations with which the students had no direct experience, Latin American education is urban-based and offers the rural

child of six or seven examples which are totally foreign
to him and his parents. Literacy is a major objective of
the first years of schooling—but the rural child who does
learn to read has only limited opportunity to use, much
less to maintain or further develop his skill, because of
the scarcity of reading material relevant to his own
situation or that of his parents. On a functional basis,
however, the rural school probably *is* relatively efficient
in selecting, albeit informally, those who are best-suited
to urban life as future rural-urban migrants. By creating
new aspirations, it may also serve as a major stimulus
to such migration—which, at the moment, is not so
desirable.

In qualitative terms, then, the overall assessment
of the contribution of educational institutions to development is rather glum.

Quantitative Aspects

The answer to the question, how much? is not much
more encouraging. The low level of educational attainment characteristic of Latin American populations is
viewed with sufficient concern that improvement in this
respect is included among the major objectives of the
Alliance for Progress. This item of the list in Title I of
the Charter of Punta del Este reads, in part:

> "To eliminate adult illiteracy and by 1970 to
> assure, as a minimum, access to six years of
> primary education for each school-age child
> in Latin America...."

There are great variations from country to country, but
in 1950, perhaps one-half of the adults of Latin America
as a whole knew how to read and write. The latest
estimates run to an average of 60 per cent illiteracy in
the rural population, a figure which is much lower in the
cities.

Literacy is a crude and minimal indicator of
education, and reporting is inclined to overstate the

ability to read and write. The number of years of schooling completed is a much more satisfactory measure. Errors in reporting this are probably much smaller, and the data show how much education the individual has had, not just how many people have achieved a certain minimum level which, in itself, is of questionable utility. If anything, the average of less than four years of schooling for adults of Latin America as a unit reflects even lower educational standards than the statistics on illiteracy. The dropout rate runs as high as 35 per cent *each* in the first and second grades in some countries. In the eleven countries for which data were available at the end of 1965, only 25 per cent of those entering the first grade finish primary school, and it is estimated that only eight per cent finish secondary school. This situation continues all the way through the system; less than four per cent of those of university age are actually enrolled in college.[1] This, in a situation where the whole system is designed primarily to benefit those who go all the way through it, and in which the system has relatively little to offer those who drop out along the way.

Educational Functions
Outside the School System

The expansion of formal school systems in Latin America in general has added to, not replaced, the educational functions of kinship and neighborhood groups. These functions, however, are weakening in two senses: first, with the growth of formal education, their proportion in the total educational function is diluted. Secondly, these groups are characteristically less effective in performing educational functions in urban than in rural society, and there is no reason to suppose that this general rule does not hold true in Latin America. There-

---

[1] *Social Progress Trust Fund: Fifth Annual Report, 1965* (Washington: Inter-American Development Bank, 1966), pp. 79-80.

fore, with growing urbanization, the proportion of local groups performing it effectively is probably declining. One reason for this reduced effectiveness is that urbanization decreases the amount of time that parents, and especially the father, can spend with their children.

While the formal educational system is ineffective for large segments of the population, and local groups are not only incapable of providing adequate education for development, but are in all probability even becoming less effective as urbanization proceeds, other mechanisms are emerging to handle part of the educational function in rural as well as in urban areas. The most important of these new elements arises from the revolution in mass communications, and most specifically from the spread of the transistor radio and its use. During the last ten years, radios have become commonplace even in the most remote parts of Latin America, and, in the cities, television has been widely adopted in spite of its high cost. These changes alone have made possible effective communication between leaders on the higher levels of society and virtually the entire population, communication which is one-way and impersonal, but nonetheless direct. The widespread adoption of radio and television receivers has also brought advertising to the masses; and whether it is esthetically desirable or not, advertising is very important in creating new material desires and thereby fomenting further commercialization of the economy. In terms of non-material innovations, the radio has become *the* major element in carrying ideas of life in more prosperous parts of the world—including domestic urban centers—to people all over Latin America. By comparison, even the recent rapid expansion of primary and secondary schooling has had a restricted impact on development because it has reached only a relatively small additional part of the population.

Health education merits examination whatever the degree of its effectiveness in Latin America, in view of the great importance attached to improved health as a component of development and the important contributions that *can* be made by a few relatively simple innovations. Some health education does take place in the schools, where in long-range terms it represents an innovation in the curriculum, and where it has had important effects whether directly, as in the case of boiling drinking water for the sake of health, or indirectly, as through increasing use of shoes as prestige symbols. Outside the school, exposure to health education is largely through public service radio broadcasts and through various types of medical installations. The latter directly reach only the people living near the installations, but the impact of their instruction has been important in some respects, particularly those relating to the care of infants.

A great deal of "vocational training" takes place informally through work experience. This is not a matter of formal on-the-job training, but of a gradual progression from the least-demanding jobs to more demanding ones. Specialized vocational training institutions for lower level workers are receiving some emphasis in Latin America, but they are beset by problems. One major difficulty is that some educational background is required for this type of training, and those who have gone far enough in the regular school system to possess it in many cases have also gone far enough to aspire to white collar jobs. Another is the financial problem of how the trainee is supported while he is in training; by the time he has reached the age for which such instruction is offered, he is able to earn something in almost any Latin American setting.

The Creole Foundation reportedly has had useful early results in Venezuela from an experimental primary-school program designed to develop mechanical aptitudes and to avoid creating unrealistic aspirations. So far, however, this program is but a novel experiment.

Nature and Effectiveness of
Efforts to Improve Education

Education is among the areas receiving greatest emphasis in Latin American development. A great deal of faith—perhaps more than is justified—is placed in its future contributions to the development process. The principal efforts fall into four groups: (1) literacy campaigns; (2) improvement of the quality of public education; (3) making primary and secondary school available to more children; and (4) improving the administration, quality, and availability of higher education.

The elimination of adult illiteracy is among the goals of the Alliance for Progress, and most countries have literacy campaigns of one sort or another. However, one may question how long the literacy is likely to last when it results from a crash program unaccompanied by other changes, and how much low-level literacy by itself is capable of contributing to Latin American development at this time.

In practice, activities aimed at improving the quality of public education most commonly take the form of efforts to improve the qualifications of teachers. Many Latin American teachers are inadequately prepared: in seven countries for which recent data are available, one-half or more of the primary school teachers had neither certification nor any systematic teacher-training. Efforts here are in the direction of providing more teachers who are better prepared to teach in traditional programs.

Many professional educationists in Latin America recognize that curriculum revision—if not a complete overhaul of the entire system—is badly needed to adapt the educational institutions to the requirements for development, and probably every ministry of education is devoting some attention to this problem. However, strong social and economic forces underlie the present qualitative defects, and the likelihood of major improvements in this respect does not seem great for the near future.

Even though strong forces oppose major changes in the nature of public education, there is little or no effective opposition to making the existing system available to ever increasing segments of the population. From 1960 to 1964, primary school enrollment in Latin America increased at an average rate of about six per cent per annum, well ahead of the rate of total population growth, and secondary school enrollment grew by about eleven per cent. This is simply a continuation, and acceleration, of a trend which started much earlier.

School enrollment, like educational attainments, is still highly concentrated in the urban population, where it is easier to provide and staff schools, where there are fewer competing demands on children's time, and where formal education offers more apparent and immediate advantages. But there is some expansion in rural areas as well, and this can be expected to increase as deficiencies in urban facilities are reduced.

Specific action programs in this area take the form of school construction and teacher training. Even in rural areas, it is relatively easy to enlist local support for school construction projects—but staffing problems are severe, and after initial enthusiasm wears off, so does attendance. Two other elements contribute at least as much to high dropout rates in rural areas. By the time he reaches school age, the child is able to produce at least as much as he consumes, and his contribution is needed in the family economy. Secondly, it is difficult for either the child or his parents to see how more schooling will do him any good.

The last of the four principal areas of action in educational development in Latin America involves the improvement of higher education. Departures from the traditional educational system have been greatest in the universities. Visiting professors from the United States and Europe have shown no hesitation, and sometimes even less diplomacy, in expressing their views about the defects of the existing system. Moreover, foreign financial and personnel support has been directed more and more to institutions with demonstrable inclinations to adapt their academic programs to the needs for development. Still another element in changing the nature of higher education is that increasing numbers of Latin American professors study abroad, either while they are still students or after they have assumed teaching duties at home, and they, too, exert pressure to improve the traditional system—particularly with respect to the number of classes they teach each week and remuneration, but also in teaching methods and other features.

This is not to say that changes in higher education to date can be qualified as radical. Preparation for the traditional professions remains predominant—on the order of twenty per cent of all university students are still to be found in law schools, while unsatisfied demands for skilled professionals in most other fields continue to rise. In some countries, manpower deficiencies are much greater at middle than at upper levels, and some types of professionals are being turned out more rapidly than they can be absorbed at home. Chile, for example, is a major "exporter" of economists.

Viewed in broad perspective, education, and particularly formal education, is a key area in development. It deals with children before their attitudes and habits become thoroughly established, whereas most other action areas deal primarily with adults who are much more resistant to changes in their established ways.

Expansion of the existing school system is making important contributions to development, but it falls far short of realizing its maximum potential. Other forces impede too-rapid change in it, and actually make it perform to some extent the function of a "balance wheel" which keeps the total change process from getting out of hand. Resistance to change in this sense arises from the segments which have the greatest vested interest in the existing social order, not from the masses of the population who only now are gaining access to schooling for the first time.

HEALTH SERVICES AND SANITATION[1]

Good health is one of the most widely accepted objectives of development. It can be defined as freedom from acute and chronic ailments, adequate nourishment, and general physical and mental well-being. Even though the case may be overstated at times, healthy workers are more productive, and healthy students are more effective learners than those who are ill. Thus, improvements in health are likely to have some direct influence in bringing about improvements in other sectors.

At the same time, development in other sectors may contribute to improved health. Improved transportation facilities, for example, may bring people who previously lived beyond the effective reach of existing health facilities into their service areas, and the increased contact with urban centers associated with improved transportation facilities may increase their desire for the benefits of modern medical services. Similarly, higher real incomes may bring scientific medical attention within financial reach of a larger proportion of the population; in addition, it may make it economically possible, for example, for more people to habitually wear shoes, and if this is accompanied by an actual change in custom toward regular use of shoes it has a very important bearing on the control of hookworm. The connections between improved health and other aspects of develop-

---

[1] Documents on environmental sanitation, the health protection services, and medical care were prepared for the 1966 Workshop on Development by Charles L. Senn, Arnold I. Kisch, and Milton I. Roemer respectively. This section, and particularly the part on medical care, draws to a much greater extent than most parts of this book on the documents prepared for the Workshop. I have added some points on the basis of recommendations made during those meetings, and both the selection of the content and the views expressed reflect my own background in sociology to a greater extent than they do Dr. Roemer's or Dr. Kisch's in

ment thus are numerous, and often they are reciprocal in nature.

Health and Disease in Latin America

Both death rates and the incidence of illness are generally higher in Latin America than in industrialized countries. This remains true even after the spectacular declines which have taken place in the death rate in recent years, and equally spectacular results in controlling a few important diseases, especially malaria. Latin American death rates are comparatively high at all ages, but the differences are greatest among the very young.

These differences in death and disease rates exist because the principles of scientific medicine which are widely applied in the industrialized countries—in the form of preventive medical programs, environmental sanitation, medical care, and even in the personal habits of the population at large—are neither as widely nor as effectively applied in Latin America. There, the application of most aspects of scientific medicine is concentrated to a greater or lesser degree in the urban population and, within it, among people living in the largest cities. Many health problems are more severe in rural than in urban areas because of this difference, even though living conditions in the cities, and especially in

medicine or Mr. Senn's in environmental sanitation. The reader interested in a more medically-oriented treatment should consult Dr. Roemer's monograph, *Medical Care in Latin America* (Washington: Pan American Union, 1964); Ernest C. Long (ed.), *Health Objectives for the Developing Society* (Durham: Duke University Press, 1965); and *Facts on Health Problems: Health in Relation to Social Improvement and Economic Development in the Americas* (Washington: Pan American Health Organization, 1961). Cultural aspects of health problems receive greater emphasis in the case materials available in Benjamin D. Paul (ed.), *Health, Culture, and Community: Case Studies of Public Reactions to Health Programs* (New York: Russell Sage Foundation, 1955).

their low-income neighborhoods, are more conducive to the spread of disease than those in the countryside.

"Tropical diseases"—particularly malaria and intestinal parasitoses—generally are of a debilitating rather than a killing type, even though malaria was once among the most important reported causes of death in many lowland areas. Since World War II, mosquito control programs have either eliminated or greatly reduced the incidence of new cases of malaria in most parts of Latin America where it was once common; yellow fever has been under control even longer.

With this control of malaria and yellow fever, the list of most common illnesses no longer includes any type which is unknown or even truly uncommon in middle latitudes. Intestinal parasites and respiratory infections invariably rank high on the list of prevalent diseases, and in many parts of the hemisphere they are among the most common causes of death. The incidence of disease in general and the proportions of the various types vary considerably from region to region within Latin America, as well as between rural and urban areas, but the variations appear to be much more closely linked to differences in levels of living than to differences in natural environment.

Modern Medicine and the Transitional Cultures

Disease and death are no novelty to traditional societies: all human groups have some sort of ideas concerning the nature, causes, and treatment of disease. In the modern urban population of the United States, those ideas are based to a very large extent on scientific medicine, but in Latin America traditional folk beliefs and practices remain common even in the cities.

Traditional explanations of the causes of disease seldom have any relationship to causes as identified by modern science. Yet some traditional treatments, such as the use of certain herbs, actually have curative functions in the scientific sense, and even the recovery, for other reasons, of many patients who receive treatments which are medically ineffective reinforces long-standing beliefs. Such concepts as the germ theory of disease remain totally foreign to many Latin Americans, and are viewed with some skepticism by countless others. Only a relatively small and sophisticated segment of the population accepts such ideas without reservation—many of those who seek modern medical services do so on a strictly empirical basis, because those services helped others suffering from the same or a similar ailment and the traditional healer simply has made no progress.

Resistance to modern explanations of the cause of familiar diseases definitely is an obstacle to the success of related health programs. Often it is difficult for the outsider to be sure whether or not the people of the community with which he is dealing have accepted his explanations, for politeness requires that they not contradict him. Thus, even though improvement in health conditions almost invariably is included among the major objectives of development, and good health is probably nearly as universal a desire as having enough to eat, traditional beliefs and practices which are still held by the majority of Latin Americans act to retard improvements in these respects. These beliefs contribute to indifference to environmental improvements which might be made through local initiative in both rural and urban areas, they restrict the demands of the populace at large for the provision of more and better medical care, and they even limit the effective utilization of existing medical resources. Nevertheless, the scarcity of human, physical, and monetary resources is more important as a limiting factor in the expansion of health programs in Latin America today than any other consideration.

Even in the face of obstacles related to traditional beliefs and practices, and others such as severe shortages of adequately trained personnel, considerable improvement has been made in health conditions throughout Latin America during the last two or three decades. This success is amply demonstrated by the falling death rates, particularly of infants, which are characteristic of all countries in the area. It reflects continuous and relatively massive efforts which as a rule have been better coordinated both nationally and internationally than those in most other sectors.

Health problems are approached through three different types of action programs: (1) environmental sanitation, (2) health protection services, and (3) medical care. Although these types are conceptually distinct, it is generally agreed that best results are attained when they are carried out simultaneously as parts of a single, well integrated health program.

Environmental Sanitation

Environmental sanitation programs are designed to control disease on a community-wide basis by breaking contact between the agents of infection and man, and to make the milieu in which man lives more healthful in other ways as, for example, by controlling pollution of the atmosphere. Several of the most important diseases in Latin America can be attacked through efforts of this type: most of them are water-borne diseases resulting from the contamination of drinking water with fecal material. Water supply and sewage disposal projects, often carried out in conjunction with one another if not as a single effort, are the most important means of dealing with such illnesses.

The control of diseases transmitted by insects, more specifically malaria and yellow fever, deserves separate attention, not so much because of the present incidence of those diseases, but because their control represents one of the most successful large-scale development efforts of all time. Other types of environmental sanitation programs which are not considered here include food and milk control; the control of rodents; and occupational health and safety programs. Housing, which is sometimes considered in connection with environmental sanitation, is treated in a separate section of this volume because of its broader implications.

Water supply and sewage disposal. Water-borne diseases are still among the principal causes of death in Latin America, even though this is one of the fields in which recent improvements have been great. As a group, they are *the* most important cause of reported infant deaths in three countries, second in seven, and third in four others. The impact of water supply and sewage disposal projects on death rates is greatest among infants; such infectious diseases are common among older children and adults, but they are not often the primary cause of death except among the very young. The Inter-American Development Bank, the principal external funding agency for water-supply and sanitation projects of this type, estimates that about 680 million dollars of foreign and domestic funds were spent on such projects from 1961 through 1965, and that about 45 million Latin Americans benefited from these investments.[1]

Water supply and sewage disposal investments have been highly concentrated in urban areas for several reasons. First, the alternatives to more or less modern systems are more unpleasant in the cities than in small villages or in the open country; secondly, such problems in urban areas are likely to come to the attention of power groups, and to be viewed by them as eyesores if not personal threats. In rural areas without toilets or privies, people go to the banana patch or its local equivalent, that is, to some site outside the immediate habitation area. In the city, if such facilities are lacking people may not literally defecate in the streets, but their excreta commonly end up there either by being thrown into the street from some container or by being washed into it by rainwater.

Similarly, rudimentary methods of water supply, which are taken for granted by rural Latin Americans, may represent true hardship in urban slums. The source

[1]*Social Progress Trust Fund: Fifth Annual Report, 1965* (Washington: Inter-American Development Bank, 1966), p. 77.

of water is a major consideration in selecting the original location for a rural settlement, which is small by definition, and usually there is ample water for domestic uses even though it may be necessary to carry it some distance. Urban slum neighborhoods without internal sources of water—there are some of this type in Latin American cities—and urban houses lacking a piped water supply can be supplied by individuals carrying their own water from the nearest public tap or by delivery in carts. Such practices may involve little or no physical effort beyond that expended by the typical rural family for similar purposes, but they are much more likely to be thought a burden in the city, and the cost is high, if not in money, at least in working time which might otherwise be used more productively. Moreover, rudimentary methods of water distribution in urban areas are highly visible signs of "backwardness."

The greater true need for modern systems and the higher visibility of deficiencies are not the only reasons that water supply and sewage disposal projects are highly concentrated in the cities. The per capita cost of providing modern services is much lower in urban than in rural areas. First, the greater population density characteristic of cities means that a smaller amount of pipe is required for each household connection or for each public facility designed to serve a given number of families. Secondly, the absolute size of the population in the service unit is much larger in the city, and economies of scale are great, especially at the lower end of the range of technically feasible installations.

The per capita cost of providing "adequate" water supply and sewage disposal facilities for urban populations depends to an important extent upon the standards adopted. Specialists in the subject are inclined to think in terms of modern plumbing in every urban dwelling, and their opinions are reflected in the recommendations of international bodies, including the World Health Organization. Actually, about sixty per cent of all urban Latin American families have running water in their homes, and the remainder for the most part live in slums.

Both water supply and sewage disposal projects and urban and village housing projects as a rule attempt to meet these standards for the areas they serve. The actual per capita cost of all the projects covered in the Inter-American Bank's data referred to above averaged about twelve dollars, as compared to a theoretical average per capita cost of sanitary facilities in the dwelling of around 20 to 25 dollars. More of the people who still lack such facilities could be provided with minimum services for the same amount of money by settling for public installations designed to serve several dwellings from a shared unit initially, and to permit individual household connections when the inhabitants can afford to install them at their own expense. This would be a more realistic approach where the people of large sections of a city do, in effect, dispose of excreta in the streets, and where the lack of modern plumbing constitutes not only an eyesore and an inconvenience to the inhabitants, but a hazard to the health of the entire city.

In large cities, the problem is not just a matter of preventing disease: it is also one of meeting absolute physiological requirements for water in extreme cases and of convenience in all cases. In rural areas, water supply and sanitation are primarily health problems. It is much less a question of convenience than in the city, for the people have long been accustomed to the existing arrangements, and in fact the place where water is obtained commonly serves an important social function as a meeting place. The basic health problem is to avoid contamination of the water supply with fecal material, but in practice the conventional source often is surface water which already has been contaminated with the waste of other communities before it arrives in the area in question. In such cases, just protecting the water supply from the community's own contamination is not enough, and the question becomes one of either purifying water from the conventional source, or seeking an entirely new source of clean water.

Rural settlements are so small and dispersed that the cost of provision of minimum facilities by the central government generally would be prohibitive. Even where the rural people live in villages, population density within the residential area usually is much lower than that in the city, and the size of the average village is so small that conventional designs for public installations would be uneconomical. Therefore, the self-help approach is the only one that is economically feasible for a large segment of the rural population. The general idea of this approach is to introduce simple but effective systems, providing a little technical guidance in key places, and to let the local people provide their own facilities on the family or the community level. Improvements of this type probably will take place in the long run in Latin America, just as they have in the United States. However, local-initiative projects work only where there is sufficient local motivation, and while resistance to this type of project is usually not great, the strength of the present desire for it in rural areas is questionable at best. Where the people are ignorant of the germ theory of disease, they see no connection between impure water and illness or infant mortality, and hence they have little interest in making a self-help effort to obtain a clean water supply.

In Mexico, it has become a common practice of centralized agencies to carry out village water supply projects only if the local community will meet one-half or more of the cost. This has proven to be a good selection mechanism, in addition to its obvious financial advantages. At least theoretically, the motivation for local participation is village pride even though in some cases it may be political in the sense that another undertaking desired much more strongly by the local leaders may be tied to a water supply project. Such projects are not truly of the local-initiative type in most cases, but the village does mobilize laborers, and sometimes it even provides some funds for materials.

Insect and malaria control. Malaria is an ideal example of the type of disease which is communicable only by way of an insect vector. One human being does not get malaria directly from another: a mosquito of the proper kind must bite an infected human, thereby become infected itself, and later bite another human to transmit the disease to him. Thus, malaria can be eliminated by breaking the cycle of transmission at any point. Some drugs will prevent malaria from striking people who do not have it, and suppress it in those who do. Technologically it would be feasible to eliminate the disease by eliminating the human reservoir—but not the human beings—through the use of such suppressive drugs. However, this approach would be expensive, and its effectiveness depends upon reaching all of the infected population and convincing most members of it to take pills regularly whether they feel ill or not. It would be very hard to accomplish the latter where the idea of preventive medication is not strong; even the United States armed forces in the Pacific, for all of the coercive powers of the military, had considerable difficulty in achieving compliance among servicemen during World War II.

It is therefore simplest and most effective to go after the mosquito instead of the human carriers, and this in fact is the approach which has produced such spectacular success in Latin America during the last two decades. This success depended upon the discovery of DDT and other insecticides and their use in regular, repetitive spraying programs embracing all houses, settlement by settlement, until the disease became inactive in most human carriers. Such programs also are expensive, and they involve some problems such as the development of DDT-resistant strains of mosquitoes which must be attacked with other insecticides. However, there is no question of acceptance or rejection by the local people: the agency responsible for the program simply sends in a brigade to spray all houses, whether the inhabitants like it or not. Once the decision has been made to allocate the necessary funds to this purpose and the required administrative structure has been created, little stands in the way of success in achieving control. By the early 1960's this had been done throughout so much of Latin America that malaria is no longer among the major killing diseases of the area.

Success of environmental sanitation projects. The most common types of effort in this field therefore are relatively free from danger of failure through rejection by the local populace, because they are customarily planned in such a way that the work is done for the community and success does not depend upon local cooperation. Moreover, the results as a rule are of such a nature that they are accepted, or even heartily welcomed, once the people have had time to become accustomed to them.

The same is not equally true of efforts in other health sectors, where action is directed at the *persons* of the local people, instead of at the physical features of their habitat. Success in these areas requires that individuals submit to treatment by strangers of another social class, and often that they themselves perform specific acts which are strange to them. Thus traditional beliefs and practices have a much stronger and more direct influence on efforts in other health fields than they do on those in environmental sanitation.

Preventive Medicine

Preventive medicine has the same final purpose as environmental sanitation—to prevent disease before it occurs. Instead of doing so through treatment of the surroundings in which the people live, however, it treats the people themselves. It is distinguished from medical care, which focuses upon those who are already ill, and it deals with well persons either on an individual or a community basis. The control of communicable diseases, nutrition, health education, and maternal and child health protection are only a few of the subdivisions of preventive medicine, and only the first two are considered here.

The control of communicable diseases. The increasing ease of transportation and the changes in social organization which normally accompany development in both rural and urban areas—quite apart from the matter of rapid urbanization of the population—facilitate the spread of contagious diseases as well as the movement of goods, services, and ideas. Because of this, the minimal health protection services characteristic of the traditional setting would not even prevent degeneration of the comparatively poor health of the traditional community once the effects of modernization have begun to be felt. Nor is the growing need to control communicable diseases one which can be met completely by the free play of market forces—financial considerations if anything are more likely to encourage the ill person to continue his normal activities than to isolate himself from others to avoid infecting them.

The identification of those suffering from contagious disease, and their isolation and treatment until they have been cured or at least have become non-infectious, therefore grow in importance as development proceeds. Some increase in efforts of this type is required to compensate for the growing number and frequency of contacts with persons beyond the limits of one's own local community, and thereby merely to *maintain* the earlier health standards. One's first inclination may be to think of this principle in terms of such spectacular diseases as smallpox and typhoid fever, but it is equally important in terms of infirmities with more gradual effects, especially such serious ones as tuberculosis and venereal disease.

Immunization has the same general purpose as isolation of infected individuals: to prevent the spread of a disease to the uninfected members of the population. Effective procedures exist for many illnesss, but no effort is made to apply all of those available to all people even in the richest of industrialized countries. Some of the considerations involved in deciding to what extent use should be made of an available procedure include the probability of exposure to the disease; the severity of the disease and the likelihood that it will spread through the entire population; the receptivity of the population to the particular immunization; and the costs in terms of alternative uses of money, personnel, and facilties. In the United States, for example, few people have been vaccinated against yellow fever, because it is extremely unlikely that those who do not travel abroad will be exposed even once in a lifetime.

Immunizations are among the preventive efforts most likely to be met with indifference or even outright rejection. Vaccination is effective against some types of influenza, a disease which causes considerable discomfort and economic loss in the population of the United States each year. Yet even though such vaccination is available, often without charge, and mass media are used to urge people to be vaccinated when important outbreaks are anticipated, many fail to take advantage of it. Similarly, a practicing physician in a large Latin American city once jokingly commented, while immunizing the author against typhoid fever, "I've had the shots, and I've had the typhoid—I'll take the typhoid." These examples both involve people who, in principle, attach great importance to preventive medicine and who accept the basic principles of scientific medicine without reservation. Immunization efforts charasteristically meet with much greater indifference, and sometimes even outright resistance, where ignorance or skepticism of the germ theory of disease, in combination with fatalistic attitudes, are .characteristic of broad segments of the population—and these latter characteristics are widespread among lower class Latin Americans.

For this and other reasons, Latin American governments have not always given highest priority to immunization campaigns within their health programs. Nevertheless, some important efforts have been made, especially against such diseases as smallpox.

Nutrition is a quite different type of effort within preventive medicine. Actually the subject extends beyond the limits of this sub-sector, where it is important primarily because the undernourished have relatively low resistance to contagious disease, and in its own right it is one of the major elements in the general well-being of a population. More than the mere amount of food is involved: a diet which is quantitatively adequate may be seriously lacking in important elements. Protein, vitamin, and mineral deficiencies are common among the poor of underdeveloped lands, and often they are simply the result of poverty.

As in the spread of contagious disease, development may bring changes of an undesirable nature in dietary patterns, although for different reasons. The changes in this case involve differences in the methods used for preparing food or the disappearance of quantitatively minor, but nutritionally important items from the traditional diet. Rice, which is a major staple in many parts of Latin America, was once milled by hand in wooden mortars. The procedure is so time-consuming in comparison to that used in modern mills that even the lowest-income peasant finds it economically advantageous to sell his rice production unmilled and to repurchase machine-milled rice if he can work as a day laborer for the same amount of time he otherwise would spend at the mortar. However, the rice mill is *too* efficient in one sense, for it removes the seed coat so thoroughly that many nutrients which formerly were eaten now are lost with the waste. This specific instance is the most important one of its type in Latin America and in the world as a whole, but it is not the only one.

No single example of such importance is available to illustrate the replacement or disappearance of an important item of the traditional diet throughout so much of Latin America. The gradual substitution of beer and other beverages for *pulque*, a rather mild alcoholic drink made from the sap of the *agave*, has had an effect on the diet of the people of Central Mexico similar to that of the adoption of modern rice milling in other areas: in addition to alcohol, *pulque* contains several vitamins which are not present in the products which are replacing it.

The general pattern of the traditional diet is among the features of any culture which are most resistant to change: this point is given some attention in the section on agricultural development. Because existing nutritional standards were developed in the middle-latitude setting of the industrialized countries, on the basis of observations in cultures which attach considerable value to eating meat, there is some room for discussion concerning the qualitative adequacy of the *unaltered* traditional diet of any present-day underdeveloped area. When a student in his class reported that a field study in southern Mexico had found that the traditional diet in the area supplied all known nutritive requirements if eaten in the preferred quantity, a physiology professor commented: "But that should be obvious! The people are alive, aren't they?"

Even if one accepts the position that traditional diets throughout the world were qualitatively adequate in their unaltered form, both qualitative changes and quantitative restrictions have had the result that many of the people of Latin America are ill-fed, in a strictly physiological sense, at the present time. Qualitative changes of this sort have almost certainly been more severe among the urban poor than elsewhere. Given existing trends in population growth and urbanization, the situation is not likely to improve of its own accord in the near future. Mathematical projection of recent rates of growth of the food supply in comparison with similar projections of population growth in fact raise alarming specters of widespread hunger. This and their value as an inexpensive source of complete protein are major reasons that so much emphasis is now being placed upon the refinement of such potentially rich food sources as fish and soy meal.

Medical Care

For both technical and economic reasons, no country in the world even attempts to completely prevent all disease; all accept that some of their people will be ill some of the time. It is therefore important to develop and maintain health services which treat the prevalent illnesses promptly and effectively.

Personnel, installations, and supplies ideally should be available for treatment of the most common illnesses and injuries in every community center, and facilities for more complex or prolonged attention should be made available to the entire population through more complete medical establishments in the major centers of broader socio-economic regions. No country in Latin America has attained such an ideal situation: none, in fact, even closely approaches it. On a national scale, the inventory of physicians and other personnel and that of hospitals, clinics, and other health facilities everywhere falls far short of meeting the existing demand for medical services even when that demand is defined in terms of the amount of medical care which actually would be "consumed" if it were immediately available to all people at present costs.

When reference is made to indifference or resistance to modern medical care in the transitional societies of present-day Latin America, then, the question is one of internal distribution of medical facilities in relation to the existing demand for them. There are more sick people who want to be treated and who could meet the present financial costs of treatment, if it were locally available, than can be effectively treated by existing medical facilities.

Nevertheless, the prevalence of traditional beliefs and practices in large segments of the population of every Latin American country detracts from the effectiveness of investments in medical care, to a large extent through postponement of treatment until the condition has become severe. Long waiting periods in crowded facilities, the high cost of medical care in relation to lower class incomes, and high-handed behavior of medical personnel toward patients whom they consider their social inferiors all have the same general effect. Thus two sets of factors limit the expansion of the use of existing medical knowledge to cure disease: (1) failure on the part of the ill to make the most effective possible use of those facilities which are available, and (2) the scarcity of modern medical facilities themselves.

Some elements of the first of these sets of factors already have been considered in general terms. Attention is now turned to the second of them, particularly as it bears upon the treatment of people who already are ill. Many of the points made here in connection with medical care also pertain to the provision of preventive services.

The provision of modern medical resources. The term, medical resources, is used here in the broadest possible sense to embrace all of the elements which enter into caring for the ill and injured. It therefore includes all of the many kinds of personnel involved in caring for the needs of the ill, providing medical supplies, and managing the operation of the various installations and the organizational structure in which they perform their services, as well as the buildings for hospitals, clinics, and laboratories and the internal equipment necessary for their operation.

While each of these resources may be treated separately for some purposes, as is done in the paragraphs below, in practice they must be brought together in proper proportions: the provision of medical care is a system made up of interdependent parts, and development of a truly effective system of this sort calls not only for highly specialized attention to each of the components, but also careful planning and coordination of the system as a whole. The latter function itself requires special aptitudes as well as more general knowledge of all of the various components, and the lack of proper planning and coordination is among the more serious defects of the medical care systems of most Latin American countries at the present time. In some of these countries, the situation is probably such that efforts toward the development of effective planning and coordination mechanisms, by increasing the effectiveness of resources which already exist, would yield a higher return than those devoted to any other aspect of the medical care system.

The development of an effective medical care system requires action on both the national and the local levels. Thus, the production of skilled personnel, certain types of centralized installations, equipment, and drugs and other supplies calls for efforts on a country-wide scale. A number of Latin American countries, in fact, are so small that it would not be economically feasible for them to produce many resources exclusively to supply their domestic systems. In such cases, the only workable alternatives are continued dependence upon external sources, or cooperation among various Latin American countries to form a "service area" large enough to support production on an efficient scale.

At the same time that action on a nationwide or broader scale is required to provide resources of more specialized types and to furnish centralized coordination, local initiative is potentially important for providing more ordinary facilities. The local level in Latin America today is technically capable of such contributions as the construction of buildings for health centers, transporting patients to more centralized installations, providing manpower for certain auxiliary functions, conducting some types of health education, and providing housing for specialized personnel from outside the community. The community can also articulate local demands for medical care and express them on the national level, and thereby it may contribute to achieving more effective territorial allocation of new resources. If local leadership is strong, it may even achieve effective collaboration on the local level among programs of the central government which are not adequately coordinated with one another on a broader scale.

The scarcity of well-trained personnel is an even more serious bottleneck in the development of medical-care systems than is the shortage of physical facilities because of the long training periods required. The physician is the key element, although not the only one, and medical doctors are being prepared in increasing numbers by university-based medical schools in nearly all major cities of Latin America. Many doctors in Latin America, unlike the majority in the United States, earn most of their income from salaried appointments, even though they usually devote a few hours a day to private practice as well. In a public clinic session, a doctor may see an average of twenty patients per hour, in contrast to only about three or four in his private office. The physician's organized service pattern in Latin America therefore makes the attention of the average doctor available to larger number of patients, but with obvious implications for the quality of medical care.

Other professional personnel in the medical fields —nurses, technicians and therapists, and pharmacists— also are scarce in Latin America. Often they are called upon to perform services reserved for the physician himself in the United States, and this is another situation which makes modern medicine available to a larger number of people at the cost of some sacrifice in quality.

Ambulatory care facilities which serve the general public or a broad segment of the population (such as persons covered by the social security system) are proportionately much more important in Latin America than in the United States. Such units take the form of health centers, health stations or posts, or mobile clinics. They can be, and usually are, organized in a network, with a hospital at the center and peripheral health centers and stations to serve people needing ambulatory care. The health centers usually are staffed by doctors, and the outlying stations by nurses or other auxiliary personnel who work under the supervision of the doctor in a health center. An ideal objective would be to have stable facilities of this type in every locality within reach of 1,000 or more people. Such an objective would be realistic only in extremely long-range terms in Latin America; meanwhile, "mobile clinics" are an expedient alternative for many communities which can be reached by motor vehicle.

Serious illness requiring bed care, numerous tests, surgery, etc. can be coped with only in hospitals, but it is not necessary, or even desirable, for all hospitals to be fully prepared to deal with all types of cases. Ideally, hospitals should be organized in a system, with large and complete facilities in major centers, "district" or "intermediate" hospitals of 100 to 200 beds to serve the most common surgical and medical cases in the next echelon, and small "rural" or "community" hospitals of from 25 to 50 beds for maternity, minor accidents, and immediate admission of any condition prior to referral, if necessary, to a larger installation. Ideally, the hospital system should operate under centralized planning and direction, with fixed standards for quality control, records, etc., but this ideal is seldom achieved in practice in Latin America.

Even though the monetary cost of many types of medical service is lower in most Latin American countries than in the United States, only a small percentage of the total population can meet those costs without severe hardship. Various types of public financing are extremely important. These include tax support from revenues of the central government for extensive programs carried out under the ministries of health, social security systems financed by contributions from the government, employers, and workers covered by the system; national lotteries; and various public charities. The multiple sources for financing national medical care facilities make centralized coordination of those facilities into efficient systems extremely difficult, for normally each funding agency operates its own installations through an independent administrative structure. In a few countries coordination gradually is being achieved.

Medical Science and the Population Problem

Even though Latin American death rates are high when compared with those of the industrialized countries, they nevertheless have fallen rapidly during recent decades. In the face of stable and high birth rates, this change has resulted in spectacular increases in the rate of population growth, which now exceeds three per cent per year in several countries. The explosive population growth now characteristic of Latin America has become a source of major concern. At the same time, medical research has led to the development, during the past decade, of contraceptive techniques which would make it technologically and even economically feasible for poorly educated low-income families in Latin America to practice birth control if the necessary knowledge and supplies were available to them.

Many more or less localized efforts have been made to introduce birth control in Latin America, but as yet these efforts have not produced any substantial change in the birth rate. One exception is in Puerto Rico, where the migration of many women in the childbearing ages to the mainland United States may have had an even greater impact on the birth rate than the family planning program. The negative attitude of the Catholic Church toward birth control is well known, and its influence as a deterrent to family planning should not be under-estimated; through its influence on the opinions of important political leaders, this set of religious attitudes is likely to at least delay the dissemination of knowledge and supplies in several countries. At the same time, the child becomes an economic asset to his family by the time he is eight or nine years old in most of rural Latin America, and one may question the extent to which motivation for family limitation is likely to be strong enough to result in effective birth control under these circumstances. Nevertheless, the scattered results of research and actual experience relating to the demand for birth control suggest that some segments of the Latin American populations, at least in the cities, would welcome any opportunity to limit the number of their dren.

Priorities

The health situation in Latin America, whether considered in terms of the availability of medical care,

the incidence of disease, or death rates, clearly is a field
in which large improvements are required in the course
of development. The same is also true of many other
fields, each in its own way, so that it is necessary to
choose among alternative uses for the scarce resources
available for development. The question is not one of
deciding whether or not there are to be any health
programs at all, but a matter of deciding how much of
the available resources should be devoted to health, and
what kinds of health programs should be carried out.
Hopefully, these decisions are made by setting priorities
on the basis of the expected results of each particular
program in relation to the expected results of alternative
uses of the same resources.

The allocation of resources available for development among the various sectors must in practice often
be somewhat arbitrary. One reason for this is that the
scarcity of personnel capable of adequately preparing
truly sound projects remains one of the major bottlenecks
in development efforts, and to a certain extent funds are
distributed on the basis of the existence of projects
which are ready to go into the field. On such grounds,
health as a rule fares rather well, for many of the
agencies and personnel involved have the benefit of
longer experience in the project approach to development than their counterparts in other sectors.

Certain technical and emotional considerations, in
addition to simple expediency, make it difficult to
determine on strictly rational grounds the priority to be
given to health within the total framework of sponsored
development. Conventional cost-benefit analysis of
health and sanitation projects is likely to be misleading,
for even though it is possible to go through the appropriate analyses for some types of projects, benefits in
this field cannot be expressed adequately in monetary
terms. If a man of fifty who has had hookworm most of
his life is freed from it, and as a result feels much better
for the remainder of his days, it is quite possible that
there will be no measurable monetary benefit either to

him or to the society in which he lives; if many people experience a similar change as a result of a particular project, no one can deny that the project has produced some benefit. The extreme humanitarian view, of course, holds that life and health are priceless, and should be given priority at any cost. Only by assigning arbitrary monetary values to life and health can the benefits of projects in this sector be compared statistically with those of projects in other fields.

Considerations of this same type are involved in setting priorities within the health fields. However, some considerations relating to allocations among the three sub-sectors of health service are of rather general applicability.

Environmental sanitation projects do not depend heavily upon public participation. They are capable of bringing noticeable changes to many people at a relatively moderate cost per person directly affected by the project and aware of it. Moreover, there is high probability that the change will be considered beneficial by the people affected, if not initially, at least within a short time. A few types of project within this field offer good possibilities for local participation and even some chance of a "demonstration effect" in other communities nearby. However, now that so much progress has been made in malaria control, most new environmental sanitation projects have their most spectacular effects in reducing infant mortality, and, inhumane or not, one must take into account the possibility that further large reductions in death rates among the very young may postpone accomplishment of some other development goals, including some related to health.

In the field of preventive medicine, the situation is more varied, but the impact usually is not so concentrated on infant mortality except for maternal-and-child-health programs, which are only one part of the total sub-sector. Nutrition programs, if they are not culturally biased but are adapted to existing food habits with only minor additions, are appealing in terms of im-

provement throughout all age groups and their general
effect of increasing resistance to contagious diseases.
All types of preventive medical efforts, however, do
involve acceptance on a personal basis, and that in
spheres which characteristically are resistant to change.
Moreover, to be effective, they must reach many people
(sometimes most of those living in a particular area),
and their per capita costs are inclined to be high.
Therefore, such programs and projects need to be
evaluated very carefully, especially in terms of the
receptivity of the proposed beneficiaries to the changes
which are contemplated.

Medical care, like preventive medicine, is a field
in which success depends upon acceptance at a personal
level. There is a major difference, however: resources
for treating the ill are so scarce in relation to the effective
demand that, in any Latin American country, local
situations exist in which "project success" is assured
even if most local people do reject the new services on
an individual basis. This feature makes medical care
projects especially attractive for use as an "opening
wedge" to promote enthusiasm for general development
in regions or communities where efforts are to be
expanded, even though medical service is quite expensive
per person effectively treated. Again, benefits are
spread throughout the life span unless emphasis is
placed upon some particular age group.

In addition to these considerations related to population policy and to public receptivity, many strictly
medical considerations enter into determining both long-
range and short-range priorities within the health fields.
The balance among various types of efforts aimed at
preventing disease, on the one hand, and providing
resources for treatment, on the other, calls for medical
policy decisions based on economic and humanitarian,
as well as strictly technical grounds. Such decisions
should aim to maximize progress toward the goal of a
population which is free from acute and chronic ailments,
is adequately nourished, and is able to enjoy general
physical and mental well-being.

RURAL DEVELOPMENT PROBLEMS[1]

Latin America is a predominantly rural part of the world—no matter how "rural" and "urban" may be defined. Even Argentina, Uruguay, and Chile, which are among the most urbanized countries in Latin America, are all quite rural in every sense when compared with industrialized nations.

Much more is involved in the concept of rural than the mere number of people living outside compact settlements of more than a given size. However, the relationship between size of settlement and degree of urbanity is sufficiently close at the lower end of the scale of size to serve as a rough index, and many national censuses in fact use this as the basis for their rural-urban definitions. The percentage of the total population living in places of fewer than 2,000 inhabitants is given below for each Latin American country for which recent

---

[1]All of the documents on rural development problems for the 1966 Workshop on Development were prepared by Peter Dorner, Director of the Land Tenure Center at the University of Wisconsin, which conducts a major program of research and training on land tenure and rural development in Latin America, and publishes many valuable items on these topics. The frame of reference used for most of this section is basically that developed by T. Lynn Smith and presented in his *Sociology of Rural Life* (New York: Harper & Brothers, Third Edition, 1953); for application of this frame of reference to particular Latin American countries, see Smith's *Brazil: People and Institutions* (Baton Rouge: Louisiana State University Press, Third Edition, 1963) and his *Colombia: Social Structures and the Process of Development* (Gainesville: University of Florida Press, forthcoming). Dwight B. Heath and Richard N. Adams (eds.), *Contemporary Cultures and Societies of Latin America* (New York: Random House, 1965) includes a section (pp. 139-254) on land, agriculture, and economics. Albert H. Moseman (ed.), *Agricultural Sciences for the Developing Nations* (Washington: American Association for the Advancement of Science, Publication No. 76, 1964) places greater emphasis on economics and various fields of technical agriculture. Many of the items listed in the bibliography at the end of this book include articles or sections on various aspects of rural development.

data are available, and for the United States and
West Germany, to show in a rough way the extent
to which most Latin American countries remain
predominantly rural.[1]

Country and Year	Per Cent
Argentina (1947)	38
Brazil (1960)	60
Costa Rica (1950)	71
Ecuador (1950)	71
El Salvador (1950)	72
Haiti (1950)	90
Honduras (1961)	77
Mexico (1960)	56
Nicaragua (1950)	72
Panama (1960)	57
Venezuela (1961)	36
United States (1960)	29
West Germany (1961)	23

Aside from a few debatable cases, such as small,
compact communities devoted to mining and fishing, the
"rural community" is virtually synonymous with the
"agricultural community" and the vast majority of the
rural population, however defined, is made up of
people who are directly dependent upon agricultural
occupations. This is true whether the farmers' houses
are closely grouped together in villages, as they
characteristically are in some parts of Latin America,
or widely scattered over the landscape as in the United
States.

Rural development is an especially important field
in Latin America, and not only because this is so rural
a part of the world. Many development problems are

---

[1] Compiled and computed from data in United Nations,
Demographic Yearbook, various issues; U. S. Bureau of the
Census, *Census of Population: 1960*, Vol. I, Part A, Table 5:
and Mexico, Dirección General de Estadística, *VIII Censo General
de Población, 1960, Resumen General*, Cuadro 5.

much more severe in rural than in urban areas and some, in fact, are relevant only in the rural context. In addition, rural people the world over are characteristically more resistant to change than city-dwellers, and this differ- ence is much greater in Latin America than in the United States.

Many different aspects of the way of life are involved in rural development. Just as development itself is an integral process, *rural* development is a sub- process in which various features are even more closely tied together in an intricate web of interrelationships, and rural life is a functioning system of parts which are more or less closely related to one another.

The connections among the various parts of a rural social system exist whether it is undergoing rapid change or not. The traditional rural society is ex- tremely stable and the relationships between the local community and the rest of world are neither very numer- ous nor very complex. Few present-day Latin Amer- ican rural communities can validly be treated as though they remain at the traditional pole of the traditional-tran- sitional continuum, however. Backward, poverty- stricken, underdeveloped, immutable, or otherwise tra- ditional though they may appear to the observer from Northwestern Europe or the United States, it would be difficult to find one single example of a rural community in Latin America that has not begun to feel the effects of the Twentieth Century, that has not, in other words, moved away from the traditional pole of that continuum in some respects.

The situation is much more complicated in the transitional than in the strictly traditional rural com- munity, because both internal and external relationships are undergoing change. In some respects, rural life itself eventually undergoes some "urbanization"—modern farmers of the United States are in a sense at least as "urban" as most city-dwellers in the world. But, in other respects, rural life remains distinct. Many things are involved in this, but one key item is the low population density that is necessarily characteristic of agriculture. This places some limitations upon the workable size of rural communities and upon the nature of the social relationships associated with the production system.

Latin American rural life, even though it has assumed a transitional character, remains very different from rural life in the United States. Its present nature holds many problems of profound significance for Latin American development, not only as it affects the rural population itself, but in the cities and in the external political and economic relationships of the Latin American countries as well. Particular action areas in sponsored rural development are barely touched upon in the next section of this text; the present one is devoted to a summary—which the expert is sure to find over-simplified—of some characteristics of rural Latin America. This is an extremely complex subject. Even though its various aspects are closely related to one another, and in practice cannot be separated, it is necessary to consider them one by one for purposes of study. The particular aspects to be treated here are land use, in a very broad sense; the manner in which the agricultural population is arranged on the land, that is, the settlement pattern; a whole set of questions related to the nature and distribution of property rights in land, referred to here as land systems; and finally, the question of agricultural technology. This by no means exhausts the list of features of rural life which are involved in the changes of rural development: it merely singles out a few closely related sets of features that are unique to rural situations.

Land Use

The limited space available here does not permit a detailed discussion of land use in terms of specific agricultural products. The patterns in Latin America in this sense are very complex, and depend upon variations in both human and natural elements at both the regional and local levels. However, some general

tendencies are true to a greater or lesser extent throughout most of Latin America, and are important enough
in relation to development to merit attention here.

First, there is the matter of a close linkage between
food habits and the selection of subsistence crops. Many
farmers the world over grow what they do simply
because it is what they eat. It would not occur to them
to produce anything else until their basic requirements
for their own food crops had been assured. For example,
the main crop in Mexican subsistence agriculture is
corn—even in regions where natural conditions are such
that manioc might produce more food per acre or per
unit of work. Why is this so? The Mexicans living in
these regions know about manioc and how to grow it,
and as a matter of fact there is some manioc production
there. However, no Mexican community uses manioc
as a mainstay in the diet, nor do Mexicans know how
to use it as a mainstay. To the Mexican in such a region,
manioc is just another vegetable for occasional use as
a minor item in the diet, like a dozen or so others.

In a large part of Brazil, however, manioc *is* a
mainstay. In these areas, it is preferred over corn, which
is also known—but tortillas are not known, and corn, like
manioc in Mexico, is just another vegetable among the
minor items of diet.

Traditional diets usually are extremely resistant to
change, and the traditional selection of subsistence
crops as a general rule is a reasonably good adaptation
to the potentials of the environment. Usually, it is
much wiser to direct development efforts related to basic
food crops toward improving the yield of traditional
crops than toward introducing new ones which would
require a change in diet. Even such improvement of
existing crops often meets resistance. One well-known
case involved an attempt to introduce high-yielding
hybrid corn in Hispanic communities in the South-
western United States. Through the use of demonstration plots, an agricultural extension agent convinced
the local Spanish-American farmers of the advantages
of the hybrid seed he wished to introduce. Many of

the men were so impressed that the project was considered a great success—within a year or so, almost
everyone had adopted the new variety. But then, even
more rapidly, they changed back to the old one, even
though it yielded much less. Why? Inquiry revealed
that, while the men were pleased with the high yield,
the women did not like the new corn. Objections cen-
tered around its qualities for making tortillas, a very important activity in the woman's life, and ultimately the
attempt at introduction failed because of relatively minor
considerations.[1]

One of the characteristics of Latin American
agriculture, then, is that many farmers produce the local
dietary mainstay as their principal crop. Another is that
those who do usually are unwilling to accept any changes
related to the production of that crop unless they can
be convinced that the risk is small and the opportunity
for improvement great. And yet another characteristic
is that these farmers can be expected to reject completely a sudden change in basic subsistence crops (which
would involve a sudden change in diet), even though
they might consider substituting some commercial crop
with which they already are familiar for part or even all
of their subsistence crop production in some circumstances.

Another general tendency which is true to a greater
or lesser extent throughout most of Latin America
relates to the emphasis placed upon livestock in relation
to that placed on crop production. Some animals—cows,
burros, llamas, pigs, chickens, and others, the particular
assortment depending upon the region—are important
in traditional small-scale farming patterns throughout
most of Latin America. This is not really "mixed farming" in the sense that this term is used in the United
States, but the same family does have both crops and
animals. In this type of small-scale operation, which is

---

[1]Anacleto Apodaca, "Corn and Custom," in Edward H.
Spicer (ed.), *Human Problems in Technological Change: A
Casebook* (New York: John Wiley & Sons, 1965), pp. 35-39.

just as characteristic of the transitional as of the traditional community in Latin America, all families in the same locality are on approximately the same socio-economic level, and the assortment of animals a family possesses is not a major element in determining its prestige.

When the focus shifts to large landholdings of traditional types, however, the situation is different. On them, in both their traditional and contemporary forms, livestock production yields much more prestige than crop production in many circumstances. In most Latin American countries, such holdings are not highly commercialized. Usually, they are owned by a member of the elite who lives in the capital or some other large city. The owner characteristically holds the land, and decides how it is to be used, in terms of considerations which may be based more on prestige than on profit motives. In this situation, it is both less troublesome and more prestigeful to raise cattle than to produce any crop.

This characteristic is very significant for development. Such holdings usually have a considerable amount of land that is of much better-than-average quality for the region in which they are located. Because of this land-use preference, some of the potentially most-productive cropland throughout Latin America is *under*-utilized as pasture, while crops grown in the same area are concentrated on second-rate land, often on slopes above fertile basin land that is in pasture.

One of the most important sets of changes in rural development in Latin America is that involving increasing dependence upon markets outside the local rural community, both to sell agricultural products and to obtain ever-greater amounts of goods from the outside world. Here we are concerned with one particular part of this general set of changes, the one which specifically involves the commercialization of agriculture itself or, in other words, increasing agricultural production intended for sale.

The commercialization of agriculture can take more

than one form. First, it may simply involve increased production of the same crops, and sale of the surplus. It may also be a matter of adding new crops produced primarily for sale to the existing combination. Both of these forms are most likely to occur among small-scale farmers. The third form is that involving the creation or expansion of specialized production units which concentrate on just one or two crops, usually on a large scale, a situation in which any home use of the product is purely incidental to market production.

Commercialization of the last type is clearly the most effective way to increase the production of particular crops as rapidly and as cheaply as possible. However, its *other* effects for development are likely to be rather limited. Most of the people involved in this last type of commercialization ordinarily are hired laborers who receive a very small share of the return —usually approximating the minimum amount required to buy food for themselves and their families— and who in other ways have but limited exposure to and participation in the change process.

The first two forms of commercialization mentioned above, however, usually involve increasing commercialization of very small production units. Sponsored change of these sorts is both much more difficult and much more costly than commercialization through large-scale specialized units—but these forms of commercialization are also much more effective in promoting other changes. The fruits of the same amount of additional production in this case are spread more or less evenly among a much larger number of producers, and although the individual increment may be rather small, it nonetheless is something above and beyond current subsistence requirements and increases the recipient's capacity to innovate. Moreover, the number and intensity of the commercial contacts of the individual producer are likely to increase significantly, and with them, his exposure to potential innovations also increases. In practice, these forms of commercialization are occurring all over Latin America, and occurring spontaneously as components of the much more general process which has already carried the communities involved from a strictly traditional situation to a transitional one.

Settlement Patterns[1]

Like food habits, the manner in which the agricultural population is arranged on the land is a characteristic of rural life which, once established, is very resistant to change. In the United States, the rural people live in houses located on the land they work, and scattered widely over the landscape. To them, this seems the only logical way of doing things. In many other parts of the world, however, the houses of the rural people are characteristically grouped together in compact villages from which the farmers commute to their fields when there is work to be done there. Again, for the particular people involved *this* seems the only logical way of doing things.

Tendencies toward dispersion of the rural population are strong enough in some areas in Latin America—as in much of Colombia—to make scattered farmsteads predominant; elsewhere, as in parts of highland Mexico, the forces of agglomeration are so strong that village settlement is the typical form, and the countryside is almost devoid of isolated dwellings.

Neither the extreme dispersion of the agricultural population characteristic of the United States, nor the extreme concentration found in some village situations elsewhere in the world, is typical of any large part of Latin America, however. Small and often amorphous

[1]The first synthesis of the work of geographers and sociologists on settlement patterns in various parts of Latin America was completed recently by the Economic Commission for Latin America (ECLA), and published as "Rural Settlement Patterns and Social Change in Latin America: Notes for a Strategy of Rural Development," *Economic Bulletin for Latin America*, Vol. X, No. 1 (March 1965), pp. 1-21.

clusters of rural houses are a major element in the settlement pattern in many areas. The houses in such a
cluster are too few in number to constitute a village in
the usual sense, but they are too close to one another and
too far removed from the land worked by the residents
to count as scattered farmsteads. Such settlements are
referred to by different terms in different parts of Latin
America—*ranchería,* the most common designation in
the part of Mexico where this was first described as a
distinct form of settlement, is used here.[1]

Settlement in rancherías is perhaps more typical of
Latin America as a whole than either of the better known
types, but there is a great deal of diversity among different regions. All gradations from the single farmhouse
standing alone in the midst of its fields, to large, compact villages with regular street patterns—but nonetheless inhabited principally by people directly dependent upon agriculture—may be present even within one
relatively small area.

There are many connections between the type of
settlement pattern and the development process. The
village pattern obviously *facilitates* contacts among
members of the local community, but it is not the only
element which enters into determining the frequency and
intensity of those contacts, and the evidence now
available is not adequate to demonstrate that interaction
really is substantially more frequent and intense in
villages than in dispersed rural communities in Latin
America. This question, or whole set of questions,
relates to development particularly in terms of features
of social organization which may be made use of to
promote semi-spontaneous diffusion of desired changes.

Village settlement involves some disadvantages in
terms of farm management. A considerable amount of
time has to be spent commuting to and from the fields,

[1]William W. Winnie, Jr., *The Lower Papaloapan Basin:
Land and People* (Ann Arbor: University Microfilms, 1956),
Chapter V. The ECLA study cited above recognizes two types—
the larger *villorrio* and the smaller *caserío*—instead of only one.

farm products have to be transported to the village even if they are for home use, and it is more difficult to make use of manure for fertilization. The village pattern also offers some advantages in terms of public services, however. Public water supply and sewage disposal systems simply are impossible in dispersed rural settlement. Many villages are large enough to make the installation of such services economically feasible, but in a sense this is a mixed blessing because the village that is large enough to *permit* such services ordinarily is large enough to *require* them on the basis of modern standards. This reservation is not applicable in the case of medical and educational facilities or electrical service, all of which can be provided more satisfactorily in a village situation.

Both village and scattered settlement offer advantages and disadvantages for the purposes of development. On balance, the difference does not appear to be very large, and even if it were, any major alteration in established settlement patterns would be very costly, in addition to being difficult because of resistance to such change on the part of the people involved. The central authorities in Latin America have attempted to gather the rural people together in villages, or larger villages, from time to time ever since the Conquest. At least the upper classes of Mediterranean societies do have some features which might be referred to as "urban ideals," and rural settlement in large villages appears to be one of them. However, efforts at out-and-out change in settlement pattern never have met with more than temporary success in this part of the world, although some shifting has taken place from time to time in the balance between tendencies toward dispersion on the one hand and agglomeration on the other—both are present throughout Latin America. As far as sponsored development in already-settled areas is concerned, then, it would appear wisest to simply accept the settlement pattern that already exists, and to concentrate efforts on features where lasting change is more likely to be attained.

This is not necessarily the case when dealing with

the colonization of new lands, however, even if all of
the colonists are to be drawn from a single region. In
such a situation, land surveys can be made in such a way
that the shape of the individual holdings allows the
houses of the farmers to be located close to one another
and, at the same time, to be located on the land worked
by the occupant. Such a pattern, commonly referred to
as a "line village" because it often takes the form of a
ribbon settlement along a transportation route, offers
some of the advantages of both dispersed and village
settlements, while minimizing their disadvantages.

The line village pattern has been used in some colonization projects, both public and private, in various
parts of Latin America. There is also some tendency
for it to appear spontaneously along newly-opened
roads, both through new agricultural settlement along
their routes and, in older areas, through a tendency for
those with land along the road to relocate their houses
at the roadside.

Land Systems

Many other features of rural life and economy are
closely related to the nature and distribution of property
rights in agricultural land. This general subject actually
involves several features which are very closely related
to one another, but yet conceptually are quite distinct:
that is, it is a group of topics, rather than a single one.
The entire group, referred to here as land systems, is
commonly treated under the general title of land tenure,
a term which is used here to refer to just one component
of the cluster for the sake of clarity.

Land tenure. In this sense, land tenure refers to
the *nature* of the individual's property rights in land,
apart from the question of how much land he has, how
it is delimited, and how his rights are recorded. Some
features which commonly are referred to as land tenure
problems, however, do not involve the nature of property rights at all, but their distribution among the population dependent upon agriculture.

Some important differences exist among the Latin American countries, and between them as a group and the United States, in the nature of property rights in land. However, there are many similarities. Land *is* subject to private ownership and control throughout the Hemisphere. Each piece of the earth's surface is considered to have an "owner" who may be an individual, some level of government, or some private organization such as a commercial corporation.

Such a system based on private, individual ownership and control of the land on a permanent basis seems to those who have grown up with it to be the only logical type of arrangement. Yet this idea seems as strange and unnatural to some of the world's peoples, who have *other* ways of dealing with land rights, as their ways appear to us. In many societies, the land is considered to belong to no one in particular, but to everyone in general—the idea that a particular plot of land might have a particular owner simply does not exist. The individual may own the house he has built on the land, or the crops growing there, but not the land itself. Systems of this general type were the only kind that existed in pre-Columbian America, and even the traditional Spanish and Portuguese land systems which were introduced at the time of the Conquest had some elements based on this concept of land rights at the same time that they were based primarily on the idea of permanent private ownership of particular tracts. It is not surprising, then, that the present land systems in Latin America include numerous survivals of communal and collective patterns of land tenure within the general framework of a system of private property rights in land.

All societies which recognize private property rights in land place some limitations upon those rights. One may "own" a particular piece of the earth's surface —but he also may lose it if he does not fulfill certain obligations (particularly relating to taxation), or simply because it is needed for some particular public purpose (the right of eminent domain). These two limitations on private property rights—taxation and eminent domain—exist throughout Latin America, although in most countries the second of them is interpreted somewhat differently than in the United States.

One concept of growing importance in Latin America would further limit private land rights. This is the idea that the land should belong to the man who works it, the idea of "the social function of land" which forms the basis of some arguments in favor of land reform. It affects the *nature* of property rights only in the sense of potentially restricting the amount of land which may be held by any one owner, and thus concerns the distribution of rights even more than their nature. Up to the present time, however, the concept of the social function of land has become an important element in actual practice, as well as a point of legal and intellectual discussion, only in Mexico, Bolivia, Venezuela, and Cuba.

It is more useful to think of the nature of land rights themselves in terms of the *farm operator* than in terms of the owner of the land for present purposes. Each farm has an owner, and the owner's original rights are quite similar from one Latin American country to another. However, the owner may temporarily transfer some of his rights to some other individual who is the one directly responsible for the day-to-day management of the affairs of the individual agricultural production unit. This individual is the farm operator.

Direct operation of the farm by the owner of the land is widely considered to be the most advantageous type of land tenure. The owner is presumed to have more interest than anyone else in maintaining or even improving the productivity of the land base. Furthermore, within the limits of this long-term consideration, he also is the one who benefits most by making the most productive possible use of the land on a year-to-year basis. Because the owner's rights are permanent but transferable, he can use them as security for long-term loans to make improvements in the land and to purchase equipment, as well as for short-term loans for operating expenses. Owner-operators are far more numerous than all other types of farm operators combined in most Latin American countries.

One of the major forms of land tenure in Mexico was created by land reform legislation associated with the Mexican Revolution. This type of tenure exists within the framework of a system based on individual private ownership. In it, the land technically remains the property of the national government, but an inalienable use-right is granted to *ejidos*, landholding rural communities which were created, or at least formally recognized, as a result of the land reform laws. In most ejidos, this use right to cultivable land is reassigned to individual members of the community, who are known as *ejidatarios*; in some, the land is worked undivided, on a collective basis.

In the Mexican ejidos operated on an individual basis, the ejidatario in practice closely resembles an owner-operator in many respects. He has a permanent use right in a particular parcel of land. However, this right is transferable only through inheritance, and therefore it cannot be used to secure loans. If the ejidatario wishes an ordinary loan, it can be secured only with growing crops, livestock, or some other collateral besides his rights in the ejido; and if he wishes to move away, he is free to do so but legally he can neither sell nor rent his parcel to others.

The rights of the individual ejidatario in a collective ejido are not at all like those of an owner-operator, but more closely resemble the rights of a factory worker who happens to own stock in the company that owns the factory. Again, the ejidatario's rights are inalienable, but they are undistributed rights which include the right to take part in arriving at operating decisions.

Farm operation by hired administrators—accompanied by absentee ownership—involves a relatively small number of production units in all parts of Latin America, and is insignificant except on large farms. It is important in terms of the amount and quality of land involved and the number of people directly dependent upon agriculture, rather than because of the number of farms operated in this fashion.

Administrator operation actually involves two different types of situation in Latin America. The first of these is the highly-commercialized, large-scale operation, the "factory-in-the-field" type of agriculture characteristic of many plantations producing for the export market. In this case, the administrator usually is a highly-qualified technician. The second type of administrator operation occurs on large estates which are held by their owners more for prestige than for profit motives. Here, the administrator commonly is of the same origin, and has had approximately the same training, as other employees on the estate; he differs from the others mainly in that he is especially trusted by the owner, and has been appointed by him to take care of things in his absence and to look after details on the occasions—often rare—when the owner himself is present. This administrator or *mayordomo* is a straw-boss without much authority or managerial competence.

The objections which are commonly raised about absentee-ownership in most cases refer particularly to this second type of arrangement. The most basic of the various issues involved is that very little management actually is applied to the operation of the unit, because the mayordomo is incapable of exercising it and the owner does not spend enough time on the ground to do so effectively.

The types of arrangements already described cover most farms and most of the land in farms in Latin America as a whole. Renting of various types occurs throughout the area, but in most places it is a minor form involving few people and but little land. Various traditional types of communal tenure are widely distributed, but they, too, are minor forms except in some areas of the Andes and in Honduras. The Mexican ejido system, which at the time of its creation drew heavily upon traditional communal arrangements, already has been mentioned; the same terms are used in

Honduras in relation to a traditional system in which members of a land-holding community rent land from the community for individual use. Squatting, in which the individual simply uses the land, with or without the owner's permission but without any property rights of even a temporary nature, is much more common in Latin America than in the United States.

Two other types of tenurial arrangements are especially important in Latin America, but involve rights which are transmitted by the operator of a larger unit to much smaller plots within that unit. The recipients of these rights are primarily farm laborers, rather than farm operators, although many of them in fact are both simultaneously. The first of these types of arrangements, sharecropping, sometimes is true renting in the form of a situation in which the sharecropper (farm operator) gives the owner of the land a fixed fraction of the crop in return for a temporary use-right, and makes the operating decisions himself. More commonly, however, the sharecropper is a farm laborer who does the owner's or administrator's bidding and, in effect, receives a share of the product of his labors as his remuneration. He differs from the ordinary hired laborer in that he is responsible for working a particular plot within the larger holding, is paid in kind, and improves his own income as well as the owner's if he is especially productive.

The second of these types of arrangement is an old Roman institution, the *colonato,* which was introduced into Latin America by the Spanish and the Portuguese. In some parts of Latin America the people involved in this system are known as *colonos,* but there are many regional differences in name: *huasipunguero* in Ecuador, *yanaconero* in Peru, and *inquilino* ("tenant") in Chile include some of the most important variants. Whatever the local name, this worker in most cases is a resident hired laborer on a large estate, and simultaneously operates on his own behalf a small plot assigned to him within the land of that estate to enable him to raise his own food. He may be, and often is,

allowed to pasture some of his own animals on grazing
land belonging to the larger unit. In most parts of Latin
America colonos are extremely poor peasants, but in
Chile many inquilinos have gained this type of secondary tenure right in so much land that they have other
inquilinos working for them within these holdings.

Even when all of the people involved in the various
types of primary and secondary tenurial arrangements
mentioned here are combined, the total number falls far
short of accounting for all of the population engaged in
agriculture. The rest of this population is made
up of laborers who have no rights at all in the
land on which they work beyond a labor claim for
unpaid wages. When reference is made to the land
tenure problem in Latin America, this is usually the
central issue: most people engaged in agriculture have
no rights at all in the land on which they work, a
problem which is more a matter of the size of agricultural holdings than of land tenure in the narrower sense
of the term.

Size of holdings. This topic concerns the distribution of property rights in land among the agricultural population, as distinct from the nature of those
rights. If the average size of holdings is very large,
then few of the people engaged in agriculture can have
a significant amount of land of their own. If it is relatively small, then many rural families have rights in at least
a small tract of land. In this sense, the size of holdings
refers more to the number of workers per production
unit than to the actual area of farms. A farm with 250
acres of very poor land may be too small to provide a
living for even one family, yet another with the same
area of top quality cropland conceivably could support
as many as 50 or 100 families of resident laborers.

Two types of large landed estates are common
throughout most of Latin America. In both cases, the
operator himself takes little or no part in performing the
labor function, and the unit is a large one employing a
substantial number of laborers who have no land of

their own. The amount of land involved characteristically is large—hundreds, or even thousands, of acres. One of these types of large estate, referred to here as the plantation, is highly commercialized. It is operated for profit motives, and ordinarily is a well-managed and very efficient production unit. Its workers most commonly are wage laborers. Often they are housed on the plantation, but few of these units provide their workers with plots on which to grow their own food crops—it is more profitable for the plantation to use its cultivable land on its own behalf, and to pay its workers enough —usually barely enough— to enable them to buy all of the food they consume. Sugar cane is perhaps the most typical plantation crop. Others include bananas, coffee, and cotton. A considerable range of social and economic relationships is involved among different types of plantations, but most tend to a greater or lesser degree toward impersonal employer-employee relationships, rather than the traditional type of paternalistic *patrón-peón* relationships for which Latin America is much better known.

The other type of large estate differs in many ways from the commercial plantation, although the two types are more distinct in theory than in practice: in reality, they grade into one another, for the *traditional*, as distinct from the *modern*, Latin American plantation was quite similar in many respects to the second type, referred to here as the *latifundio*. Only during the last 100 years has the present sharp distinction between the two emerged as a result of the gradual modernization of many plantations and the creation of new, up-to-date units. Today, some older plantations remain relatively unaffected by this modernization process, and they now more closely resemble the traditional latifundio in some respects than the modern factory-in-the-field.

The owner of the latifundio is motivated more by prestige than by profit. He may receive some income from his agricultural operations, but usually this is not his only source of income and it may not even be the most important one. Commonly, he is a practicing profes-

sional in the capital or some other large city. This is
the type of holding on which the preference for livestock specialization mentioned earlier is strongest. The
work force generally is made up of resident laborers,
and each family is allotted a small plot for use on its
own behalf, most commonly in some variant of the colono
system but sometimes as sharecropper. The population
of most of these units is very stable, and relationships
between "management" (the owner and his representative, the administrator or mayordomo) and the workers are highly personalized and paternalistic. While the
plantation is entirely dependent upon external markets
both to supply food for its own population and to dispose
of virtually its entire production, the latifundio is marked
by a high degree of internal self-sufficiency. The
workers characteristically produce most of their own
food, and because they devote so much of their effort
to doing so, the amount of product per worker which
enters commercial channels is small. In return for this
"exported" part of the total production of the latifundio,
it depends upon external markets for most of its tools
and clothing, in addition to providing cash income for
the owner.

On both the latifundio and the plantation, the
resident labor force is commonly a large enough
population unit, and is sufficiently supplied with services, including food distribution mechanisms on plantations, to be considered a community in terms of
locality-group structure. However, authority in this unit
is highly concentrated in the owner and his representatives, and many of the features of structure and
internal relationships which are characteristic of independent communities are either poorly developed or
entirely lacking. Thus, while the large landed estate
often is co-terminous with a type of rural community in
one sense, in another its resident population does *not*
make up a well-developed rural community.

It is correct only in a very limited sense to think of
Latin America as a land of large estates. To be sure,
the latifundio and the plantation together account for

the majority of all land in agricultural holdings—but they make up only a minute fraction of the total *number* of holdings. Most of the rest are extremely tiny units of the sort that has been referred to as "pocket-handker-chief-plots" in some studies. These latter holdings are not "small farms" in the sense that the term is used in the United States—they are much smaller. The operator of such a unit does not have enough land to provide an effective outlet for his and his family's labor potential even with extremely rudimentary technology—such a unit with a total of as much as five acres of land is considered well-off if the quality of the land is at all decent. This type of holding is referred to in much of Latin America as a *minifundio,* and its operator is known as a *minifundista.*

The minifundista may be no better off economically, and may rate very little higher socially, than the landless laborer on a large estate. He has some land of his own, but he does not have a patrón to help out in an emergency—this function is performed to some extent by the local merchant, and in part by stronger family support. In practice, there is little difference between the colono, on the one hand, and the minifundista who works a day or two a week on a nearby large estate, on the other.

Mechanization is out of the question on the minifundio, unless many separate units are combined and worked jointly. The plots simply are too small to permit efficient use of agricultural machinery—and pooling units is far from being as simple as it sounds. Other technological improvements, of the sort most commonly introduced through extension practices in the United States, are also very difficult and costly, because it is necessary to reach an extremely large number of individuals to produce change on any substantial area of cropland; individual adoptions are perfectly feasible in a technical sense, but they involve great economic risk for the minifundista and run counter to his traditional conservatism.

Minifundistas usually do not occur singly in Latin

America, but in "community lots"—as a rule, either the
entire rural community is made up of minifundistas, or,
with the limitations on its nature which were previously
mentioned, it is involved in a large-estate situation.
In the former, a true community usually does exist in
every sense. Informal leadership patterns are well
developed, and all of the internal and external structural
relationships which serve to set the community apart as
a separate unit of social structure are present.

Communities of minifundistas most often occur as
villages in Latin America, although this is not universally the case. A rule of equal inheritance by all children
continously rearranges the pattern of land ownership in
the direction of producing minifundia which consist of
an ever-increasing number of extremely tiny parcels
scattered over the entire territory occupied by the community. As long as this inheritance rule continues, the
marriage pattern guarantees that such fragmentation
will also occur—and if eliminated through special legal
measures, will reappear within two generations. In
addition to involving a *total* amount of land which is too
small to permit efficient agricultural operations, then,
this small total area of the minifundio typically is divided
into at least two, and usually a much larger number, of
non-contiguous plots.

Land rights are signally important to both the
minifundista and the owner of a large estate. In both
cases, they are commonly the family's most valuable
single asset. Nevertheless, the situation relating to land
surveys and titles approaches total confusion in most
parts of Latin America. This is less a problem of
registration of property rights, than of vague and impermanent land boundaries which cannot be adequately
described for purposes of registration. Herein lies a major
source of conflict in rural Latin America, and a major
factor making an effective land tax virtually impossible
to administer. In Chile and some parts of Central
America, aerial photography has been used as a tool to
locate and record property boundaries, but this is a slow
and expensive undertaking.

Agricultural Technology

The major reason that levels of living are abysmally low in rural Latin America is that per capita production in agriculture is extremely small. To be sure, large landowners and the merchants who serve as the commercial links between rural producers and the national and international markets for agricultural products enjoy incomes far above the average for the rural population—but even if the distribution of the total income arising from agriculture were to change in such a way that each family dependent upon agriculture received exactly the same share, these average "shares" would be but little larger than the present real income of the average member of the rural lower class. Land redistribution and improved markets for agricultural products can contribute directly to rural development —but *not* by markedly changing rural income levels themselves. Such a change depends primarily upon changing agricultural technology in such a way that production per worker increases substantially. With the notable exception of a few highly commercialized plantations, farming in Latin America is characterized by a most rudimentary technology, and there is a great deal of room for increasing productivity per worker simply through adoption of technological improvements which already exist, and in many cases have already been introduced on a few farms throughout Latin America.

The broad subject of agricultural technology may be divided into two general areas, each of which is related to the productivity of agricultural labor in a different way. One of these is referred to here as *systems of cultivation*: this is a matter of the tools and the power used for working the land and caring for and harvesting the crop. The general effect of improvements in this area is to substitute capital goods for labor in the productive process, thereby increasing the amount of production per unit of labor *and* reducing the number of workers supported by a given area of cultivated land.

The other general area of agricultural technology involves application of scientific principles, mainly from the fields of plant genetics and plant physiology, to increase agricultural yields under whatever system of cultivation happens to be used to work the land. Improvements of this type do *not* greatly affect the number of workers supported by a given area of cultivated land, but they *are* capable of greatly increasing the yield per unit of labor through spectacularly raising the yield per acre.

Systems of cultivation. The full range from the most rudimentary imaginable systems of cultivation to the most advanced mechanized agriculture occurs in Latin America, again with great regional and local differences. However, only four basic types of system are of major importance. Three of these are quite rudimentary and the fourth, mechanized farming, is still of rather limited importance in terms of total production as well as in terms of the number of workers involved.

Fire agriculture, the simplest of these four systems, was very widespread before the Conquest, and actually was the basic type everywhere outside the areas of highest civilization in the Andes and Central Mexico. This system often is referred to as shifting cultivation, for one of its basic characteristics is that the farmer abandons one field after it has been used for only a year or two, and moves on to another. In practice the system usually involves sedentary residence in more or less stable settlements, with fields which are shifted from place to place over a large surrounding area.

To prepare the land for planting under this system, one simply cuts down the smaller plants and girdles the largest trees during the dry season, and sets fire to the debris after it has dried out for several weeks (hence also the term "slash-and-burn" agriculture). Once the field has cooled off, he simply plants his crop, usually without any further preparation of the soil. He may make some effort to control weeds during the growing period, but if he does, it usually is a very minor one. The principal tool in this system before the Conquest was the digging stick, a long pole sharpened on one end and hardened in the fire. The machete was added later, and with its addition there was probably some increase in efforts to control weeds during the growing period; but otherwise the system remained substantially intact—where it survived. It is still common on steep slopes outside the area of Andean hoe culture, and remains the basic system in many tropical lowland areas.

Aside from the fact that very little labor is devoted to preparation of the land for planting and care of the crop once it is in the ground, the key feature of this system is that after only a few harvests the original field is abandoned and a new one is brought into use. After each period under cultivation, the land is left idle long enough for more or less complete regeneration of the wild vegetation, that is, for a period which under ideal conditions may amount to twenty years or more. If it is re-used for crops too frequently, the eventual result is to create an area of artificial grassland which cannot be cultivated in this way; but if the period between successive uses remains long enough, the system can continue permanently without damaging its own land base. This feature and its consequences, then, mean that fire agriculture requires a great deal of land per person, even though only a very small fraction of that land is under cultivation at any given time. The yield per man-day of labor under this system is roughly comparable to that of the traditional plow-farming system discussed below. However, the yield per acre in the long run is very much lower, because it must be taken into account that in any given year *at least* 80 to 90 per cent of the land is "resting"—the minimum may well be more like 95 per cent if this type of use is to be sustained for centuries.

The major departures from this system before the Conquest occurred in a relatively small area of Central Mexico, and in a much larger one in the Andes.

Irrigation had been developed in both. Only the Andean system will be considered here; the one in Central Mexico is not of major importance today, and was not at all similar to the Andean one.

The Andean system included extensive terracing of steep slopes. Entire mountainsides were in appearance practically converted into a series of stair-steps, and where irrigated the water was carried down from one level to another by gravity. Many of these terraces remain in use today—but the techniques for building them appear to have been lost.

The Andean foot plow is the characteristic implement in this system. In appearance, it more closely resembles an extremely heavy, small-bladed spade than a plow; in its effects, it is more like a hoe, and because of this the system is most commonly referred to as Andean hoe culture. It is an especially labor-intensive form of cultivation, involving continuous use of the same land in a well-developed rotation system. Because the same land is cultivated year after year, its yields per acre of usable land are many times as great as those characteristic of fire agriculture. Production per man-day of labor may be about the same in Andean hoe culture as in fire agriculture where the land in the former system is not fully irrigated, and somewhat higher where it is. The traditional Andean system, in only slightly-modified form, is still the major form of cultivation on steep slopes, whether terraced or otherwise, in much of highland Ecuador, Peru, and Bolivia.

With the Conquest, the Spanish and Portuguese introduced in the Western Hemisphere a system of farming which was already old in the Middle East at the time of Christ. This system involves permanent cultivation of the same land, based on the Egyptian plow drawn by oxen. The same plow is used to prepare the field for planting and to control weeds during the growing season. It is sometimes referred to as a rooting plow, in contrast to more modern turning plows, because it simply scrapes a small trench in the surface without overturning the soil.

Metal tools including the machete and the axe had been added to this system before it was introduced in the Western Hemisphere, but its main outlines had remained stable for centuries, and have remained so in the Americas during the four centuries since its introduction. This system of rudimentary plow farming is now the most common one throughout most of Latin America; it works with or without irrigation, on flat to moderately steep land, but not on extremely steep slopes. Yields per acre are low by modern standards, but they would be little if any higher with mechanized farming unless other changes were made along with those in the system of cultivation. Yields per man-day of labor are very low compared to those of mechanized farming, which has the primary effect of replacing human and animal labor with inanimate energy and more sophisticated tools, but they are roughly comparable to those obtained in fire agriculture and Andean hoe farming.

The type of "advanced plow" culture developed principally in the United States a century ago never has been significant in Latin America outside a few very limited areas. A change from the Egyptian plow to the metal turning plow, unaccompanied by other changes in the system, has been accomplished to some extent in a few parts of Latin America, most notably in Mexico, but this change alone does not make a major difference in the effectiveness of the system of cultivation. The lighter metal plow is somewhat easier to handle, and is more effective at weed control, but these advantages are offset by its greater effectiveness in inducing destructive soil erosion.

Mechanized agriculture based on the tractor and a large assortment of specialized implements used in conjunction with it has been adopted on many plantations and quite a few large prestige holdings all over Latin America. The effect of this change is to replace human labor, an especially abundant element now in rural Latin America, with capital, which is very scarce. Economically, mechanized farming may offer some advantage over traditional systems—how much, if any, depends upon the particular crop and the type of land. Socially, however, the desirability of further mechanization in the immediate future is highly questionable, given the existing situation with respect to alternative uses of capital and labor.

Seed improvement, fertilization, and irrigation. Present agricultural yields in Latin America are notoriously low, whether expressed on a man-day or an acre basis. The yield per man-day is low partly because so many man-days are required to produce each acre of crops; this is a matter of systems of cultivation. It is also low because the yield per acre, quite apart from the system of cultivation, is low when compared to yields in the industrialized countries. Parenthetically, it may be added that it is also low in comparison to the yield of Oriental agriculture, but for different reasons.

Yields per acre characteristically are low in Latin America because the traditional varieties of each crop grown are *not* high-yielding ones, and because fertilization, where practiced at all, usually is of a traditional variety which falls far short of being as effective as similar practices associated with scientific agriculture. In most parts of Latin America, failure to realize the full potential offered by irrigation could also be counted among the reasons for comparatively low yields, but the differences in this respect are much smaller than those previously mentioned.

Seed improvement and fertilization are the particular fields in which the greatest advances have been made in "industrialized agriculture" during the last fifty to sixty years. In reality, the comparatively low per-acre yields of Latin American agriculture are not so much the result of the use of seed varieties and fertilization techniques which are of low productivity when compared with other traditional agricultural technology, as they are the result of the fact that recent innovations in scientific agriculture have greatly increased yields in some other parts of the world—but have not been widely adopted in Latin America.

One reason that these technological innovations have not been more widely incorporated into Latin American agriculture is that they were developed in climatic regions which are very different from most of those to be found in the tropical portions of the Hemisphere, and biological reasons alone make it impossible to directly transplant many technological improvements of this sort. In addition, many cultural barriers impede technological improvements in the areas of seed improvement, fertilization, and irrigation, all of which involve direct adoption at the level of the individual farm. Here, cultural problems of the sort mentioned in connection with food habits, and economic factors related to the fact that many Latin American farmers live near the bare subsistence level, work together to discourage trying the unknown.

Viewed in broad perspective, many features of rural life in Latin America function to maintain the status quo. Traditional patterns of land use are reinforced by other features of the rural sub-cultures, especially by existing dietary patterns; the present land systems operate to discourage innovation in many ways; and the areas of agricultural technology in which improvements appear to be most desirable and feasible from the technical and macro-economic points of view are the very ones in which human resistance to change is likely to be greatest.

ACTION AREAS IN RURAL DEVELOPMENT[1]

The many types of specific activity which have been undertaken in the Latin American countries to promote development in rural areas may be grouped together in five general classes: (1) land reclamation and improvement (including irrigation); (2) colonization and settlement; (3) agrarian reform; (4) agricultural

---

[1] More detailed treatment of some of the points mentioned here, especially those relating to agricultural research and agricultural extension, is available in Moseman, *op. cit.,* and particularly in the articles there by Erven J. Long and F. F. Hill.

research and agricultural extension; and (5) rural community development. These classes overlap to some
extent in practice. Most experts in agrarian reform, for
example, believe that agricultural extension and the
provision of farm credit should be included in any land
redistribution or colonization project; and irrigation
commonly involves colonization on the newly irrigated
land.

Colonization and settlement refer to the establishment of agricultural population in areas which were
previously more sparsely inhabited. Although sometimes used when a large estate is subdivided and the
resulting units become separate farms which together
support more people than the original one, colonization
more commonly refers to the peopling of land which has
recently been reclaimed or improved, or which lies outside the densely-settled parts of a country. When
colonization and *settlement* are not used synonymously
—and they sometimes are—the first refers to the sponsored establishment of population on new land, and the
second refers to spontaneous movements of people onto
previously unoccupied land.

Agrarian reform. The Charter of Punta del Este
not only favors agrarian reform in principle, but
specifically sets transformation of the existing systems
as an objective of the Alliance. Mexico, Bolivia, Cuba,
and Venezuela had already carried out or started
substantial land reform programs in 1961, but further
efforts since that time have been disappointing. In 1964,
the Inter-American Economic and Social Council
appraised results of the first three years of the Alliance
in this respect in the following terms:[1]

> "... in general, efforts made to date have
> been insufficient to achieve the objectives of
> agrarian reform..."

---

[1] *Third Annual Meeting of the Inter-American Economic and
Social Council at the Ministerial Level: Final Report* (Washing-
ton: Pan American Union, OAS Official Records, Doc. OEA/
Ser.H/XII.9), Resolution 6-M/64, paragraphs 3-5.

"... expansion of agricultural production and colonization are not acceptable substitutes for agrarian reform, for, as the Charter of Punta del Este declares, reform must be directed toward the effective transformation of structures, eliminating unjust systems of ownership and exploitation of land."

Of all the objectives of the Alliance, those relating to agrarian reform are the ones which most directly attack the existing socio-economic systems and which call for the most fundamental changes in social organization. It is not surprising that the legal changes which must precede effective action have been slow in forthcoming.

Agricultural research and agricultural extension. The present agricultural extension system of the United States has evolved to its present form over a period of about a century as part and parcel of this country's system of family-size farms. Extension activities are closely interwoven with agricultural teaching and research in a cohesive system for developing agricultural technology and getting it into use on the country's farms. Most of the professionals involved in this system are themselves of agricultural origins, and the farmers toward whom extension efforts are directed are both highly educated and, as rural people go, very receptive to change.

The assumption at the beginning of United States technical assistance programs after World War II was that this country has a great store of technical knowledge in agriculture which could be transferred more or less directly to other countries. This assumption has since been proven incorrect, not only with respect to details of the knowledge itself but with respect to the methods of transmitting agricultural technology to farmers. The idea of agricultural extension has been appealing from the start in Latin America, but for several reasons it has never gone far in practice. One of these reasons is that scientific agriculture is adapted to the environmental conditions of the countries in which it was developed, and a large part of its technology does not work well on the tropical soils characteristic of Latin America. The Latin American countries themselves have not yet developed agricultural research activities to the extent required to support an extension system, and therefore the nascent agricultural extension services which have been established in Latin America have had little to offer local farmers that they could actually apply. Moreover, the professionals in even the agricultural fields in Latin America are drawn from the middle and upper sectors of society in most cases, and are separated from the people who actually work the land by a vast social distance and a lack of appreciation for their day-to-day problems. At the same time, those people have had little or no formal education, are fearful of and resistant to outside influences, and often live in such precarious economic conditions that they risk going hungry if they attempt a new technique and it fails. Only the large commercialized plantations can be reached easily by extension efforts at the present time, and these are the units on which the gap between actual and optimum technology is smallest.

Community development. There is no single clear-cut definition of community development. Generally, the term implies local grass-roots programs based on stimulating local people to get together to help themselves; it usually further implies a broad effort relating to more than one, and commonly to almost all, aspects of local life. It is not so much an action area, then, as a particular approach to development, and it is treated as such in Chapter 4.

The most effective community development projects in rural Latin America have been carried out in places where strong community organization and structure already exist. This is probably the basic reason that indigenous communities commonly have proven more responsive than mestizo communities of minifundistas.

Apart from activities which bring previously uncultivated land into agricultural use for the first time or provide irrigation water for previously unirrigated cropland, then, the major action areas in rural develop- ment are all subject to severe problems. Except for agrarian reform activities which were begun on domestic initiative before the Charter of Punta del Este was adopted, the programs which have been most suc- cessful in introducing important improvements in agriculture in most cases have been of very localized territorial scope, and too costly to permit simultaneous replication in most communities of any Latin American country.

On the other hand, important changes are taking place in the countryside. Small-scale agriculture gradually is becoming more commercialized, and rural people are selectively adopting some of the innovations to which they are exposed through better transportation facilities and the expansion of mass communications. One of the major tasks of planning in Latin America during the next few years should be to identify those matters in which the rural people of each region are most inclined to change in desired directions in their own right, and the actions which can be taken to stimulate and facilitate those changes.

URBANIZATION AND URBAN DEVELOPMENT[1]

The influx of rural people to the cities of develop- ing countries throughout the world has been the greatest

[1] I gratefully acknowledge the collaboration of Francis Violich in the preparation of this section. The monograph by him and Juan B. Astica, *Community Development and the Urban Planning Process in Latin America* (Los Angeles: UCLA Latin American Center, forthcoming, 1967) provides a much more com- prehensive treatment of these topics. A somewhat different ap- proach on a world-wide scale is available in Gerald Breese, *Ur- banization in Newly Developing Countries* (Englewood Cliffs; Prentice-Hall, Modernization of Traditional Societies Series, 1966). Citations in these two sources will lead the reader to the bulk of the recent literature dealing specifically with this subject.

spontaneous change associated with the development process since the end of World War II. In Latin America, this rural-to-urban migration is partly a response to an imbalance between rural population growth and the availability of developed agricultural land. Even though this great region is as yet sparsely populated, demographic growth in many individual rural communities has more than filled the land base actually available to the local people in terms of distance from the settlement and the control of local land rights.

Perhaps to an even greater degree, the movement of rural Latin Americans to the cities is a major tangible expression of the "revolution of rising expectations," the growing hope on the part of many for a better life than that of their parents. Advances in urban living are far ahead of those in rural areas, and this all-too-marked gap in meeting national development needs has made the cities symbols in the minds of rural people of the place for greater opportunities for the social change they strive to achieve. The cities offer educational, health, and other services which are not available in the rural communities and, above all, they offer hope for upward socio-economic mobility.

Large-scale migration to the cities, together with the population explosion, is having a major impact on urban areas, even though the rate of natural increase characteristically is higher in the countryside. In 1950, about 39 per cent of the population of Latin America lived in cities of more than 20,000 inhabitants; by 1960, this ratio had increased to 46 per cent, and it is estimated that by 1975 some 54 per cent, or 171 million of the expected 315 million persons in Latin America will be living in towns of that size or larger.[1] Expressed in another way and for one specific country, while the total population of Mexico increased by 35 per cent between 1950 and 1960, the number of people living in places with 2,500 or more inhabitants expanded 61 per cent

---

[1] *Economic Bulletin for Latin America*, 1961.

and the number in smaller places grew only 16 per cent.

The actual *rate* of growth of many of the smaller cities is considerably higher than that of the larger "primate" cities, even though the latter absorb the greatest number of migrants from the rural areas. For example, some smaller Venezuelan cities like Valencia and San Cristobal are growing faster than Caracas today, even though Caracas itself has tripled in population since 1940. A similar situation is notable in Brazil and some of the other countries. In this connection it is preferable to consider the processes of urbanization in Latin America in terms of the growth of whole systems of cities, more with relation to advancing regional economies and related regional transportation systems than with relation to the growing central cities seen as single entities. This is, of course, happening in varying degrees from one country to another, depending on size and degree of development.

During the last two decades a vast amount of economic expansion has taken place in many of the major Latin American cities or, more precisely, in the entire regions of which these cities are the focal points. São Paulo, Caracas, Bogotá, and Santiago are among the many examples. It is this actual growth, together with building booms that have accompanied it, that characteristically has attracted the migrants.

However, the number of migrants and their technical skills bear no relation to the number of workers that can be immediately and effectively absorbed by the urban economy. In a sense, the migration is a response to the expectation of future social and economic betterment, while in actuality unemployment and underemployment, in both overt and hidden forms, have become the problematic consequences of such migration in the rapidly expanding major cities of Latin America. Moreover, migrants are arriving in the cities at a rate faster than can be satisfactorily absorbed by the normal expansion of physical facilities to provide for their needs, especially with respect to housing, and as a result the old centrally-located slums—the *conventillos* and the *casas de vecindad*—have become more congested than ever, and mushrooming shacktowns like those that cover vast expanses of such metropolitan areas as Santiago and Lima have become characteristic of every capital city and of some of the other major centers throughout the region.

This expansion of urban population is a spontaneous component of the total development process, and in this restricted sense urbanization is a source of problems which call for solution through official policies and action. Yet urban development involves much more than either demographic growth or efforts to solve problems associated with it, or both of these together. It is one of the major sub-processes of development. As such, it is extremely complex—more so, perhaps, than rural development—and it involves vast social and economic changes which, while they originate in the cities, ultimately reach out to affect all segments of the society. Even if urbanization is viewed in its narrowest sense, to refer to the physical growth of cities, it is part of a complex process including interrelated changes of a social and economic nature. Here the term is used to refer to the entire process.

Because urbanization is so complex a system of change, a similarly complex procedure for decision-making must be established in attempting to plan for urban development. In this sense, urban and regional planning are directed toward establishing policies and organizing implementation programs into strategies, both long-term and short-term. Such strategies for decision-making and action attempt to guide the growth of urban socio-economic systems along lines which are considered desirable, at the same time that they seek to overcome existing features which are regarded as problems and to avoid or minimize the creation of such conditions in the future.

With respect to smaller cities and towns where there is more room for growth than in the already-congested major urban centers, urban and regional planning strategies can work toward developing sounder economies to attract new migrants. In this way, future pressure on the larger cities may in time be reduced, and development of the areas dependent upon the smaller centers may be stimulated.

When viewed in this light, planning for urban betterment is forced to look beyond the single city as an isolated agglomeration of population. It has begun to approach urban problems in regional terms—that is, it deals increasingly with whole *systems of cities*. In doing so, it is concerned with the relationships of cities to one another and to the hinterlands they serve, as well as the internal matters of each city.

Urban planning thus embraces a broad series of interrelated changes. Ideally it starts with the establishment of goals in economic and social terms, and works throughout with a series of interdependent elements. An industrial project, for example, may be planned as much on the basis of its influence on future urban growth as from the standpoint of its future contribution to the economy. Numerous types of projects, whether they are actually treated as integral parts of a comprehensive plan for urban development or, at the other extreme, are carried out in virtual isolation from efforts in other sectors, are specifically intended to improve conditions in a particular city. Many programs and projects in the health and educational fields, for example, are intended specifically to alleviate shortages of facilities in the urban slums. Of all the widely-recognized sectors, however, housing, now generally defined broadly to include all elements needed for satisfactory community life rather than mere shelter alone, is the one which is most typically urban in its focus, and in practice it is often the one around which most other efforts at urban development revolve.

Urbanization as a Social Problem

Shortages of physical facilities associated with the rapid growth of cities are so striking and so specific that

it may appear relatively easy to the uninitiated to conceive of measures to alleviate them. Yet, to the responsible and informed authorities, some of the more
ephemeral characteristics of urbanization have created
great concern. Increasingly, the needs for physical facilities are being approached in terms of the underlying social features related to them. Each social need calls for
some type of physical facility to serve it, and guiding
the urbanization process calls for an understanding of
both social and physical requirements—in terms of one
another.

Migration involves much more than mere movement from one place to another. Even the person who
moves from one city to another leaves behind him an
established network of social relationships through which
he has been accustomed to satisfying his material and
psychological needs, and, even if he already has friends
and relatives in the new place of residence, some time is
required to establish a complete new set of such relationships there.

More is involved than just finding a job and locat-
ing a good butcher: man is a social animal, and only
part of his dependence upon other human beings is of
an economic nature. One's more personal relationships
with others of his kind have a great deal to do with his
general state of contentment, and they are extremely
important in guiding his conduct along socially acceptable lines. Crime and delinquency rates often are higher
in populations in which the number of migrants is large,
and one reason is that the types of inter-personal relationships which ordinarily act to restrain disapproved behavior were broken by the migrants when they left their
places of origin and have not yet been fully re-estab-
lished. To what extent the symptoms of social disorientation and disorganization reach such extreme
pathological proportions among recent rural-urban migrants in Latin America is not yet clear, however.

The problems faced by the city-to-city migrant are
much less severe than those to which the rural-to-urban
migrant must adjust. One must establish a complete

new set of social relationships of the type to which he was previously accustomed; the other not only must establish a complete set of relationships, but he must also become accustomed to the less-personalized social system characteristic of urban life.

Moreover, the rustic finds it impossible, when he moves to the city, to continue to live as he did before; many of the needs he previously satisfied by application of his own labor to locally available resources must be satisfied by purchases in the market economy after he moves to the city. At the same time that he becomes more dependent upon others who supply him with goods and services in return for money, he must in another sense become more self-reliant because the kinship and other systems which carry out an informal social insurance function in the rural community are no longer so readily accessible if indeed they continue to function at all in this respect.

Nor is the rural migrant's ability to produce money income likely to increase markedly when he moves to an urban area: any specialized skills he possesses normally are those of agriculture or some rural handicraft industry, and therefore unmarketable in the city. The recent rural-urban migrant most commonly enters the city's labor market as an unskilled laborer, and whatever the shortages may be for highly-trained manpower, unskilled labor is a super-abundant element in today's labor markets throughout Latin America.

To some as yet unmeasured degree, the continuation of extended family relationships in the city[1] and the development of new bonds based on common place of origin, as exemplified in "regional associations" among new migrants to major cities,[2] serve accommodative

---

[1]See, in this connection, the works of Oscar Lewis resulting from his research with people from Tepoztlán in Mexico City, especially his *Five Families: Mexican Case Studies in the Culture of Poverty* (New York: Basic Books, 1959).

[2]Lewis, *op. cit.,* and William P. Mangin, "The Role of Regional Associations in the Adaptation of Rural Migrants to

functions which ease the change from rural to urban ways of life. Too often, the difficulties of accommodation, which are relatively well-known because they are easy to identify through theory developed in North America and Europe, are stressed to such a degree that more positive features characteristic of Latin American situations receive less attention than they deserve.

Not all migrants who leave the rural communities of Latin America go directly to the major metropolitan centers. To some extent, rural-urban migration takes place by stages. A farmer moves to a nearby market town, someone from there migrates to a larger regional center, and yet another person goes from there to the national capital. To what extent the rural-urban migration takes place in this pattern, rather than in the form of direct movement from rural community to major city, is uncertain. Some migrants from the countryside do move directly to metropolitan centers, and in some cases those from a particular rural community band together in the city and establish a miniature replica of the social structure of the rural community. Again however, the relative importance of the latter situation in the total migration pattern is uncertain.

Whether the new migrants to a metropolitan center come predominantly from smaller cities or direct from rural areas, the problems arising from rapid urban population growth through migration are numerous and complex. Those of a socio-cultural nature—unemployment and underemployment, crime and juvenile delinquency, illegitimacy and family instability, and disorientation and normlessness in general—are more perplexing to the authorities than those which can be attacked through the provision of physical installations. It is not surprising, then, that most efforts to deal with

---

Cities," in Dwight B. Heath and Richard N. Adams (eds). *Contemporary Cultures and Societies of Latin America* (New York: Random House, 1965), pp. 311-323 both deal with such associations.

urban problems in the early years of major population explosion in the metropolitan centers following World War II were concerned with providing housing and related services of a primarily physical nature.

No substantive reason makes it necessary, or even desirable, to treat housing primarily as an urban sector; unsatisfactory housing conditions, in fact, are characteristic of an even larger percentage of the rural than of the urban population of Latin America. For several reasons, however, most Latin American housing programs deal exclusively with urban areas. To the extent that rural housing problems are dealt with at all—and often they are not, because they are considered to be of such a magnitude and nature that available resources could make no appreciable difference—they are not even assigned to the regular housing agencies.

In a more positive sense, many of the problems which urban development activities are intended to alleviate are associated with overcrowded conditions in the cities, and this overcrowding is most pronounced with respect to residential facilities. Therefore, it is perfectly logical that efforts to provide acceptable housing and related services should form the core of most urban development programs.

Today, the most progressive housing programs in Latin America recognize that the provision of housing, seen as shelter alone, is no longer the main issue in urban areas. Rather, the provision of services and community facilities as the basic elements of urbanization has become a major feature of some recent housing projects, since the availability of these elements is expected to more rapidly induce social change and community formation and structuring. Emphasis is thus upon building a broader social framework within which there will emerge a motivation for securing better housing clearly identified with local requirements, and one which, it is assumed, will assure more gainful participation in the economic system in the long run.

Nature and Magnitude of
  the Urban Housing Problem

The arrival of migrants in Latin American cities at a rate greater than that at which new housing facilities have been produced has led to a situation approaching crisis proportions in many cases. Today, the magnitude of the housing problem alone is one of the region's most pressing development problems: it has been estimated that the inadequately housed urban poor account for about one out of every six Latin Americans, and that the elimination of the housing shortage during the next thirty years would require construction of about three million new dwellings per year. The precise manner in which "adequate" housing is defined has a major effect on statistics on the magnitude of the housing problem, but, whatever the definition, a very large segment of the urban population of Latin America is ill-housed *even by its own standards,* and the particular people involved are the very ones who have the least financial capacity to provide improvements for themselves.

Slums are of two distinct types in Latin America. Those of longest standing—the *conventillos, casas de vecindad,* and similar types of dwellings—are found in the the central parts of the major cities. They are not unlike tenement neighborhoods in other parts of the world. Most of the structures are now old, and the original dwelling units in them, which were far from satisfactory by modern standards when new, have deteriorated and have been subdivided so that the building now houses more families than it was intended to. "Sanitary" installations are shared by many families; often cooking facilities are shared, and sometimes even the same accommodations—which are not always beds—are used in turn by two or more shifts of sleepers.

The poorest of rural shacks could scarcely be as unsanitary or as crowded as the living quarters of the typical family of the central slums of a large Latin American city—yet it is in these areas that the typical new lower-class migrant first lives when he moves to the city. The population of the central slums, while unstable in the sense that these are way-stations for the newly-arrived poor, is probably quite stable numerically. These areas already are saturated, and if they are expanding at all, their growth is negligible when contrasted with that of the newer slums on the margins of Latin American cities.

The peripheral shantytowns are quite different from the tenements of the central city. Here, hundreds or even thousands of families have built improvised shelters of any materials at hand—scrap lumber, used bricks, or even flattened tin cans or cardboard cartons. The land on which they are erected belongs to others or to the government. Sometimes the shacks are built with the owners' prior knowledge and consent, but more often they simply appear without it. Sometimes such a settlement literally is created overnight: this is the organized *invasión*, in which a group formed in the central tenement areas quietly plans well in advance to occupy a given tract of land, assembles its materials, and, on a particular night, moves in.

When such settlements first began to appear on the outskirts of the major Latin American cities at about the end of World War II, it was widely assumed that their inhabitants were new rural-urban migrants. Recent studies have shown that, in some places at least, they typically have lived in the central slums of the same city for some time, and while living there have become acquainted with their future neighbors of the peripheral shantytown. That is, some elements of a new social organization appear *before* the *invasión* takes place. The migrant who, in his home community, took for granted the conventional web of social relationships of which he became a part from the day he was born, in the city may find himself actively and perhaps even somewhat consciously engaged in creating a new social organization for the specific purpose of carrying out an *invasión*. This dynamic quality which has emerged in connection with urbanization in Latin America suggests that a large potential for positive and constructive

social change may be inherent in the whole phenomenon of urban migration.

The move from central to peripheral slum represents
some improvement in living conditions.   This is true even
if the new quarters initially have to be supplied with
water hauled a considerable distance in trucks or carts,
and even though they are totally devoid of sanitary facilities.   Over the course of several years, however,
considerable improvement occurs.   As they are able, individual families make improvements in their own shelters and, in older neighborhoods of this origin, many
have built reasonably substantial permanent homes. Community organization within the shantytown, present in
at least nascent form from the time of the *invasión* or
even earlier, becomes stronger and, in many cases, it
soon gains sufficient influence to persuade the authorities to install water, sewer, and electrical services.
The shared desire for these facilities may, in fact, be
among the most important elements involved in producing
a strong enough community organization to attain them.

Initially, however, the peripheral slum is fully as
unsightly as that at the core of the city, and this plus the
growing use of automobiles for Sunday excursions by
influential Latin Americans perhaps did more to call
attention to the housing problem in the early postwar
years than the more miserable living conditions of the
central slums.   Without the strong political support
for housing improvement which had materialized in most
countries by the end of the 1950's, the responsible and
dedicated technicians of the housing authorities would
have had little opportunity to test their ideas in action programs.   As it became clear, during the 1950's,
that the squatter settlements had grown so large that
they could not conceivably be replaced by new housing
developments, there also developed a more realistic
approach to the social realities involved.

Early Housing Projects

The goverments of two Latin American countries
—Argentina and Chile—began to take official interest

in low-income housing just before World War I. Other countries joined in this movement in the 1920's and 1930's. The first efforts, although intended to benefit the lowest-income groups, produced housing more costly than those groups could afford, and the new dwellings actually were occupied by more prosperous families, usually representing the lower middle class. It was not until the 1950's that effective efforts were made to provide improved housing for those living in the worst slum conditions.

Early housing projects in Latin America—those of the 1930's and 1940's—were strongly influenced by the British, German, and Swedish pioneer efforts in this field which began after World War I. Often, these projects were too small in scale to effectively reduce building costs, and they provided for housing standards that were considerably above the level of living of the slum dweller. Furthermore, certain social considerations such as housing management programs, identification on the part of the resident with the design of the buildings, and relation to places of employment and cultural needs often were overlooked in favor of sheer architectural considerations.

By the 1950's, countries which, like Venezuela, Colombia, and Mexico, had established major housing programs earlier, realized that by resorting to building massive, large-scale housing projects in planned community settings, economies of scale would result and greater attention could be given to community requirements. This marked the beginning of the second major period in the Latin American housing movement, a period characterized in these countries and in others by projects of two types, both of which went further toward solving the problems than their predecessors in terms of physical planning and design, yet not far enough in terms of social organization.

One of these two types, particularly characteristic of Chile, consisted of mass-produced one story dwellings put together in colonies by the thousands. This type produced a low density of dwellings per block; the units were widely spread out horizontally. The other type was the multi-storied structure rising above the land with a very high density of dwellings per acre, and dependent upon vertical organization of communication and services. Venezuela particularly experimented with this type of housing on a large scale.

Neither of these types of project gave much attention to features other than those of the individual apartment as an independent unit. Selection of the new occupants of these structures was haphazard in terms of present criteria, and little or no attempt was made to create a new community structure among them. Often, one year's ambitious project was a new slum the following year: the people misused installations to which they were unaccustomed, and failed to show any interest in performing their own maintenance. Financial problems were severe in many cases, because so large a percentage of the beneficiaries of the project soon were in arrears that forclosure and expulsion of all those who were would have been politically unthinkable. A detailed post-project analysis was made of one of the largest projects of this type, the "Super-Bloques" of Caracas.[1]

The conclusions of this study are consistent with the results of studies of housing activities in other countries as well. Many of the residents of the Super-Bloques had recently migrated to Caracas from rural areas, and they were unequipped culturally, socially, and emotionally for urban life. Special guidance and orientation should have been provided for them, but it was not. Disinterest in maintenance could be ascribed in part to this, and also to the lack of any consistent management program or educational policies or incentives. Similarly, clearcut principles and standards necessary for the provision of adequate community facilities were lacking: schools were insufficient, employment was distant, and

---

[1] A brief summary of the complete report has been published by Eric Carlson as "High-Rise Management, Design Problems as Found in Caracas, Studied by International Team," *The Journal of Housing,* October 1959, pp. 311-314.

tenant associations which might have been created as an instrument to build moral and material responsibility and civic pride were completely omitted from the early operation of the project. This early experience in Caracas and the results of the follow-up study were instrumental in fomenting the greater emphasis now placed on these features in most countries, in fact.

The nature of the housing and the selection of tenants were themselves sources of some problems. A different type of housing, allowing greater variety of dwellings and therefore greater identification of the inhabitants with their own particular units, would have been more suitable on both social and economic grounds. By adapting the type of housing to the desires of the people themselves and providing for such individual identification, both Panama and Chile, for example, have successfully involved the future occupants in building their own dwellings. In the earlier experience in Caracas, more than eighty per cent of the families legally occupying apartments in the Super-Bloques had been moved forcibly into them from their former residences in hillside shacks. In general, these *"rancho"* dwellers of Venezuela and their counterparts in the *barriadas* of Peru, the *callampas of* Chile, and the *favelas* of Brazil prefer their shacks to government-built houses because of the greater freedom they enjoy in the improvised shelters they have built for themselves, and their greater opportunity for flexible community relationships.

More Comprehensive Programs

This experience in the 1950's has led to a far more comprehensive approach to the housing problem in more recent years. The work of CINVA, the Inter-American Housing Center in Bogotá, has had a major effect in introducing social considerations into housing programs. The whole architectural field in Latin America has broadened its point of view, and social scientists are becoming part of inter-disciplinary teams that now approach the housing problem in a concerted, interrelated way. Difficulties experienced in connection with early projects, in combination with increasing contact among Latin American housing experts and between them and similar experts from other regions where public housing activities are of longer standing, thus gradually led to changes which are still taking place in the entire philosophy of public housing programs in Latin America.

No longer is it considered sufficient to produce "four walls and a ceiling" with certain basic physical installations. The location of dwellings in relation to one another and in relation to external features came to be an important design element, and both it and internal features have become better and better adapted to lower-class living patterns. As increasing attention is paid to the people themselves, both for the design of facilities and for the selection of future occcupants, it becomes increasingly clear that the beneficiaries, with a minimum of guidance, can and will do some of the simpler work themselves. In addition, new designs make possible the construction of minimum basic units to which the occupants may later add improvements.

Gradually, the same type of community development approach previously applied in rural areas has become incorporated into urban development efforts, the most advanced of which no longer seek to provide only housing, or even carefully integrated physical installations of all types. They go a step further, and incorporate in their plans elements intended to produce a well-organized local social structure capable of mobilizing the resources of the local community to perform functions for its own improvement. To be sure, this approach still is far from universal, and there remains a great deal of room for improvement even in the latest projects in which it has been applied. Yet it has produced demonstrably greater benefits per dollar of public investment in housing than any other type of project. However, it does require some financial capacity on the part of the beneficiaries, and thus is inapplicable in dealing with the housing problems of typical new lower-class migrants to the city.

Urban Planning: *Problems and Prospects*

Public housing and city planning developed as parallel but separate fields. Both were accepted as a normal part of government activities intended to solve urbanization problems in Latin America. During the last few years, under pressure arising from these unsolved problems and recognition of their complexity, these efforts have converged in some measure in some countries—especially Chile, Colombia, Venezuela, and Brazil. Elsewhere, greater coordination would be advantageous.

Urban planning developed in Latin America as a specialized branch of architecture, and even today it is taught principally in schools of architecture. Concerned with the physical design quality of cities, its approach to urban planning was primarily oriented toward public works. Indeed, in many of the countries the first urban planning agencies were created within the Ministry of Public Works, and there—as in Chile, up to the recent formation of the Ministry of Housing and Urban Planning—a *plano regulador* was prepared for every major city in the country.

Few of these plans were based on adequate study of socio-economic realities. They bore little relation to public investment budgets and fiscal policies, they permitted little participation of the residents of a given city in the preparation of its plan, and very few of them were implemented in any systematic way as a part of a continuous process of local planning. Zoning controls over private development, together with building restrictions, have been non-existent or only loosely enforced in most countries. However, as the scale of urban development has increased, some of the more complex procedures of public administration are coming into use, and changes are occurring especially rapidly in this respect in the field of urban and regional planning in Latin America.[1]

---

[1]In the United States, the field developed quite apart from

After many years of limited effectiveness in any contemporary social sense, the field in Latin America is taking on a multi-disciplinary character. Changes have been especially rapid in recent years. Urban planning now involves many specialties besides architecture, and it has come to be concerned with many issues of the city other than those of a physical or similar nature.

Most urban planners in Latin America today are fully aware of the need for establishing long-range development policies that serve as guides for short-range public investment programs intended to bring about specific improvements each year. For example, new approaches to urban planning now being practiced in Chile are providing models by which major strides can be achieved throughout Latin America in identifying this field with the frontiers of social and economic change. The *plano regulador* is now being described as the "general development plan" and its components are concerned with the social, economic, and institutional aspects of urban development, as well as with the physical. These features in turn are closely tied to development at the regional level, and regional development in turn is tied to national urbanization needs. Thus, comprehensive urban and regional planning is taking the place of the earlier, more limited models, and is becoming directly involved not only in the formulation of long-range goals, but in the execution of programs and projects. Even today, it must forsee the time when seventy per cent of all Latin Americans will live in cities, so as to avoid the creation for future generations of problems which could be even greater than those of the present.

----

architecture. Rather, it was the pioneering among early landscape architects, civil engineers, and public administrators, all of them interested in municipal reforms, that led to the establishment of urban and regional planning as an interdisciplinary field from the outset.

INTEGRATION OF THE SECTORS

The subjects considered in this chapter do not exhaust the list of sectors and sub-sectors in which development programs and projects are designed and carried out, but they do include most of the principal ones. Maximum effectiveness of sectoral development efforts can be achieved only when there is close and effective coordination among the sectors, but such coordination is still lacking in the Latin American countries. Apart from this defect, there is considerable tendency for development action to be concentrated on features at the urban and national levels, without facing the problems of reaching the more traditional and rural segments of the economy and society because the costs are considered too high to solve these problems by direct measures. Yet observed changes in some aspects of rural life suggest that even highly conservative peasants may be quick to respond to new opportunities, provided they are perceived as advantageous and feasible.

The emphasis which has been placed on the creation of strong national planning organizations in recent years represents one set of efforts to achieve closer coordination and a better balance among action programs in the various sectors. Although some progress has been achieved along these lines, the obstacles are great because success would require that older agencies relinquish some of their authority to new planning organisms and that some long-standing inter-agency rivalries be resolved. Moreover, successful national planning depends, among other things, upon the effective formulation, selection, and execution of action programs and projects in sectoral agencies, and no Latin American country has yet developed a fully satisfactory capacity in this respect. In other words, a superstructure for planning has been created, but it cannot perform effectively until the corresponding substructure comes into being.

The advantages inherent in close coordination among sectoral programs become more readily apparent when one particular aspect of development is considered in the light of relationships between it and action programs in other sectors. The commercialization of traditional exchange systems and of the economy in general has been mentioned in several earlier sections, but has not been treated separately up to this point; it is an especially suitable topic for consideration in such terms.

Linkages between the traditional exchange systems of rural communities and the urban commercial super-structure are apparent at several points. Even the most self-sufficient rural people in Latin America are now dependent upon the outside world for some necessities; most communities receive factory-made clothing, or at least textiles, as well as tools, matches, and other less-frequently purchased items, from national commercial channels. In turn, their members obtain the money required to purchase these goods by selling food and other surplus local products which are consumed in the cities. Even in the present transitional systems, the rural and urban components are closely interdependent. Each small increase in the commercialization of the traditional external exchange system binds it more closely into an intricate web of commercial relationships at the national level and is associated with some further development, however small, in urban commercial institutions.

This commercialization does not take place as an isolated process, but is connected with many other aspects of development. Roads, for example, ordinarily are conceived of on the macro-economic level as infra-structure investments. As such, their primary aim is to join urban centers to one another and to outlying sources of raw materials. Through this, they stimulate industrial development by facilitating the supply of raw materials to factories, and by connecting urban centers with one another, they improve access to markets for the products of industry. However, roads necessarily pass through or near smaller towns and rural settlements between the cities. The rapidity with which people begin to make use of the bus and trucking services which appear almost as soon as a new road is opened suggests that the lack of adequate transportation may be the immediate factor which limits many types of rural change, change which is perceived as desirable, but without realistic hope of attainment before the improvement in transportation takes place. The emphasis in most Latin American countries still is heavily in the direction of completing and improving basic inter-regional and inter-city road systems, but even where feeder roads are lacking, first trucks and later buses reach out to communities near the basic routes wherever terrain and vegetation permit.

Commercialization of the traditional exchange systems, whatever the stimulus, is a gradual process which may be marked by occasional spurts in rate. It exposes the rural people to more and more potential innovations, and these additional changes in turn are often conducive to further commercialization and to ever-closer integration into the national economy and society through increasing participation in educational, health, political, and other national-level institutions. Like commercialization itself, many of these accompanying changes are conducive to changes in attitudes and values, and in social institutions and customs, in the direction of ever-increasing departures from the traditional mold and greater and greater similarities to the modernized societies of the more industrialized countries.

In a broader view of the sectoral approach to the development problem, commercialization of the exchange system is clearly a key element. Its linkages to some types of infrastructure are direct and obvious; to others, they are less so, but nonetheless present. Industrialization, whatever the temporal sequence, is connected to commercialization both through food requirements of industrial workers and through the marketing requirements inherent in large-scale production. As the traditional segments of the population become more and more integrated into the national society through commercialization and other processes, the national educational system comes to offer something more meaningful, not only as an avenue of upward social mobility, but also because the knowledge and skills it imparts come to be viewed as truly useful. Similarly, improved health and sanitation — perhaps desirable in the traditional situation, but beyond attainment — come to be viewed as attainable.

The different aspects of rural development are linked to commercialization in various ways. Traditional land systems involve many features which are potential limiting factors in commercialization, factors which may be diminished or removed through agrarian reform. The characteristics of traditional agricultural technology likewise may restrain commercialization— but the demands created by commercialization may prove to be the very stimuli which produce change in those characteristics.

Commercialization and its concomitants appear on both the cause and effect sides of urbanization. The development of the urban components of a national market system makes the city more attractive to the potential migrant from rural areas—and requires more urban population as an ever-greater percentage of the labor force is engaged in trade. But these changes, in turn, contribute to accentuating the set of urban problems which are the object of other types of development action.

Any sector could be examined in this light—with the same type of results. Change in any one is related in one way or another, directly or indirectly, to change in all others. Consideration of the development problem in terms of a sectoral approach thus does not detract from the view that development is an integral process. On the contrary, it reinforces this view and demonstrates that, if sectoral programs are to make their maximum possible contribution, each must be closely coordinated with programs in all other sectors.

CHAPTER 4

OPERATIONAL APPROACH

On the operating level, efforts to accelerate or guide the development process consist of a host of concrete actions, each accomplished at some specific place and time. A different principle is therefore involved in dealing with development operations than in abstract analytical study of development as a system of change, a whole which is greater than the sum of its various parts yet so complex that it must be subdivided into simpler units of study. Instead of analysis, synthesis is necessary to arrange the many individual actions of sponsored development into larger units which, while omitting much extraneous detail, make it possible to consider these efforts in relation to one another and to the total process.

Actually, highly specific actions of the type referred to here normally come into being as parts of more comprehensive efforts—projects which themselves are of a rather specific nature. The individual development project, in fact, is so specific that some further synthesis beyond the project level is indispensable in studying sponsored development, whether the purpose is to assure that resources are used as effectively as possible, or to examine in more academic terms the question of how efforts to sponsor development are carried out.

The same type of sectoral classification presented in Chapter 3 is widely used as a basis both for designing development projects and for grouping them together—synthesizing—into broader units. It is not the only possible classification for these purposes, however. Some projects are designed to involve coordinated action, at the project level, in several sectors simultaneously, and these projects of course will fit into a sectoral classification only if one or more cross-sectoral classes are created especially to accommodate them. If development action is considered in terms of a classification based on broad levels of social integration[1] instead of on the basis of a sectoral approach, almost all projects and programs fall very neatly into one or another of four broad classes:

1. Grass-roots development
2. Integrated regional development programs
3. Programs of national scope
4. Programs cutting across national boundaries, more specifically, when reference is to Latin America, those aimed at inter-American integration

Each of these classes is considered further in the pages that follow, with by far the greatest emphasis on the first two. Much that might be said in connection with programs of national scope already appears in Chapter 3, and only centralized planning of national development is considered here. International programs as such are scarcely more than mentioned in passing, for they either relate to efforts of types discussed elsewhere in this volume, or have to do with specialized economic matters of types which purposely have been avoided. The final section of the chapter and of the book returns to the question of the role of sponsored development within the total process.

---

[1] See "Locality Group Structure," pp. 51-54.

GRASS ROOTS DEVELOPMENT

The term used here to designate action of the type most commonly referred to as community development reflects past concentration of such efforts almost exclusively in rural settings, and particularly in agricultural villages. More recently, some of the same techniques have been applied in the slums of large cities, especially in Latin America but also in other parts of the world. Even though there are some major differences in orientation between rural and urban community development programs, this general approach is now important in both types of setting.

Community development may be interpreted in at least two ways: development of a strong local community where some elements of its organization are weak or lacking, or secondly, assisting a community to make improvements in local living conditions through its own efforts. Most community development programs have emphasized the second of these concepts, often almost to the exclusion of the first. Such programs have been most successful where the community already was well organized; where it was not, results often have been disappointing. Indigenous communities characteristically are among the strongest in this sense, and their importance in Mexico and in the Andean republics is one reason that the number of successful grass roots programs has been much greater in those countries than other parts of Latin America.

Behavioral scientists have been much more active in community development than in any other type of development action. Often they have served primarily as administrators, but even so their knowledge of behavior patterns and their sensitivity to problems of a social and cultural nature have resulted in the application to practical development problems of existing knowledge and belief in the social sciences to a far greater extent than has been characteristic in any other approach.

Typically, the grass roots program involves carefully coordinated efforts by a team of specialists seeking to introduce several different types of improvement simultaneously. There usually is considerable flexibility 'in adapting actions to the felt needs of the local people in such a way that the program, in fact as well as in theory, may be designed to help those people bring about changes which they themselves strongly desire. Herein lies much of the strength of the grass-roots approach. Its weaknesses are that well-trained social scientists are scarce and the per capita costs in both money and skilled manpower are rather high. Specialized training aimed at transmitting the required skills rapidly to middle-level field personnel has been partially successful in overcoming the first of these problems, but as yet little progress has been achieved in developing programs which have a widespread effect on the national scale, or in creating linkages between such programs and those of other types so that the various kinds of development action may become mutually reinforcing.

On a strictly local level, it is easy for community development workers to become so absorbed in their efforts to achieve near-term material objectives that they lose sight of the more lasting benefits which would arise from developing an organization and spirit through which the local people will continue to make improvements on their own behalf long after the outsiders have departed. Some grass-roots programs work intensively in a given community only a short while—two or three years—before being terminated or moving on to a new site. Those which move on to other communities nearby are able to follow results and to continue to provide assistance, although at a much less intensive level, where they worked before. This provides a valuable element of continuity which could be decisive in encouraging the local people to make new efforts on their own behalf; it also facilitates longer-term evaluation of response to project efforts.

Perhaps the greatest handicap of all in grass-roots development in Latin America, whether viewed on the local or some broader level, is that the local government

characteristically is almost powerless either to finance or
to administer development action. Even where community organization is strong for some purposes—for example, for conducting the traditional festivals or keeping the
local trails open—and where mutual aid practices are important at the neighborhood level for such things as building houses and tending crops, the county-level governments—municipios in most Latin American countries—
are unaccustomed to taking action on their own account
to bring about local improvements. They generally do
not collect enough taxes to finance any substantial efforts, and in some of the countries they are not even legally empowered to do so. The local initiative which
has contributed to the success of past community development work in Latin America only rarely arises in
the local government.

No effort is made here to present a survey of all
community development activities in Latin America. Instead, the number of specific cases considered has been
kept at a minimum, to make it possible to deal with each
in more detail than otherwise would be possible. All
of the three relating to rural community development
are drawn from the Andean Highlands, and are dealt
with in terms of a broader effort directed at integration of
the indigenous population of the entire region into
the respective national societies.

The Andean Indian Program[1]

The highland region from Colombia to northern
Chile was the home of the Inca Empire, one of the more
advanced civilizations of the entire world at the time
of European contact. Today, this same area is one

[1]The literature on the Andean Indian Program and efforts
related to it is vast. This section is based primarily on sum-
maries in recent mimeographed papers which, unfortunately, are
not widely available: Carlos d'Ugard, "Experience in the
Andean Region," in Inter-American Development Bank, *Community Development* (Mexico: VII Meeting of the Board of

of the most backward in the Americas. Per capita income is extremely low, death and disease rates are high,
and literacy is unusual. Predominantly Indian in race,
many of the people of the Andean Highlands speak only
the language used by their ancestors at the time of the
Conquest. Everything about their lives is strongly
oriented toward local affairs; relatively few are more
than dimly aware of the existence of the nation in which
they live as a territorial or socio-economic unit.

The way of life of the rural people is remarkably
homogeneous throughout the region. The indigenous
economy is based on a combination of farming and
grazing. Cultivation takes place in extremely small
plots, either by the traditional system of Andean hoe
culture (pp. 141-142) or with wooden plows drawn by
oxen. The same basic patterns prevail both in independent indigenous communities and on the large
estates, where the Indians live in *colono* arrangements
(pp. 133-134) and, in addition to tending their own
crops and herds, work several days a week on the land
operated on behalf of the estate for token wages at best.

One feature of major significance for community
development is that in pre-Columbian times, the Indian
commoners worked in not-strictly-voluntary community
work parties to carry out public works of benefit for the
local community and for broader levels of the political
organization. This custom continued, with modifica-

Governors of the IADB, April 1966) Section AB-52-7; Henry
F. Dobyns, Paul L. Doughty, and Allan R. Holmberg, *Peace
Corps Program Impact in the Andes: Final Report* (Ithaca:
Cornell University, Department of Anthropology, Cornell Peru
Project, 1966), which is referred to in in-text citations here as
"Cornell Report;" and International Labour Organization, *Panel
of Consultants on Indigenous and Tribal Populations,* First Ses-
sion, Geneva, 15-26 October 1962, Second Item on the Agenda,
"Appraisal of the Achievements of the Andean Indian Pro-
gramme" (ILO Doc. PCITP/1962/1/2). Recent statements in
English, which are more easily accessible but unfortunately are
limited to the Vicos and Pillapi programs, appear in Arthur H.
Niehoff, *A Casebook of Social Change* (Chicago: Aldine
Publishing Company, 1966), pp. 42-76.

tions, in the colonial period. In many places it remains in use today, even though it is no longer channeled through the formal political organization.

Efforts to integrate the Andean Indians into the national culture, largely through grass-roots programs, are of major concern in the development of all the Andean republics. While the planning and execution of projects to accomplish this is a national responsibility in each country, the various national undertakings are linked together by a broader effort, the Andean Indian Program, which provides technical assistance and, through the exchange of information and experience, a certain amount of informal coordination among the national programs. Initiated in Bolivia, Peru, and Ecuador between 1954 and 1956, this program has since been expanded to include Colombia and the northern parts of Argentina and Chile. Together, these areas have an indigenous population of about seven million, making this program the farthest-reaching community development effort in the world. It merits consideration if only because it includes so large a part of all community development work in Latin America; it is even more worthy of study for the lessons of experience it offers.

The large territorial scope of the Andean Indian Program is matched by the variety of agencies which, formally or informally, collaborate in its efforts. The International Labour Organization, a specialized agency of the United Nations, is responsible for general coordination; three other specialized agencies—the FAO, UNESCO, and the World Health Organization—participate in their own fields, and the United Nations Special Fund, UNICEF, and the World Food Program have taken part in financing particular projects. The various national agencies involved have been encouraged to make use of the bilateral and regional international assistance available to them, and the Organization of American States, the Inter-American Development Bank, the U.S. Agency for International Development, and the Peace Corps, among official

bodies, all have been involved in one way or another.
Even a major university in the United States, Cornell,
has concentrated much of its research effort in Latin
America on one community development operation closely connected with the Andean Indian Program. On
the national level, a variety of agencies representing a
number of sectors participate, but few effective linkages
have been established between the community development efforts related to the Andean Indian Program, and
the conventional projects of the sectoral agencies.

The objectives, working methods, technical and administrative organization, and systems of financing are
similar among all of the national programs. The topical
scope of these programs is as comprehensive as the
Andean Indian Program's territorial coverage and their
support by national and international agencies, but all
components focus on the same central objectives: "to
promote an increase in labor productivity and an improvement in the standard of living of the indigenous
rural populations, with a view to their progressive integration into modern society" (d'Ugard, p. 5). The specific fields of activity include agriculture, stock raising,
forestation, vocational training, handicrafts and small industry, agricultural and consumers' cooperatives, food,
housing, home improvement, health, education, community organization, recreation, infrastructure works,
and community services. Not all of these are necessarily represented at any one locality, of course. As of
1966, field programs were being carried out in 31 areas,
many of which include several individual communities.
About 250,000 rural Indians are directly affected by
these projects, and it is estimated that about 430,000
others live in areas which receive indirect benefits.
That is, on the order of one-tenth of the Andean Indian
population is now being reached directly or indirectly
by the program.

In brief, then, this is a comprehensive program extending throughout a major cultural region made up of
parts of no less than six nations. Many national and in-

ternational agencies take part, but the individual projects all have the same general objectives and all follow
the same general patterns. Only one project of the Andean Indian Program itself—Pillapi—is considered here.
Two others related to it, the Vicos Project and the work
of a Peace Corps group at Cuyo Chico, offer somewhat
different types of experience in the same general type
of setting.

The Pillapi Project.[1] One of the first efforts of the
Andean Indian Program was initiated at Pillapi, Bolivia near the southern end of Lake Titicaca, in March,
1954. The Revolution of 1952 was only two years in
the past, and there was still a great deal of unrest in the
countryside. Large landed estates were making little
or no effort at crop production and, indeed, the cropland
of some had been appropriated by the colonos for their
own use. The Agrarian Reform Decree of 1953 had
been in force only seven months, too little time to have
become effective.

The Pillapi estate on which the project was established consisted of nine "farms" with a total area of
10,800 hectares, of which about 3,100 were cultivated.
Some 500 Aymará Indians lived on Pillapi as colonos,
and cultivated about 250 hectares on their own behalf.
The estate was well-stocked with machinery and pure-
bred livestock, and was considered advanced although
yields were low even by local standards. Before the Revolution, it produced large quantities of potatoes, meat
animals, butter, cheese, and wool for the market; it was

---

[1] The summary on the early experience of this project is
based on Lorand D. Schweng, "An Indian Community Development Project in Bolivia," *América Indígena*, Vol. XXII, No. 8
(April 1962), pp. 13-19, reprinted in Niehoff, *op. cit.*, pp. 44-57,
with comments on pp. 42-43. Schweng was director of the project
in its first two years of operation, and these sources refer only to
that period. Information on later experience at Pillapi is drawn
from d'Ugard, *op. cit.*, from the *Social Progress Trust Fund:
Third Annual Report, 1963* (Washington: Inter-American Development Bank, 1964), pp. 19-20 and 154-156; and from I.L.O.,
op. cit.

already connected to La Paz, 88 kilometers away, by
both road and railroad.

The owners of the Pillapi estate donated eight of
their nine farms to a "Foundation for the Development
of the Andean Peoples" the month before the project
was established. A Bolivian organization with official
backing, the Foundation had just been created to promote the cultural and economic development of the Indians. The owners retained title to the central farm and
the headquarters house, but the Foundation was to enjoy
the use of the headquarters buildings for a fixed period,
during which it was to operate the central farm for the
mutual benefit of the owners and itself. The Pillapi Project was then established at the invitation of the Foundation.

Soon after taking over, the ILO expert in charge
of the project filed a petition to have the provisions of
the Land Reform Law applied to the estate, but actual
application was beset with difficulties. The colonos on
three of the farms refused to admit the technical commission sent by the Government to prepare the required
plans, and even after plans had been prepared and ap-
proved by the authorities, the Indians would not observe
them. A substantial area technically became the property of the Foundation, but its control was tenuous even
over the outlying buildings of the hacienda headquarters. As far as implementation of the legal provisions
for land redistribution was concerned, the project was
viewed with hostility by the Indians, who considered it
an agent of the original owners because of the nature of
the arrangements with them. The project appears to
have been beset with a continuous series of conflicts and
readjustments over land rights and their redistribution
during the first two years of its existence, and perhaps
because of this the evaluations by Niehoff and Schweng
are characterized by neutral to negative overtones.

Nevertheless, some success was achieved in other
respects. Producers' cooperatives were established on
the land of each of the six farms which at least nominally were operated by the project. The plots operated

individually by the Indians were strongly subsistence-oriented and produced virtually nothing for sale, but the cooperatives were intended to yield cash income for the local people at the same time that they contributed to solving the shortage of domestically-produced food for Bolivia's urban population. To be sure, this effort too involved some difficulties. Suitable leaders were lacking, because most campesinos were illiterate and those who were not lacked other leadership qualities. The project attempted to collect thirty per cent of the production to offset the cost of the services it performed for the cooperatives, but found that the best it could do was to obtain reimbursement of its direct out-of-pocket expenses for specific services. In spite of these and other difficulties, however, the area cultivated on a co-operative basis expanded from only 142 hectares in the first year to 600 in the second. Two of the larger coop-eratives, on their own inititive, purchased tractors with the proceeds of the sale of their crops in the spring of 1956, and began doing contract work for others. Even though the project was almost immediately successful in promoting cooperatives to cultivate the estate's cropland, however, the Indians could not be persuaded to partici-pate in the government's program for cooperatives or to start a cooperative dairy farm using the buildings, equip-ment, and even some animals of the former estate. Niehoff (p. 43) comments:

> "The idea of co-operatives was not at all contrary to the values of the Indians so long as these were truly advantageous and as long as the Indians could participate fully in planning and running them. In fact, in those co-opera-tives where their interests were truly served, the Indians took the initiative...."

Efforts in the field of health were less successful. Previously, there had been no scientific medical services at all on the estate, but the project established a small dispensary and stationed a doctor and two nurses at

Pillapi. Initial efforts emphasized preventive rather than curative medicine, and included a house-to-house health and family survey. The recipients of this aid resented what they regarded as useless and inquisitive questioning, and did not understand why those who appeared to be healthy should be molested by the health personnel. In brief, the campesinos preferred their own healers to the medical doctor, and this part of the project's initial efforts was suspended almost as soon as it started.

Education was much better received, although there was some friction between the project and the teachers provided by the Government, and the schools were seriously handicapped by their use of Spanish instead of Aymará, the only language spoken by many of the local people and the one used universally in their homes.

> "After the first school was built in 1955 at the expense of the project, the other schools were built by the *campesinos* themselves. They made the adobe bricks, levelled the ground, dug the foundations and provided all the unskilled labor. The project furnished the plans, provided supervision and the services of a mason and a carpenter, bought the material that could not be produced locally and had it transported to the building site in each instance.
>
> "In the school year 1954-55 the number of enrolled pupils was 113. In 1955-56 their number rose to 479, of whom 190 were adults attending evening literacy classes. Some 350 pupils attended school regularly and 290 completed the courses. In 1956-57 enrollment remained at about the same level. It was estimated that about 70 percent of the children of school age were attending school. The ratio was much higher for boys than for girls." (Schweng, in Niehoff, p. 54)

In its first two years, then, the Pillapi project provided some successes—none of which was without complications—and some serious disappointments. Its

radius of action did not then extend beyond the limits
of the six farms of the former estate which accepted its
attentions, although after 1956 it began to operate in
other communities nearby. It did not immediately spark
of a number of "little Pillapis" and itself become a training center for workers who would carry its ideas all
over the Altiplano of Bolivia during this period, as had
been hoped.

Schweng's account ends as of 1956, when he was
replaced with an Aymará-speaking director; he himself
attributes the early difficulties of the project in part to
the need for its personnel to rely upon interpreters, most
of whom had been foremen on the former estate, for
communication with the local people. The general tenor
of one's impression, gained from Schweng's article, is
that the project

> "...can be viewed as having limited success
> primarily because of the powerful vested inter-
> ests existing, the lack of good communication
> techniques by the innovators, and their failure
> to use the existing motivations for change or
> the potential leaders. There does not appear
> to be any simple solution that would have
> helped save this project...." (Niehoff, p. 43)

Nevertheless, the Pillapi Project remains in operation today. It has, in fact, become one of the most important centers in Bolivia's expanding community development program and has had effects reaching beyond
the borders of that country not only through the Andean Indian Program, but also through an OAS-spon-
sored training program in rural community development
started there in 1963. The experience gained in Pillapi
and two other centers established in Bolivia in connection
with the Andean Indian Program served as a basis for
the country's ten-year rural development plan prepared
in 1962 and the two-year action program drawn up
within the framework of that plan the following year.
The 1962 plan calls for establishing a total of fifty centers similar to that at Pillapi, and the action program

was to expand the centers already in existence at Pillapi and Otavi, on the Altiplano, to start one new one at Paracaya, in the Cochabamba Valley, and to establish two others at places which were yet to be selected.

It therefore appears that the Pillapi Project has been reasonably successful in the long run, even though there was some room for doubt about its future after it had been in operation for only two years. This suggests that, at least in certain circumstances, it is necessary to view community development as an extremely long-range type of effort—the impact of Pillapi and other efforts in the Bolivian Altiplano, after a dozen years, has been minor if not entirely negligible outside their immediate areas of operation. Their principal result in national terms has been to establish a sound basis for a broader program which itself will take many more than the ten years of the rural development plan to introduce truly major changes in the level of living and other aspects of the way of life of the local people. This raises serious questions concerning the value of shorter-range efforts that are not carefully integrated into broader, continuing programs to influence the same communities.

The Vicos Project is the most widely known community development effort in the world. It has been reported upon to the general public of many lands through a popular magazine,[1] and the bibliography of the professional literature on it has become voluminous.[2]

---

[1]L. Stowe, "Miracle at Vicos," *Reader's Digest,* Vol. 82 (April 1963), pp. 222-226.

[2]Recent items which contain references to many earlier works include Allan R. Holmberg, *et al.,* "The Vicos Case: Peasant Society in Transition," Special Issue. *The American Beheviorial Scientist,* Vol. VIII, No. 7 (March 1965), which is quoted below with the permission of the publisher; Dobyns, Doughty, and Holmberg, *Peace Corps Program Impact in the Peruvian Andes, op. cit.,* includes an extensive bibliography. Two articles first published in 1962 are reproduced with comments in Niehoff, *op cit.,* pp. 58-76.

Its purpose and methods were quite different from those of the Pillapi Project, and it did not form part of the Andean Indian Program as such. However, it worked closely with that program and the national program in Peru which is operated in conjunction with it, and, since completion of the original project, Vicos has become one of the four centers of operations of the national program.

The Vicos project itself was conducted jointly by Cornell University and the Government of Peru, more as a research project than as an effort directed primarily toward promoting change for its own sake. The spirit behind it is best shown through the words of its founder, Allan R. Holmberg:

> "In the natural sciences, research and development are inseparable. Scientific discovery is sooner or later inevitably put to the test of success or failure through the application of research results in engineering and technology. Research and development work in behavioral science are seldom joined as they were to some extent in Vicos, for the systematic exploitation of their reciprocal benefits. To get the feedback necessary for rapid advance in a behavioral science like anthropology, policy is needed, even if policy does not need science."[1]

Thus Vicos was designed more to learn, than to serve as a model community development project which might be replicated over a large area. The resources involved per inhabitant, especially in the form of highly-trained anthropologists, would, in fact, make it impossible to carry out such intensive projects in more than a few dozen of all the world's localities at any one time.

Vicos was an Andean hacienda owned by a Peru-

---

[1] Quoted in John Lear, "Reaching the Heart of South America," *Saturday Review*, Nov. 3, 1962, pp. 55-58 and reprinted in Niehoff, *op. cit.*, pp. 60-67.

vian "Public Benefit Society" and rented out on a ten-year lease to a private operator. This particular hacienda was not a profitable one for the operator who, in fact, had gone bankrupt halfway through the period of his lease. Holmberg, a young American anthropologist, was then in Peru on behalf of Cornell University to study the impact of industrial civilization on agrarian communities. He knew of the situation at Vicos and, when the opportunity to sublet the hacienda for five years presented itself in 1952, he was eager to seize upon it to conduct

> "an experimental program of induced technical and social change which was focused on the problem of transforming one of Peru's most unproductive, highly dependent manor systems into a productive, independent, self-governing community adapted to the reality of the modern Peruvian state." (Holmberg 1965, p. 3)

Arrangements were made with the Institute of Indigenous Affairs of the Government of Peru to make the experiment a joint venture between it and Cornell University, and the Cornell Peru Project at Vicos became a reality.

A Peruvian anthropologist already was conducting a very detailed study of this particular estate when the project began, and several months were spent drawing up a plan of operations before the project assumed operation of Vicos. This plan

> "was focused on the promotion of human dignity rather than indignity and the formation of institutions at Vicos which would allow for a wide rather than a narrow shaping and sharing of values for all the participants in the social process. The principal goals of this plan thus became the devolution of power to the community, the production and broad sharing of greater wealth, the introduction and diffusion of new and modern skills, the promo-

tion of health and well being, the enlargement
of the status and role structure, and the formation of a modern system of enlightenment
through schools and other media. It was
hoped that by focusing on institutions specialized to these values as independent variables
this would also have some modernizing effect
on the more dependent variables, namely, the
institutions specialized to affection (family and
kinship) and rectitude (religion and ethics),
which are sensitive areas of culture in which it
is generally more hazardous to intervene directly." (Holmberg 1965, p. 5)

Because of the earlier research, it was not necessary
to spend a prolonged period studying the local situation
before taking action. The colonos already were permitted to cultivate small plots of the hacienda's
land to produce their own food crops, and to pasture
their animals on its range. In return, each family
was required to furnish one *peón* to work for the
hacienda three days a week at a nominal wage
of about three cents a week, a wage which had not
been paid for about three years. There was not even nominal pay for the domestic and similar services performed
for the hacienda headquarters. The system is typical of
Andean estates. The most important complaint of the
serfs against it involved their obligation to provide free
services to the manor, not the requirement that they furnish a peón for three days a week.

Because the project, like any patrón in similar circumstances, was in a position of near-absolute power, it
was able to make a strong start by replacing the system
of compulsory domestic services with one of voluntary
paid services, and further to weaken resistance by ob-
taining from the former operators and itself paying to
the Indians the back wages which were due them.
Through such relatively small changes, and the collaboration of the Peruvian anthropologist who had been
studying Vicos and was known to and trusted by almost

every one of the 380 families of the community, the project was able to overcome almost immediately much of the suspicion and hostility normally directed toward the patrón.

The Vicos project began at a time when the goal of increasing agricultural productivity was especially meaningful to the community: the potato crop had just failed due to blight, and many of the poor were actually starving. Yet the land was in bad condition after decades of exploitation, and the project controlled no funds for capital investment.

In consultation with the Indian leaders, it was decided that no immediate changes would be made in the day-to-day operations of the hacienda. However, instead of being removed from the area as had previously been done, the profits were retained in the local community. There, they were used primarly to improve productivity by introducing the use of fertilizer, pesticides, improved seed stock, and more effective practices in general. Part went to construct health and educational facilities, to develop a wider range of skills among the Indian population, and to reconstruct the previously abandoned administrative center of the estate. The same techniques initiated on the hacienda's cropland were soon adopted by the Indians on their subsistence plots.

Economic improvement was one area of interest in the project. The diffusion among the populace at large of the power which had been concentrated in the patrón, and the development of effective leadership mechanisms within the community itself, were even more important. The existing Indian leaders—officeholders in the traditional internal civil-religious hierarchy of the community (see pp. 35-37, 47) —were so occupied with religious affairs during their terms of office that they were considered unsatisfactory for accomplishing the transfer of power to the community itself. It was decided that the hacienda foremen would be more suitable for this purpose, in spite of the disadvantages of their position in the hacienda power structure and the fact that all incumbents were old and therefore more resistant to innovations than younger men would have been. Over the years, retiring members of this group were replaced by appointing younger men more committed to the goals of modernization.

At the end of the project's five-year sub-lease, decision-making and other skills had developed to such an extent that responsibility for the affairs of the community was largely in indigenous hands. At that point responsibility was shifted to a ten-member council, elected annually by the people instead of being appointed by the project, and the community began renting the estate on its own behalf. Five years later, after considerable difficulty, the community purchased the land; thereafter, the project's role was only of a research and advisory nature.

The Vicos project did not produce spectacular changes in many of the material elements which commonly are stressed in development. The people still live in adobe huts without bathrooms and drink impure water. However, changes in agricultural technology have increased their production. They have enough to eat, and their commerce with the outside world, formerly minimal, has become substantial. And especially, they have become economically independent, responsible for their own affairs, and accustomed to working together for their own benefit.

Other communities nearby have been enthusiastic over the social and economic results achieved at Vicos. The Peruvian community development and educational program started in Vicos in conjunction with the Cornell Peru Project has subsequently been extended to nine nearby communities, and the Vicosinos themselves have begun to furnish technical assistance to their neighbors. Thus, even though it was not designed as a pilot project for widespread replication, or even primarily to produce change, the Cornell Peru work at Vicos was a successful community development project in the sense that changes it introduced were institutionalized and are now diffusing to surrounding communities. Little by little, its scientific results are being applied in more conventional grass-roots programs, not only in the Andes but throughout the world.

The Peace Corps. The Andean Indian Program is an especially propitious setting for Peace Corps activity, for it offers an opportunity to incorporate the two-year tours of service of individual volunteers into longer-range efforts in such a way as to make maximum possible use of the lessons of past experience and to provide a strong element of continuity of action in particular groups of communities. Even where no conscious effort is made to do so, the fact that the volunteers work within the framework of a continuing program in the immediate areas in which they serve, and at least informally learn something of past experience there, probably has an important effect in this direction.

One Peace Corps research project, conducted under contract by Cornell University, evaluated the performance of the third group of Peace Corps volunteers sent to Peru.[1] This group of about sixty volunteers arrived there in 1962, very little later than the first two groups. It received its training at Cornell, and many of its instructors themselves had taken part in the field work of the Vicos project, which in turn worked in close collaboration with the Peruvian agencies and individual experts involved in the Andean Indian Program. Therefore, it may be assumed that these volunteers received the best possible substantive and area-studies instruction which could be made available to them at the time of their departure, within the time limitations of their training period.

In Peru, these volunteers were assigned to particular communities within the four areas in which the Peruvian National Plan for Integration of the Aboriginal Population (PNIPA) operates departmental (major administrative division) sub-programs. One of

---

[1] Dobyns, Doughty, and Holmberg, *op. cit.,* is the final report of this project.

these is the Cuzco Program, which was established in 1959 as a cooperative venture between the PNIPA and the University of Cuzco to apply in another densely populated Andean area the experience of the Vicos Project and of the Puno-Tambopato departmental program. Originally planned to conduct research and to promote improvements in the local economy, education, recreation, homemaking, and sanitation, the Cuzco Program has its principal operations in Cuyo Chico, some 32 kilometers from Cuzco. This village of less than 400 inhabitants was selected because its zone of influence extends over several neighboring communities, and because it can be reached fairly easily from Cuzco.

In all, nine volunteers were involved in the program in and around Cuyo Chico, not counting two stationed in Pisac, a larger center nearby.[1] Their individual performance levels seem to have varied over a wide range. One girl, Carmen (the names are disguised), a teacher who spoke Spanish fluently on arrival, took part in a great many activities, collaborating with fellow volunteers, Peruvians of the Cuzco Program, and local people. At the other extreme, four men are merely mentioned in passing in the Cornell evaluation—Clem, Clyde, Curt, and Conrad, who left Peru a year ahead of schedule. Parker, an experienced farmer and one of the most effective volunteers at Cuyo Chico, was transferred there from the Puno-Tambopato area after the original group had been in the field several months. The other two volunteers, Carol and Charles, appear to have performed well in their respective activities, although their efforts were limited to a smaller range of

---

[1] The Cornell Report, in its introductory statement on the Cuzco Program (p. 114), indicates that seven volunteers were assigned to Cuyo Chico to reinforce the Peruvian staff, and that three of those were reassigned immediately. However, in describing the work done by Peace Corps volunteers, the report (pp. 117-126) mentions nine including the three who were reassigned at the beginning of the period but who later returned to Cuyo Chico.

undertakings than Carmen's. Four other volunteers, including Cecilia, who worked out of nearby Pisac and made considerable impact by supervising a school pupil feeding program in thirteen localities, are mentioned in connection with work in the Cuzco region, but outside the immediate vicinity of Cuyo Chico; they are not considered here.

Four of the nine volunteers at Cuyo Chico were of questionable effectiveness. There is nothing in the Cornell report to suggest whether the reason was related to selection, training, assignment, orientation in the field, or some combination of shortcomings. The other five, however, appear to have performed remarkably well for this early stage of Peace Corps history, and the Cuyo Chico group as a whole may well have been one of the most productive ones, not only among the various subgroups which comprised this operation in Peru, about which the Cornell report leaves little room for doubt, but in all Peace Corps operations in Latin America to date. Enthusiasm and dedication, which unquestionably are indispensable in this type of operation, with or without salary, apparently were combined in these five cases with a sincere desire to cooperate with national technicians as well as with the local poor and with one another, a certain reasonable minimum level of technical competence, and some development of capacities of adaptability, initiative, and responsibility.

Carmen's principal activity during the first six months of her assignment was to organize and teach sewing classes in Masc'a, a ten minute walk from Cuyo Chico, using a treadle-operated sewing machine furnished by the Cuzco Program. Forty women registered, and thirty actually attended the classes during this six-month period. Carmen bought cloth and thread to start instruction. but thereafter her students bought their own supplies. When Carmen took up her teaching assignment in the Cuyo Chico school, the instruction was transferred to one of the Cuzco Program's regular workers stationed in Cuyo Chico. The latter was unwilling to walk to Masc'a to give classes, however, and only ten of the students continued.

The Cuyo Chico school previously had never offered more than the first two grades. At the start of the new school year in April, 1963, Carmen started a third-grade group with eleven pupils, introducing many innovations in teaching methods and so impressing her superiors that she was taken to Pisac to demonstrate classroom techniques in the Cuzco Program's "nuclear school" there. Because there normally is serious regression in the level of learning of rural Indian students during the long summer vacation, Carmen later joined forces with Parker to organize and teach a three-week summer course which started with only six students but ended with 25. She also took part in a number of efforts by other volunteers, and clearly was the key performer in the entire operation.

Charles was one of the three volunteers who were initially reassigned to work in remote Indian communities to the north of Cuyo Chico, where they spent three months attempting to introduce sheep-dipping practices, with disappointing results. After he returned to Cuyo Chico, Charles worked with Carmen to prepare the third-grade classroom, with another volunteer to promote the installation of latrines, and with yet another to vaccinate animals against hoof and mouth disease and to assist in resettlement of a nearby hamlet on a new site. His most important activity, however, was to reactivate the construction of an irrigation canal. The Indians had started this job, but they had become disheartened when they reached a massive rock outcrop that a Peruvian engineer had estimated it would take them two years to cut through. Charles was able to obtain help from the AID representative in Cuzco in purchasing a portable air hammer for the Cuyo Chico program, and to train the Indians in its use. Progress on the canal increased from a foot and a half per day by hand, to sixteen feet per day with the jack hammer. While these efforts did not initiate a new self-help activity, they rekindled waning enthusiasm for the value of local self-help efforts and reactivated the one earlier activity besides the production of roof tiles which is likely to have an important impact in expanding Cuyo Chico's economic base. Charles was important in demonstrating the need for resourcefulness and perseverance, while Carmen's contribution was more in the direction of generating enthusiasm and introducing new ideas.

Cliff was perhaps more specialized than any of the other volunteers who worked at Cuyo Chico during this period. An English major in college, he had worked three summers in a hospital before joining the Peace Corps. In Cuyo Chico, he took over the medical post, which previously had been open only when the physician who worked half-time for the Cuzco Program went to the community to hold clinics. Cliff provided emergency treatment for the people of Cuyo Chico and nearby settlements on an around-the-clock, seven-day-a-week basis, working as first aid dispenser under the physician's supervision. He had learned Spanish during prior residence in Peru, and learned some Quechua during his Peace Corps training and more in the field; he was able to communicate with the Indians well enough to carry out his more technical functions. This and his willingness to make house calls day or night were important elements in the excellent rapport he established with his patients. The system of medical records he established for the clinic showed a patient load of up to 75 per day, with an average of twelve. His efforts in preventive medicine included vaccinations, taking the school children to Cuzco for chest X-rays and other examinations, work with Charles to promote the adoption of latrines, and talks to the school children on intestinal parasites that resulted in a few families starting to boil their drinking water.

Carol's work as a "social science analyst" to a large extent was independent of that of the other volunteers at Cuyo Chico, and while it apparently was very useful in other respects, it did not involve direct efforts to introduce change in the village. Carol's only role there was to collect new information under the supervision of the anthropologist who directs the Cuzco Program, and to organize a summer field session there for her anthropology students at the University of Cuzco.

In general, the group of volunteers at Cuyo Chico carried out a reasonably cohesive program within the framework of long-range community development work related to the Andean Indian Program. Their most obvious efforts were concentrated in the fields of education, health, and irrigation, along lines on which the broader program already had begun work and on which it continued after their departure.

Unlike many of their fellows in the Vicos area and in the Puno-Tambopato sub-program, the volunteers at Cuyo Chico spent considerable time with their Peruvian counterparts, both socially and at work. As a group, they can be rated as successful in achieving the three functions Peace Corps community development projects can be expected to perform, even though not all individuals were equally successful: (a) effective and worthwhile innovation of a lasting nature in the local scene; (b) fomenting better understanding of the United States through their dealings with local people; and (c) the broadening experience of foreign service from which the volunteers themselves benefit. The second and third functions obviously are characteristic only of such operations as the Peace Corps. The first, in reality, is sufficiently broad to embody all of the goals of community development. It may be stated more clearly in terms of its various elements. The first of these is the introduction of worthwhile innovations. However, if a program merely makes a few changes, and the community thereafter stagnates, or even retrogresses, the changes would have to be important ones indeed to justify their cost. Thus the second element is institutionalization of the innovations. To this one may add, as yet a third item, the institutionalization of the *means* for bringing about local improvements through local effort, or what amounts to a "multiplier effect" in terms of the project investment. Finally, and a point not mentioned in the already-complex statement of Peace Corps objectives, these first three elements should involve a "demonstration effect" as they did at Vicos, that is, their nature should be such that the changes spread spontaneously to neighboring communities.

Urban Community Development

Grass roots development, as an approach to rural problems, depends to an important extent upon stimulating local people to make use of their own resources to bring about improvements on their own behalf. One may think of present rural community development practices as having evolved from two types or sets of efforts, both of which depend heavily upon this principle. One of these is the agricultural extension approach, mentioned in the section on rural development in Chapter 3. Since this has not been of major direct importance in Latin America except in some colonization and settlement projects, it is not represented as such in the case materials summarized in the preceding sections of this chapter. Beginning with the introduction of innovations in agricultural technology, agricultural extension programs expanded to include home economics and eventually became broad enough in scope, at least in some cases, to be considered full-fledged community development in the sense that they deal with many different features of life on the local level. Rural sociology has been the most active social field in this line of evolution, and rural sociologists and agricultural economists often have collaborated even more closely with one another than with technicians from agricultural and other fields in programs of this type. Social work has no doubt contributed too, through the participation of sociologists who were not themselves social workers but were acquainted with that field, if in no more direct way.

The other of the two main lines of evolution of rural community development activity is the one represented in the case materials summarized in the earlier sections of this chapter. Unlike the agricultural extension type, this one has been closely identified with a social field, anthropology, practically from the start—so closely, in fact, that much of the literature labelled "applied anthropology" deals with community development. There has been considerable convergence of these two lines of evolution of community development in recent years, in part as a result of the increasing spontaneous exchange of personnel between them resulting from increased activity in each.

Urban community development in one sense has been an outgrowth of the evolution of rural community development techniques. Anthropologists with prior knowledge and experience in rural community development have been especially active in creating urban programs, and many of those programs have involved conscious application of the known approach in a new set of circumstances.

In another sense, however, some of the most successful urban community development projects in Latin America represent such an important departure from the earlier emphasis on utilization of the labor potential of lower-class beneficiaries themselves, that this work deserves a place as yet a third type of approach to community development. These projects emphasize the slum dweller's initiative and ability to organize and supervise the actual work on improvements, contributions which are far more important than that of his own labor, which may be relatively small except in a low-level managerial capacity. The interdependence characteristic of urban life may have been instrumental in the emergence of this new orientation.

This emphasis on skills characteristic of the management function is particularly significant. Both of the older grass roots approaches, as they operate in Latin America, seek to promote material or technological innovations, to mobilize the potential labor of lower-class people for their own good, or both. Hopefully, they may bring about some degree of institutionalization of the change processes involved, in such a way that adoptions and the growth of local-production-for-local-benefit continues after the change agents have departed. They introduce technological change and they mobilize latent lower-class labor for productive purposes. They may even lead to some change in social culture in the long run. But the program of this type which is directly concerned with introducing change in features of the social culture of major significance for development *in the field as well as in its statements of purpose* is rare indeed.

Perhaps the single most important feature of the more theoretical phase of the work at Vicos was that it attempted to do precisely this, apparently with some measure of success. Most rural community development projects, however, must content themselves with introducing technological innovations, broadly defined to include some aspects of health, into the peasant culture in which they work, and with stimulating collective action within more or less conventional patterns to make physical improvements through the application of local labor. If unusually effective, they may bring about a lasting increase in such local group efforts to make local improvements, strengthening local leadership among the peasants themselves; and their educational activities, again broadly defined, may accelerate integration of the local community into the national culture. But they do this within the basic patterns of the lower-class rural culture, which normally remains exactly that.

In contrast, the new type of urban community development, as it has been practiced up to now, first identifies an emerging middle-class characteristic among people of lower-class origin, and then facilitates further development and application of that and related characteristics in their daily activities. This cluster of traits— initiative, responsibility, and the combination of managerial and labor functions in the same individual—is of major importance in distinguishing between lower and middle classes in a sociological sense, and some might even go so far as to accept it as *the* key diagnostic element. It seems logical even to expect that the new approach might eventually reach the point at which it can devlop these characteristics in lower-class groups where they have not yet emerged spontaneously.

The new type of approach resulted first from recognition that the residents of squatter settlements on the fringes of large cities could make major improvements by themselves and organize themselves effectively to carry out these tasks. Later, it became clear that, at least in some areas, these people personally perform relatively little of the physical work involved in making the improvements; they function as their own "contractors" in having it done, little by little, as they are financially able to do so. The Peruvian experience summarized below illustrates this evolutionary pattern, as well as the nature of urban community development work in one of the Latin American countries where this approach has emerged during the past ten years.

Community development programs have been undertaken with some success in urban areas in several other Latin American countries as well. The participation of national housing technicians in training programs of CINVA (the Inter-American Housing Center in Bogotá) and in international meetings, and the work of technicians of international technical assistance and financing agencies with those responsible for project preparation on the national level, have provided effective channels for a rapid exchange of experiences among the various countries. Therefore the national efforts have not been independent of one another, even though there has been little or no formal coordination as such among them. Chile, Colombia, Peru, and Venezuela have been especially active in urban community development, and in these countries the needed institutions have been formed to make possible the coordination of such local programs on the national level.[1]

---

[1] Francis Violich and Juan B. Astica, *Community Development and the Urban Planning Process in Latin America* (Los Angeles: UCLA Latin American Center, forthcoming, 1967) summarizes these efforts, and treats the application of community development techniques to urban problems throughout Latin America.

Peruvian experience.[1] The growth of peripheral shantytowns, already mentioned in more general terms in Chapter 3, has been one of the major postwar trends in Peru, where such settlements are referred to as *barriadas.* The individual settlements of this type have followed a fairly uniform pattern of development. A group of families is organized well in advance to "invade" a particular tract of land. When the selected time arrives, they move in with materials they already have obtained for the purpose. Each family hastily erects a temporary shelter, usually made of straw mats; often this is accomplished literally overnight. Soon thereafter, property lines are laid out, even though no one in the group has any legal claim to the land, and each family is assigned its own plot. As a rule, this subdivision follows a regular block pattern, terrain permitting, but no immediate provision is made for installing electricity, water lines, or sewers. Soon the family builds a wall around its lot, thus securing possession and privacy. Several years may elapse before a permanent house is started, and during this period the family itself or a caretaker lives within these walls, usually in a section enclosed by additional wall and roofed over with straw mats. Characteristically, the house is built little by little, as the family is able to pay for the work and materials—it actually provides relatively little labor, usually hiring artisans to do the various jobs and closely supervising their work.

In barriadas which have been in existence for several years, there are houses at all stages of construction, but few of them are finished. "Indispensable" public services may still be lacking: if so, water is distributed by truck and stored in drums, and most families use latrines. Many families first buy electricity from local generators driven by gasoline motors—more permanent electrical connections usually are installed before sewer lines, which are more expensive and more difficult to

---

[1]This summary is based on John C. Turner (ed.), "Dwelling Resources in South America", *Architectural Design,* Vol. XXXIII (August 1963), pp. 360-393.

construct. Gradually, however, the oldest barriadas have taken on the character of established lower-middle-class neighborhoods as more and more houses have been completed, utilities have been installed, and streets paved.

The barriadas of Lima first began to receive serious official attention about 1958. In 1961, a law was passed to regularize land titles in existing settlements of this type and to improve conditions in them. Intended to prevent the formation of new barriadas, it made no provision for those which appeared after it was adopted. However, it recognized that some of the existing ones were of such a nature that they could not be improved, and it empowered the housing agency to acquire land near the city to resettle the families from such neighborhoods.

This part of the agency's work was started with the relocation of a single barriada. Since the families were poorer than most, and would be required to pay at least part of the cost of the new settlement, it was decided to provide only the absolute minimum of land and facilities for them within the resettlement area: 1600 square feet of land, a temporary dwelling, and drinking water taps near each site. Sewers, electricity, and paving were not provided. This "planned squatter settlement" was successful—in general, it was well-received by the relocated families and, while it followed the conventional process of barriada formation, it provided a more satisfactory layout than is characteristic of most spontaneous barriadas and made better provisions for future improvements.

Thereafter, the same agency was able to partially supervise the establishment of an entirely new squatter settlement, recognizing the occupancy of the land but persuading the invaders in return to adjust to the plan it had prepared and to give it some control over future development. In this type of approach, the government's role is to direct and coordinate existing forces and resources, rather than to do the work for the people in need of improved housing. Only minimum utilities are provided at the outset, and others are postponed until the majority of the residents have built at least a minimum house and are sufficiently well-off economically to pay the extra cost of piped water in the dwelling and water-borne sewage disposal. Credit can greatly accelerate construction, for the lack of funds is the principal, and perhaps the only, element which delays completion of the first rooms of the barriada house. At first, loans for this purpose were made in kind, partly on the basis of the assumption that the occupant's major contribution is his labor. The administration of such a program was found to be excessively complicated, and more recently credit has been extended in small successive amounts, in cash, upon completion of each stage of the work.

By shifting from more conventional efforts to provide housing for low-income groups to this type of approach, it has become possible for the housing agency to use the same resources repeatedly, reinvesting loan repayments from older projects in new ones. The effect is to shorten the period from the time settlement of a new urban neighborhood begins to the time that most of the houses have been completed and reasonably complete public services have been installed. Moreover, the guidance provided at early stages can reduce the cost of later improvements, improve the design of the houses within the framework of patterns which are truly acceptable to the occupants, and assure that the new neighborhood meets accepted housing and community standards. Its assistance in developing a community structure may be rather superfluous in dealing with a group which already has organized itself to form a new barriada, but it can serve at least as a clearing-house of information to help new groups organize themselves, and it can assist them in providing for community services which, as shown by experience in older barriadas, are likely to be desired after the group's most pressing housing needs have been satisfied.

In this fashion, the official agency neither attempts to provide housing *for* the urban poor, nor requires them to accept its initiative in providing for their own needs. It simply assists them in exercising their own initiative to make improvements on their own behalf by making credit and some technical guidance available to them.

It should not be assumed that this approach to urban housing and community development has completely replaced other orientations. Indeed, it has not done any more than gain a foothold in a few countries. In the words of John Turner,

> "In spite of monumental evidence of the capacity of ordinary people in building their houses, the authorities (decision-makers of the executive agencies) tend to have little faith in the initiative and organizing ability of such people, whom the agencies are meant to serve. The few available field-workers on a project must gain the confidence and respect of the participants. This essentially close contact creates a mutual bond between them that the project's managers and functionaries—often reluctant to listen to their own field staff, and even more reluctant to leave their offices and see things for themselves—fail to profit from.
>
> "Field-workers in building programmes of this kind are not only the spokesmen of government agencies, but also their eyes and ears: until managers learn to use them they cannot hope to learn the real nature of a situation, adopt proper attitudes or take effective decisions. But the projects... show that an increasing number of managers carry out their jobs satisfactorily in this way, and community and local development in housing and other fields can be promoted effectively by government agencies only insofar as this trend continues.
>
> "For it is a trend towards recognition of the ordinary family's capacity, given the right help at the right time, to solve its own prob-

lems; and at the same time recognition of the scope and nature of government action that enables such help to be given. This changing attitude—the essential basis for cooperation between people and their government—can unlock resources and energies hitherto too often frustrated or ignored and equip them for the rapid development of these countries." (Turner, p. 393)

The emergence of this new approach to community development could conceivably lead to a major breakthrough in development operations, not only in the explosive urban areas of Latin America in which it first appeared, but in rural areas as well. It is one type of development action of importance in Latin America that directly embodies, as a major feature, fundamental social change in the direction of conversion from a two-class to a middle-class society.

INTEGRATED REGIONAL DEVELOPMENT

The principles emerging from recent urban community development experience in time may have considerable impact on rural community development programs as well. Even if the grass-roots approach becomes much more effective than it has been in the past in developing latent individual initiative and in unlocking previously underutilized or ignored resources, however, the most important single limitation on this type of approach to development action still remains. It is a relatively intensive approach, and the amount of money and technical competence necessary to apply it effectively is so high on a per capita basis that it cannot deal directly with more than a small fraction of the total population.

Development efforts of national scope, on the other hand, suffer from limitations of quite a different nature. Most are of types which have no need to deal directly with a large percentage of the people who benefit from the results, and even those which do are of a specialized nature; on the operational level, they make no pretense of dealing with the total way of life of the people they reach. Because they are planned and directed by the central government, such programs seldom have at their disposal intimate first-hand knowledge of the settings in which they are to be implemented. As a result, the scarce resources available to sponsor development are sometimes allocated less effectively than they might be in terms of both type of activity and territorial distribution. Moreover, the number of individual activities is so great, and they are of such diverse types, that it is extremely difficult to achieve adequate coordination among them.

The problems and the limitations characteristic of grass-roots development, on the one hand, and of centralized national efforts, on the other, suggest that territorial units intermediate between the local community and the entire nation would be advantageous for some types of planning and action. This line of reasoning holds that development might be more effectively sponsored if approached as a regional, as distinct from a national or local problem.

The region to be developed under such an approach ideally should be of one or the other of two distinct types, not just a segment of a nation chosen without regard for its own characteristics or those of the people living in it. It may be selected and delimited in such a way that conditions are relatively uniform throughout its extent; or it may be a socio-economic unit of the type discussed in relation to locality-group structure (pp. 51-54), in which case emphasis is upon functional interdependence of differing parts within an area characterized by an internal system of social and economic bonds which both unify it and set it apart from its neighbors. In practice, such a region based on social and economic characteristics often exhibits a high degree of homogeneity with respect to many of its natural and cultural features as well or, if not, it consists of parts of only two or three regions based on natural and cultural homogeneity. Conversely, the region established on grounds of natural and cultural homogeneity is independent of territorial patterns of socio-economic relationships, although when contrasts between adjoining regions are marked it is fairly common to find a socio-economic unit lying astride, and in fact focusing upon some center in, the boundary zone between them.

By dealing with a sub-national unit of fairly large territorial extent, whatever the basis for regional delimitation, the functions which on the national level are diffused among many different administrative units may be brought together in a single integrated agency responsible for planning and carrying out a cohesive development program for and within the particular region. This feature contributes to overcoming the coordination problems characteristic of programs on the national level, although not as completely as may occur in the grass-roots approach. Similarly, the people responsible for a regional development program—assuming they actually are stationed in the region and are not reassigned too frequently—have an opportunity for first-hand familiarity with the problems of their area and the relationships among them to a far greater degree than is possible in programs of national scope, even though their knowledge of local detail is necessarily less intimate than is possible in community development. Thus the regional approach should overcome at least partially two of the major problems of development efforts on the national level. It should also be relatively free from two of the most serious limitations of grass-roots development, one of the them the highly localized nature of the immediate results, no matter how successful, inherent in the limited territorial scope of community development, and the other, which is especially pronounced in Latin America, the lack of capacity on the local level for mobilizing the managerial, technical, and financial resources required to plan and conduct major projects.

The Tennessee Valley program (TVA) initiated in the United States shortly before World War II was not the first integrated regional development program ever to be undertaken, but it did far more than any of its predecessors to call attention to this approach to development planning and action. It was a direct source of ideas leading to the creation of Mexico's river-basin commissions and the São Francisco Valley project in Brazil, both of which are considered later in this section, as well as many similar undertakings elsewhere. It was this historical antecedent, rather than any technical consideration, that accounts for the strong focus of many early regional programs on questions related to water resources. Integrated regional development might equally well focus upon improvements in agriculture or the provision of adequate basic transportation and educational systems, for example. One key characteristic of this approach, however, is that its planning seriously considers many aspects of the area in which the particular program operates, and its action extends over a broad array of problems. Programs which have been in existence for several years cannot be expected to fulfill the latest theoretical ideals, for once established on the basis of a given theoretical framework, operating plans can seldom be modified to take into account new developments. Because of this, it is not surprising that few existing regional development programs take full advantage of present theory concerning regional delimitation, locality-group structure, or the role of cities as focal points of growth—all of these are points on which there has been considerable research in the last few years.

The two sets of regional development efforts which have been selected for consideration in this section thus represent case studies of actual practice rather than theoretical ideals. The first of them is the Papaloapan Project, one of Mexico's river-basin programs initiated in 1947. The second is the long series of efforts focusing on the problem of recurrent drought in Northeastern Brazil.

The Papaloapan Project[1]

The Papaloapan Project at least nominally deals with the entire hydrographic basin which drains into the Gulf of Mexico not far south of the city of Veracruz, a total area only slightly smaller than the entire Republic of Costa Rica. Politically it embraces parts of the states of Veracruz, Oaxaca, and Puebla; physically, it includes parts of three strikingly different regions, the low-lying Gulf Coastal Plain, the extremely rugged ranges of the Sierra Madre, and a rather arid portion of the plateau of Central Mexico. Although for a time increasing attention was paid to the last two regions, most activities of the Papaloapan Commission have been concentrated in the coastal lowlands. To a considerable degree, even the projects carried out in the highlands were regarded as necessary for development of the lowlands as well as for development of the highlands, for such problems as the silting of the major lowland streams are due principally to land use practices in the mountains. Thus the territory with which the program was most concerned is much smaller than the entire hydrographic basin.

Strictly speaking, even the *Lower Papaloapan Basin*, that is, the portion lying in the coastal plain, is not a region in terms of either of the concepts mentioned above. There are several central places upon which social and economic relationships focus within its limits. Tierra Blanca, Cosamaloapan, Tuxtepec, and Alvarado are the major ones and, on the same level, San Andrés Tuxtla and Acayucan, which lie just beyond the drain-

---

[1] This section is based primarily on Thomas T. Poleman, *The Papaloapan Project: Agricultural Development in the Mexican Tropics* (Stanford: Stanford University Press, 1964); William W. Winnie, Jr., "The Papaloapan Project: An Experiment in Tropical Development," *Economic Geography*, Vol. 34 (1958), pp. 227-249 and *The Lower Papaloapan Basin: Land and People* (Ann Arbor: University Microfilms, 1956); a brief re-visit to the area in 1964; and occasional conversations over the last decade with Mexican economists and officials and former officials of the Papaloapan Commission.

age divides which mark the limits of the basin, serve as central places for some of its communities. But all of these are relatively minor centers. The Lower Papaloapan Basin thus includes all of several, and part of a few other, sub-regions at the first level above the local community, but these together do not constitute any sort of cohesive socio-economic unit within the larger one for which the city of Veracruz (as a commercial center) and the state capital at Jalapa are central places.

Nor is this a homogeneous region in either natural or cultural terms; differences within it are at least as great as those between it and adjacent parts of the coastal plain. There are marked contrasts in physical environment, contrasts which probably arise partly from differences in surface geology, but which at least have been accentuated by man's use of the land over the centuries. Present vegetation ranges from treeless grassland to tall, dense tropical forest. The climate throughout is tropical, with a pronounced dry season from December through May.

Agriculture and stock raising are the principal economic activities: the Lower Papaloapan Basin basically is a rural area, and its urban and semi-urban places are trade, service, and processing centers for the surrounding countryside. In 1947, sugar refining was the only manufacturing industry operated on any scale, and even by then it was done mostly in very large and efficient modern mills. Bananas, a major commercial crop little more than a decade earlier, had been all but wiped out by disease and had been replaced by sugar cane and pineapples. Commercial agriculture based on these products has long been concentrated along the banks of the major steams, especially the Papaloapan; when the program began, those streams were still the main internal transportation routes, even though a railroad had been built across the area decades earlier.

The people of the Lower Papaloapan Basin, like its commercial agriculture, are highly concentrated along a few of the largest rivers. Like similar streams

throughout the world, the Papaloapan and its major
tributaries spread out over a wide area beyond their
banks (the floodplain) during periods of maximum flow,
and this flooding had become much more severe during
recent decades because of deforestation in the mountains.   The major immediate stimulus for creating the
Papaloapan Commission was, in fact, an especially
severe flood in 1944 which caused large economic losses
and much human suffering.

It therefore was to be expected that the early efforts
of the Commission would emphasize flood control. The
original proposals called for comprehensive studies of
the entire Papaloapan Basin as a basis for preparation
of a long-range, multi-purpose development program.
A great deal of time obviously would be required to
complete these research and planning functions, but
meanwhile several pressing problems were so important
that it was clear that projects designed to solve them
would have to form part of any conceivable program
for the region's development.

Several such projects were undertaken almost as
soon as the Commission was created in 1947. The largest of them was a major dam on a tributary of the Papaloapan: it would go far in controlling the floods along
the main stream, it would generate more electricity than
was then being consumed within a reasonable transmission distance, and it would irrigate a large area in the
lowlands. Named for Miguel Alemán, the President of
Mexico when the project was begun, this dam has many
characteristics of "showcase projects." It is still one
of the largest and most expensive structures of its kind
in all of Latin America. It required a huge investment
of public funds, and in fact accounted for 44 per cent
of the Commission's entire budget from 1947 through
1953 (Poleman, Table 10, pp. 104-105). Even before
it was completed, it had become clear that the early emphasis on irrigation was more a result of the engineers'
previous experience in the arid lands of northern Mexico than of the existing or future needs of the region's
agriculture. Only a small part of the design capacity

for generating electricity was installed when the dam was completed, partly because the market could not then absorb the total potential output. Even the merits of this one dam for flood control, as opposed to those of a smaller aggregate investment in several less-spectacular projects, can be seriously questioned. By 1954, the year in which the Alemán Dam was officially completed, some highly qualified technicians were willing to express in private the realistic opinion that Mexico had become prosperous enough to be able to afford some ostentatious luxuries, and that the Alemán Dam was among them.

Other early projects also were in infrastructure fields. The main ones were a series of cuts across meanders in the Papaloapan itself, which increased the runoff rate of floodwaters; the construction of levees in the zone most subject to flood damage; and the construction of paved highways from the Córdoba-Veracruz highway to the Papaloapan and along the levee on the north side of the main stream through the principal area of commercial agriculture. These infrastructure projects absorbed so much of the effort of the Commission during the Alemán administration (1947-1952) that little was left even for the research function which was to form the basis for laying out long-range plans. Nevertheless, the Lower Papaloapan Basin by 1952 was served by good basic through highways, and no longer was in danger of serious flood losses. Already among the most favored territorial units of its size in Latin America when the program began, two of its most pressing problems—recurrent floods and the lack of basic highways connecting its commercial core to the major centers of the country—had been satisfactorily solved five years later.

In Mexico, the orderly transfer of power from one president to the next every six years often is accompanied by changes in policy emphasis—and in key personnel in government agencies. That which took place at the end of 1952 was especially noteworthy in two respects related to development. Earlier administrations

had emphasized major infrastructure projects almost to
the exclusion of efforts with more immediate and direct
effects. The Ruiz Cortines administration which took
office in that year reversed this emphasis and, perhaps
more than ever before, its beginning was marked by a
"professionalization" of the civil service in some agencies through appointment of career technicians of demonstrated capacity to key management positions.

In the Papaloapan Basin, a new and vigorous *Vocal
Ejecutivo* (Executive Director) of the Commission was
appointed late in 1952, and the entire emphasis of the
action program changed. The Alemán Dam was near-
ing completion and progress on it and other flood control projects and the major trunk highways made it possible to concentrate action more and more on work which
would produce more direct and immediate results.
Studies to support the planning function, including detailed mapping, also received increasing attention beginning at this time. Nearly ten years after the Commission was established, it was clear that one of the
most important lessons it could offer to any development
program in the American tropics is that a large portion
of the early part of the program must be given over to
research on the natural resources and the people of the
region to be developed. By then, the Commission's director who had assumed office four years earlier was
more convinced than ever

> "that any effort to develop new tropical lands
> in Mexico or any other Latin American country
> must be begun with work of this sort, even though
> other obviously useful projects may be under-
> taken at the same time." (Sandoval, as quoted
> in Winnie 1958:240)

The Commission had made considerable progress
by 1956 in a wide variety of such "obviously useful projects," even though minimum basic research was still
far from complete. The major fields of activity
besides flood control and irrigation included health,
transportation, education, colonization, and agricultural

experimentation. Eighty per cent of the houses in the entire Lower Papaloapan Basin had been sprayed at least once with residual DDT, and the region was well ahead rest of lowland Mexico in malaria control. Local water supply and sanitation projects carried out cooperatively with the towns and larger villages were a regular feature of the program, and already had directly benefitted one-fifth of the population of the lowlands. Peripheral highways built by other agencies and the 168 kilometers of internal highways built by the Commission had been completed by the end of 1952, and emphasis thereafter was placed upon less-spectacular types of road construction. By late 1956, 369 kilometers of graded secondary highways and 262 kilometers of feeder roads had been opened. The provision of schools was closely linked to this road construction, and the "road-school combination" had come to be regarded as a major opening wedge for promoting social and economic change. Two major colonies and several minor ones had been established: the high cost ($US 2,000 per family) limited the possibilities of colonization for peopling the empty lands of the region, but the colonies were important as demonstration units for introducing improved practices, and for further testing of practices and seed varieties developed in the three agricultural experiment stations which had been established by the Commission.

By late 1956, it appeared

> "very likely that the long-range program of the Papaloapan Commission will be highly successful in raising the levels of living of the inhabitants of the Lower Papaloapan Basin and will greatly increase the contribution of that area to the market economy of Mexico. Probably it will also stimulate the settlement of sparsely inhabited parts of the area." (Winnie 1958:246)

Before that statement was printed, however, a friend wrote its author, "all of this Basin is in mourning:"

an aircraft accident had taken the life of the director
who had vastly changed the Papaloapan Commission
to make this one of the most promising regional programs ever undertaken in Latin America.

Almost immediately, what had become a truly integrated program was

> "forced to terminate or curtail its peripheral
> activities drastically and to concentrate more
> and more on road construction and the develop-
> ment of water resources . . . . In early 1957,
> the Commission's agricultural stations were
> transferred to the Ministry of Agriculture, and
> many of its medico-sanitary operations were
> transferred to the Ministry of Public Health...."
> (Poleman, p. 109)

After the end of the Ruiz Cortines administration, the
Commission's budget was drastically reduced. In
1964, a skeleton staff, including several technicians who
had worked in the program in its heyday, complained of
having operated for six years on a "maintenance budget"
which scarcely permitted adequate upkeep of the
physical facilities that had been installed during the
twelve years when the program was in presidential favor.

For the moment, at least, the Papaloapan Project
must be evaluated in terms of its accomplishments to
date. Originally proposed as a twenty-year program,
it was for all practical purposes abandoned after only a
decade of strong support. These twenty years have
been prosperous ones in Mexico. The country during
this period has come to be recognized as one of the most
progressive of all those labelled "underdeveloped" at
the end of World War II. Has there been more progress in the Lower Papaloapan Basin than in Mexico as
a whole, or less? The answer has not been determined.

The most spectacular change which took place between 1954 and 1964 was totally unrelated to the work
of the Commission. Sugar acreage expanded rapidly
following the Cuban Revolution, and this expansion is
almost certain to have further aggravated some of the

socio-economic problems that already characterized the zone of sugar monoculture. Otherwise, however, about as many negative as positive signs of change could be seen on a short visit in 1964. To the late director's emphasis on the need for systematic study we may add, as the second major lesson offered by the Papaloapan Project to other development efforts, the need for continuity. Personalism—in the person of one still fondly recalled and highly respected by many friends and colleagues in and outside of Mexico—was a key to the promising prospects of the program over a decade ago. Personalism was also a key to the program's virtual abandonment, beginning in 1957.

Declining support for the Papaloapan Commission was not symptomatic of abandonment of the regional approach to development, however. The other regional commissions which were established under the Ministry of Hydraulic Resources at about the same time as the Papaloapan Commission have continued in operation, and others have been created since that time. In the Grijalva Basin, for which a regional commission was established in 1951, the long-range development program is to be carried out in seven phases. The first of these is the El Limón pilot project in 52,000 hectares of the total area of 350,000 hectares of the basin. Basically a colonization project, this part of the program includes the following as principal undertakings:[1]

> *Basic engineering works*: drainage, protective dikes, irrigation, and access roads.
>
> *Works preparatory to farm operation*: internal roads, land clearing, grading, and irrigation and drainage within parcels.
>
> *Agricultural development*: organization of cooperatives, agricultural research, instruction, extension services, experimental and dem-

---

[1] As summarized in *Social Progress Trust Fund: Third Annual Report, 1963* (Washington: Inter-American Development Bank, 1964), p. 36.

onstration farms, and heavy and light machinery stations.

Urbanization and social improvement: rural
housing, including water supply, sanitation,
and electrification.

Social operations and civic services in general:
medical, sanitation, and assitance services;
government and communications offices;
community centers; etc.

The El Limón project thus represents a continuation of the general concept of regional development as
it was emerging in the Papaloapan project in 1956, but
with considerably more concentration of action, at
least in the first stage, within a single sub-region.

The lowlands along the northern part of the west
coast of mainland Mexico have been the most rapidly-
growing part of the country in recent years, to a large
extent as a result of rapid agricultural expansion based
on irrigation of land previously too dry for cultivation.
Much of the past development of this type has been associated with irrigation projects operated directly by the
Ministry of Hydraulic Resources in what amounts to a
fusion, in terms of the types of development action under
consideration here, of conventional sectoral projects for
irrigation and power development, with a grass-roots
approach to development for colonization of each newly-
opened irrigation district. In one part of the area, however, the Río Fuerte Basin, a regional commission was
established and has operated along lines similar to those
of the Papaloapan and Grijalva commissions with integration at the regional level of several sectoral functions.
Expansion of this approach to cover most of the northwestern part of the country as a unit is now under consideration.

The Lerma-Chapala-Santiago Commission, and the
Lerma Plan closely associated with it, conduct basic
research and integrated planning, and formulate investment projects in all sectors. Execution functions are
performed by other agencies along sectoral lines, but

the Commission is responsible for equitable distribution of available water within the region. This program merits study as a test of the effectiveness of a regional body in coordinating projects of public agencies over which it exercises no direct control into a cohesive program to sponsor development, and in stimulating private-sector activities along such lines that they reinforce the official program.

All of these regional commissions operate as semi-autonomous agencies under the Ministry of Hydraulic Resources. While this arrangement may have involved some inter-agency conflicts detrimental to the regional programs—as appears to have been the case in the Papaloapan (Poleman, p. 109)—it has made possible an effective exchange of experience among the various programs and a high degree of continuity in the evolution of the general philosophy of the approach.

Northeastern Brazil and SUDENE[1]

Brazil's Northeast has long been recognized as a region apart from the rest of the country. Sometimes a distinction is made between the "Humid Northeast" along the coast, which became a sugar-producing region in the sixteenth century and has remained one ever since, and the "Arid Northeast" of the interior, the *sertão,* a land subjected to recurrent drought, covered with scrubby brush and supporting, at least in the more humid years, a population which is dense for this type of land through the range cattle industry, scattered subsistence agriculture, and the collection of wild vegetable products.

---

[1]This summary is based more on Albert O. Hirschman's analysis of development activities ·in Northeastern Brazil in his *Journeys Toward Progress* (New York: Twentieth Century Fund, 1963) than on any other single source. Hirschman's treatment of political factors and their bearing on development activities in the region is especially illuminating. Information for the period since publication of that study is drawn in part from an unpublished report by two internationally-recognized experts on regional development who visited the region together early in

But the Northeast, as a socio-economic unit, embraces both of these physical regions.

As presently defined for official purposes in terms of entire states, the Northeast includes nine of the 28 major territorial divisions of Brazil. Together, these nine states account for 32 per cent of the country's population and nearly one-fifth of its area. Only two Latin American countries, Mexico and Argentina, are larger in area, and only Mexico has more people.

Even though it is so large a region, the Northeast would not have received so much international attention during the last few years because of size alone. It is one of the major poverty areas of the Hemisphere, with estimated per capita income of only 140 dollars per year (Robock, p. 66) and, when drought strikes the arid portion, as it did in 1958, this becomes a major and widely publicized disaster area. Moreover, while violence and unrest have occurred sporadically in the Northeast ever since colonial times, the peasant leagues that arose there in the late 1950's and the disturbances in which they were involved were linked to international communism, in part because of visits of their principal leader, Francisco Julião, to Cuba. Because of this, there was considerable alarm in Washington beginning in 1960 over the possible threat of a Castro-type rebellion in this region.

The Northeast, then, has become rather widely known outside of Brazil during the last few years largely because of the severity of the 1958 drought in

---

1966. The reader interested in examining the subject in more detail should also consult T. Lynn Smith, *Brazil: People and Institutions* (Baton Rouge: Louisiana State University Press, Third Edition, 1963), *passim;* Charles Wagley, *An Introduction to Brazil* (New York: Columbia University Press, 1963), pp. 33-53; and Stefan H. Robock, "Recent Economic Trends in Northeast Brazil," *Inter-American Economic Affairs,* Vol. 16, No. 3 (Winter 1962), pp. 65-89. References to several works by Brazilian authors which have become classics and are available in English translation will be found in the bibliographies of these sources.

association with the growth of international concern with development, and also because of the alarm over the possibility of another communist revolution within the Hemisphere. Its problems are not new, however. Rural poverty has long characterized the arid portion, and has been accentuated every few years by severe drought accompanied by waves of migration to the coast of the Northeast itself and to other regions of Brazil. Neither is the humid Northeast lacking in problems, even though they are of a different type. The long-standing sugar industry remains basically a plantation system operated with landless labor, and even though the family-owned mill has been replaced by more modern installations, the industry as a whole remains rather inefficient. For the rural laborer, the major change associated with the advent of larger mills was some diminishment of the paternalism which had characterized the older system.

The coastal cities—Fortaleza, Natal, João Pessoa, Recife, Maceió, and Salvador, each with more than 100,000 people, are the principal ones—in some respects are symbols of modernity in contrast to the backwardness of the countryside either along the coast or in the interior. Yet, within these cities, slums are as characteristic an accompaniment of modernization as they are elsewhere in urban Latin America, and many relics of the past—for example, the primitive fishing industry in Fortaleza—exist side by side with features of modern industry and commerce.

As a problem area, however, the region is best known in other parts of Brazil and to the world at large as one in which recurrent severe droughts bring suffering and even death from starvation to some of those who remain in the sertão, and give rise to a great exodus of *sertanejos* to more humid lands. In this sense, the Northeast refers to the arid Northeast, and the area subject to drought disaster has been officially delimited in Brazilian law as the "Drought Polygon." Until recently, official programs were concentrated on this smaller area; only during the last ten years has the development of the Northeast come to be approached in terms of systematic, long-range efforts to foster and guide change in both major subdivisions of this vast socio-economic region through an integrated program. The many activities to promote development of the area are now coordinated through a single agency, SUDENE, the Superintendency for the Development of the Northeast.

Because of the large size of the Northeast, it is a special case in regional development. One might first be inclined to the view that, in practice, a regional program here would more closely parallel work at the national than at the regional level in other parts of Latin America. However, in some important respects, the Northeast's character as a sub-national instead of a national unit has been of utmost importance.

> "It is likely that if the Northeast were a sovereign country, so reform-minded an agency as SUDENE could not have been established without a major socio-political upheaval. But as shown also by the history of land reform in Southern Italy and desegregation in the United States South, the chances of evolutionary change in a non-sovereign region are better than in a sovereign country for a very simple reason: the required decisions can be taken by enlisting behind them political forces from other regions." (Hirschman, pp. 85-86)

SUDENE was established at the end of 1959 with the support of strong interests in São Paulo and other southern states. Powerful interests within the Northeast itself were opposed to at least some of the ideas involved: SUDENE was to be not only an agency for integrated regional development, but a reform agency which was expected, in the long run, to produce important changes in the region's socio-political structure— at the expense of the existing power elite.

SUDENE was not the first agency created by the national government of Brazil to deal with problems in the Northeast on a regional basis. There has been a long series of programs. SUDENE differs from its predecessors in several important ways, however. It was planned by a professional economist as a long-range development program, not by politicians to provide public relief in an emergency situation resulting from drought. Its Board of Directors from the start has included the governors of the states in which it operates, and representatives of the states and the program itself outnumber those of the central government—previous programs were fundamentally creations of the central government, and operated as such. And, instead of creating yet another unit of bureaucratic structure to compete in overlapping functions with its predecessors, SUDENE was given specific power over the other agencies which had been created in the past. Before considering SUDENE itself, it is therefore necessary to briefly review the earlier programs.

Precursors of SUDENE. The "Big Drought" of 1877-1879 marked the end of an exceptionally long period—thirty years—of adequate rainfall during which both population and economic activity in Ceará had expanded rapidly. "The failure of the rains to come in 1877, or in the next two years, had all the effectiveness of a surprise attack...." (Hirschman, p. 22) Emergency relief measures were woefully inadequate, and

> "In the interior many died of hunger and thirst, or because they took to eating poisonous roots. Even larger numbers who reached the cities perished there from exhaustion or from epidemic diseases as smallpox, yellow fever and typhoid swept the improvised encampments. Banditry and crime were rife, and several incidents of cannibalism were reported." (Hirschman, p. 22)

This drought marked the beginning of serious official concern over conditions in the Northeast. However, the results of initial efforts at port, railroad, and dam construction, as well as those of more direct relief

measures in general in the droughts of 1888-1889 and
1900, were disappointing. The first permanent federal
agency to deal with the drought problem of the Northeast in a unified manner was established in 1909. More
than poor administration and lack of continuity and professional competence were involved:

> "At least equally disturbing had been the abuses
> that invariably accompanied the distribution
> of relief funds and their use for individual
> enrichment and political advantage." (Hirsch-
> man, p. 24)

After slight changes in name the new agency became the present DNOCS (*Departamento Nacional de
Obras Contra as Sêcas,* the National Department of
Works Against the Droughts). It was established
within the Ministry of Public Works, and had its headquarters in Rio de Janeiro, some thousand miles from
the drought zone. Its creation was inspired not only by
the hope of overcoming the inefficiency and abuses
which had characterized earlier efforts, but also by the
desire for better maintenance and for a "systematic plan"
and scientific studies.

Even by the time the original agency was created,
there was considerable faith in the construction of storage reservoirs, or *açudes,* as the key solution to the
drought problem. The terrain offers many favorable
sites for both small and large dams which, when built,
keep the rain water from running out to sea; the primary function of the açude is the retention of water, not
only for supply in case of drought, but also for use
during the dry season in normal years.

> "From the beginning, the larger açudes
> were meant to serve as 'strong points' of re-
> sistance against drought in the sertão itself,
> thus making the exhausting and humiliating
> migrations to the coast unnecessary for the
> sertanejos and sparing the cities contact with

the miserable and occasionally mutinous fla-
gelados." (Hirschman, p. 27)
Storage of water through the construction of more and
more dams was to remain the principal official answer
to drought emergencies, as far as the victim was concerned, until at least 1960.

The work, by statute, was to be directed by engineers; in addition to building dams, which "was clearly
the kingpin of the contemplated solution" (Hirschman,
p. 27), it was to include the construction of roads and
railroads and various research functions.

The new agency was not notably successful, either
in eliminating the shortcomings which characterized
earlier efforts or in providing continuity of action in the
Northeast. It began serious studies and actually started
construction on some dams in its early years, but soon
the forces of bureaucratization made themselves felt.
The original team of engineers and scientists which had
been assembled soon dispersed, and data collection
functions were discontinued. When for the first time a
Northeasterner assumed the presidency of Brazil in
1919, that at the time of a severe drought, a vast array
of projects was initiated almost simultaneously; but
when he left office in 1922, his successor almost immediately began suspending work on many of them and,
in 1925, all public works in Brazil were suspended—
and stayed suspended for the next six years.

In the thirties, however, many of the unfinished
dams were completed; 31 new dams, most of the them
large, quadrupled the storage capacity that had been
available in the 92 public açudes already in existence in
1930. There was also considerable progress in highway
construction at this time: some 2,000 kilometers of
main highways and 1,000 of secondary roads were built,
about one-half of the total mileage in 1932, when many
drought refugees were absorbed in road construction.
But perhaps the outstanding achievement was the absence of large-scale corruption in the distribution of relief funds during this period, the time of maximum accomplishment by the agency.

Later, the interest of the agency shifted for a time to the São Francisco Valley, farther south and with different types of problems than those of Ceará, Rio Grande do Norte, and Paraíba where most of its dam and road construction had been concentrated, only to return again when the São Francisco Valley Commission was created in 1948. During this period, there were no major droughts, and, when one occurred in 1951, the past concentration on açudes was "criticized as a narrow strictly engineering approach to the problem which ought to be replaced by a real plan of broader economic and social planning...." (Hirschman, p. 59) This, together with renewed accusations of graft, encouraged the central government to try a new approach. The Bank of the Northeast, and eventually SUDENE, were results of this change in orientation. Nevertheless, DNOCS was the only existing agency prepared to handle direct drought relief measures in 1951, and when the rains failed again in 1953, the newly-created Bank had little to contribute. DNOCS received increased resources, and it was able to initiate and continue a number of new projects. The 1958 drought gave further impulse to its renewed activity, so that the years immediately preceding and following the creation of SUDENE were marked by accomplishments more substantial than those of any other period except the early 1930's. However, alleged abuses also expanded greatly, and "no drought had ever proved so devastating for public confidence in the agency as that of 1958." (Hirschman, p. 70) When SUDENE was created, the DNOCS was large and bureaucratically well entrenched, but publicly it was largely discredited both in terms of the nature of its principal type of projects and in terms of the integrity of its staff.

The São Francisco Valley Commission, created in 1948,

> "engaged in what was officially called 'a great policy of small services' such as access roads, building of infirmaries and small

> hospitals, provision of water and power supply in small towns, and so on." (Hirschman, pp. 53-54)

Its work in practice consisted of an agglomeration of small projects which could easily be executed, rather than an integrated regional development program for the São Francisco Basin. In 1956, when it was decided to build a major multi-purpose dam on the upper São Francisco, planning and organization of the project were turned over to a state power utility company which was considered to be a far more efficient and less "political" organization, and the Commission was simply instructed to devote part of its resources to financing the project. From the start, the major power project at Paulo Afonso Falls had been assigned to another agency created especially for that purpose, the São Francisco Hydroelectric Company.

The Bank of the Northeast, created in 1952, represented a major innovation in the approach to the problems of the Northeast. DNOCS, which had merely built dams and roads, not even providing irrigation even though much had earlier been made of proposals to do so, was out of favor and it had, moreover, suffered much loss of prestige since its greatest period of accomplishment in the thirties, in part through graft by some members of the staff. Thought regarding preferred solutions to the area's problems had shifted from emphasis on water storage, first alone and much later in combination with irrigation of subsistence crops, to promotion of agricultural activities based on native perennial xerophilous species. These crops require several years of growth before they begin to produce a return, and therefore their production could be stimulated by making credit available. Moreover, completion of the Paulo Afonso hydroelectric station was imminent, and ample credit would be required if the resulting industrial opportunities were to be realized. A new regional development bank for the Northeast could be endowed with resources merely by transferring to it

the lendable portion of a "Special Drought Fund"
which previously had been created within the Bank
of Brazil.

Unlike the agencies already in existence, all of
which had their headquarters in Rio de Janeiro, the new
Bank of the Northeast was established at Fortaleza,
within the region it was to serve. Once established, the
Bank found that it could rapidly commit its resources
only by investing heavily in short-term operations; this
was entirely consistent with the purposes of the Special
Drought Fund, whose resources were to be readily
available at any time to deal with drought emergencies,
but it is not, of course, a major function of development
banking. At the time the law creating SUDENE was
passed in 1959, such "general credit" still accounted
for 75 per cent of the Bank's outstanding loans, but during the next two years, whether due to the Bank's own
past efforts or to the requirement of the SUDENE law
that at least seventy per cent of the Bank's resources be
devoted to specialized medium and long-term credits,
loans of the latter type had grown from 25 per cent to
one-half of the entire portfolio.

The Bank of the Northeast also differed from the
agencies established before it in that, for an official organization, it remained relatively apolitical. It made a
considerable effort to assemble a qualified staff, and as
a result of this effort, utilization of external technical assistance resources, and its own subsequent research efforts, it firmly established the field of economics within
the Northeast itself as a tool for studying and solving
the region's development problems. In time, it was able
to make a major contribution to the establishment of new
industries in the Northeastern cities through its credit
and advisory operations.

By 1959, then, some four different national agencies had been established to deal, each in its own way,
with the problems of Northeastern Brazil. The DNOCS
had approached the problem through the construction
of dams in the drought region itself, and in later years
had begun to think seriously of installing irrigation works

in connection with the dams, even though there was little reflection of this new thought in its action programs. The São Francisco Valley Commission, while in words concerned with an integrated program which was, "if anything, more multi-purposeful than the TVA" (Hirschman, p. 53), in practice devoted its energies to many small projects which had little relation to one another, and was throughout its history ridden with political considerations. The São Francisco Hydroelectric Company, in contrast, was highly specialized in the single function of power development at Paulo Afonso Falls, which it carried out on a highly professional basis. Finally, the Bank of the Northeast, also professionalized, was specialized in financial functions. All of these agencies were still in operation in 1959, and each operated more or less independently of all of the others, although there was some overlap of functions among them.

SUDENE. The recommendations which formed the basis for the creation of SUDENE were made in a report prepared by Celso Furtado in 1958 and 1959, shortly after his appointment as Director of the National Bank for Economic Development. Himself a native of the Northeast, Furtado had worked for some years as an economist with ECLA; he had just returned to Brazil after spending a year at the University of Cambridge. On the basis of the data collected by the Bank since 1956 and the thought he had already given to the problems of the Northeast, he was able to prepare an analysis of the region's problems and a plan for action in record time.

> "His principal interest was... to develop a few specific lines of economic policy for the Northeast. His basic reasoning ran as follows: The Northeast needs a new dynamic center of growth and reinvestment. What growth has taken place had been due to export crops such as sugar and cotton, and the free access to the rapidly growing Center-South

makes the appearance of new dynamic
'exports' conceivable. But to take advantage
of these opportunities, the Northeast must rely
on its principal comparative advantage, i.e.,
cheap labor. The full use of this 'asset' through
industrialization a la Japan or Puerto Rico is
held back by the high price of food. The latter is caused in turn by a supply of locally
grown foodstuffs which is not only unstable
because of the droughts but is inadequate, in-
elastic, and burdened with unnecessarily high
transport and other costs, even in normal
times.

"The general nature of this diagnosis then
permitted Furtado to strike out in three directions. First, of course, the dammed-up waters
of the açudes should be used for irrigation in
such a way that the irrigated basins will become a permanent food reserve for the sertão;
secondly, organized colonization should be
undertaken in the humid lands and tropical
rain forests of the neighboring State of Mar-
anhão; and, finally, to the east, a major effort should be made at achieving better utilization of the richest lands of the Northeast, the
zona da mata along the Atlantic Coast."
(Hirschman, p. 75)

"The competence, freshness and vigor of
the Furtado Report and the promise of its
many new approaches made a profound impression. Its inescapable conclusion was not
only that agencies working in the Northeast
had failed to carry out satisfactorily their
assigned tasks, but that a number of crucial policy lines had yet to be tried and mapped out.
Thus began to take shape a new agency, which
was to have the dual task of co-ordinating existing agencies and of initiating entirely new
policies under its own authority." (Hirschman,
p. 78)

The law creating SUDENE was passed late in 1959 over strong opposition, but in the end without crippling amendments, and Furtado was appointed to head the new agency. Far from being neglected after President Kubitscheck left office in 1960, SUDENE was elevated to cabinet rank by his successor, and Furtado was confirmed as its director.

The first large-scale appropriations bill for SUDENE, about thirty million dollars, was passed late in 1961, together with the agency's "Guiding Plan" of proposed expenditures. A few months later, an agreement was signed with the United States Government for $131 million in Alliance for Progress support during the next four years, and meanwhile the Inter-American Development Bank had approved agreements with SUDENE for several loans in the Northeast. Thus, exceptionally strong funding was available to SUDENE itself virtually from the time it was created; in addition, it was given authority to approve substantial tax exemptions for industrial investment in the region.

The early operations of SUDENE were concentrated in non-controversial fields such as highway transportation, water supply, and industrialization. It did not immediately undertake to introduce fundamental changes in land use and land institutions, in part because it was awaiting congressional action on a national agrarian reform law, and in part because it already was fully occupied with other efforts.

The interplay of political forces which resulted in the creation of SUDENE continued, and although no specific projects were carried out to promote change along the lines of the more controversial aspects of the original proposal, some changes of this type—for example, increased production of food crops in the sugar zone—began to be introduced by the opposing interests themselves. Thus, by mid-1962, when Hirschman's account ends.

" . . . the Northeast exhibited a highly improbable conjuction of circumstances. On the

one hand, an upsurge in public investment
and private industrial activity was definitely
underway. On the other, the region's traditional elites were subjected to a wide range
of pressures, from revolutionary threats and
direct local actions to gentle, face-saving per-
suasion and advice. Investment boom and
profound social transformation were seem-
ingly both in the making, and both were pro-
moted and 'administered' in various ways by
by the same agency, SUDENE. The two-
pronged undertaking was by no means assured
of success, yet the chances for substantial economic and social progress of the region looked
brighter than at any previous time in this century." (Hirschman, p. 91)

Five years later, SUDENE is widely considered to
be one of the most effective development agencies in
Latin America. Celso Furtado eventually was replaced
as Director of SUDENE by João Gonçalves de Souza,
an official of the Secretariat of the OAS, and he, in turn,
was succeeded by Rubens Costa who previously had
earned a reputation as one of the most capable technicians on the staff of the Inter-American Development
Bank. All are natives of the Northeast, and, while the
changes of director have not been entirely free from political considerations, continuity of SUDENE's programs
has nonetheless been maintained throughout a period
marked by considerable instability in Brazilian national
politics.

Yet appraisals of actual achievements in the Northeast remain mixed. Little change has taken place in
rural areas, and in spite of the creation of spectacular
new industries, some reports are underlain by a tone
of pessimism. *U. S. News and World Report* has
stated, for example:[1]

---

[1] In a copyrighted article, "Close-Up of South America's
Worst Trouble Spot," September 6, 1965, p, 68.

"It's much too early to tell whether all this effort and money will have any major impact. But an observor traveling the region cannot escape some doubts. One is about the seeming lack of basic agreement, particularly among Brazilian officials, on development strategy.

"... Many of the planners seem to pin their hopes almost solely on industrialization, which outside economists say cannot possibly be pushed fast enough to achieve needed growth. These economists feel that agriculture must serve as the development base in the years just ahead.

"The biggest doubt of all concerns the Northeast's population explosion. Some authorities insist there's simply no hope for the region without an intensive birth-control campaign or massive migration to other parts of Brazil—or both.

"So far, however, resettlement efforts have achieved little. And in Catholic Brazil, birth control is discussed only with great caution."

Vision's more optimistic appraisal is more representative both of reports in the press and of professional opinions:[1]

"...SUDENE's initiative and incentives are rapidly altering the traditionally sugar-based economy of the Northeast. The coastal sugar capital of Recife is, itself, the site of 40 new manufacturing operations ....

"The Northeast is still a long way behind the industrial hub of the country's south-central region— and no one dreams of closing the gap entirely. What SUDENE and the private

---

[1]"New Hope for the Northeast," *Latin America '67: The Annual Review of Latin American Business and Development* (New York: Visión Incorporated, 1967), pp. 102-105.

investors that go there are doing is to bring hope and opportunity where there had been none at the beginning of the decade and to at least narrow the economic and social disparity between the prosperous south and the forgotten north."

As in the Papaloapan project, early emphasis in SUDENE was on infrastructure investments. Up to 1966 about one-half of the public funds, including external assistance, went into roads, dams, power projects schools, housing, health facilities, etc.; the remainder was used for agricultural improvements, food distribution, and the development of human and natural resources. The third, and current, three-year development plan for the Northeast shows some shift away from the earlier emphasis on infrastructure in the direction of increasing investments in projects with greater near-term impact in agriculture and industry. It also greatly increases the stress on human resources development, especially with respect to people engaged in actual production.

The changes in policy and in budgetary allocations introduced in the third three-year plan might lead one to expect that industrial growth will be even more rapid during this period than in the preceding six years. However, it should be kept in mind that, while official activities now place greater emphasis than they did before on short-range benefits likely to attract new industrial investment, there has undoubtedly been some degree of selectivity in the establishment of new industries in response to tax and other incentives during the last six years in the direction of taking advantage of the region's most attractive opportunities for private investment. Moreover, special financial concessions have been, and are almost certain to continue to be, more important in stimulating private investment than any of the official projects. Thus the change in emphasis in the public investment program may be no more than enough to offset the fact that most remaining opportunities for private investment are inherently somewhat less attractive than those which accounted for the rapid industrial growth during the first six years of the program.

In some important respects, SUDENE has failed to achieve the presumed advantages of the regional approach to development. A lack of adequate coordination and control has been observed even within the agency's own operations—a shortcoming which perhaps is to be expected in so large a program dealing with so vast a territory. SUDENE is akin to national-level operations in smaller countries in more than scale alone: its administrative structure is laid out along conventional sectoral lines, and it is precisely in the relations among sectoral sub-programs that these internal deficiencies have been reported.

Moreover, the notion that SUDENE should serve as the focal point of all development activities in the Northeast has been less-than-completely realized. Some national programs—health is a major example, but not the only one—apparently continue to be conducted independently within the region, almost as though no regional program existed. Similarly, even though the governors of the states in which SUDENE operates are members of its board, collaboration between regional and local efforts is but poorly developed, if not completely absent, on the operating level.

One suggestion which has been made for improving the effectiveness of SUDENE's operations is that a few small areas within the Northeast be selected and concentrated upon as focal points for development. In one sense, this is tantamount to saying that the entire Northeast, as a unit, is too large for application of a regional approach in the usual sense, and that it should be dealt with in terms of territorial divisions of more manageable size. Presumably some urban center would be the focal point of each such subdivision, so that this suggestion would be entirely consistent with reducing the concentration of industrial growth in Recife itself.

Neither the administrative weaknesses of SUDENE as a regional program nor its relative inaction in some

fields of critical importance, however, should be allowed
to obscure its genuine success in other respects. Easily
the most ambitious regional program in Latin America,
its achievements in carrying out infrastructure projects
and in promoting industrial development make it one of
the most successful as well. Its focus upon the Northeast, as a region within the national framework, has been
one of the elements behind this success.

NATIONAL-LEVEL PROGRAMS
AND NATIONAL PLANNING

Both regional and grass-roots development programs characteristically act simultaneously in several of
the sectors discussed in Chapter 3; just as characteristically, however, each of these sectors also represents the
field activity of one or more specialized agencies on the
national level. It is to these national level sectoral
efforts, which are broader in geographical scope but
topically more restricted than regional and community
development programs, that our attention is now turned.

In a sense, the distinction made here relates more
to the level at which planning and integrative functions
are performed than to action itself, for any specific action
of course occurs at some specific place. While the
community development program consists of an array of
actions of a wide variety of types, all conducted in one
locale under the same management, the sectoral program
in contrast is made up numerous activities of the same
or similar types conducted in a number of specific places
which is usually, but not always, large and widely
disseminated over the national territory.

The nature of the particular problems involved in
planning and carrying out specific projects depends upon
the sector involved and the type of effort within it. A
number of individual sectors have been considered at
some length in Chapter 3, and therefore the focus here is
upon the integration of action in the various sectors into
a cohesive national program to sponsor development,

rather than on activities in any given sector.[1]

Lack of coordination among the increasing volume of official programs and projects related to development was a matter of growing concern among those studying Latin America in the early postwar years. Signs of inter-agency rivalry were much more evident than those of cooperation; the expansion of official action was accompanied by an expansion in the number of agencies responsible for conducting it, and it was not unusual for two or more agencies within the same Latin American country to have approximately the same responsibilities. In such situations, each agency was jealous of its own prerogatives and, far from seeking to work with others to avoid duplication of efforts, it more characteristically attempted to prevent its competitors from stealing its ideas. Parenthetically, it may be pointed out that use of the past tense is not entirely justified here, even though a great deal of improvement has taken place in recent years in some countries, nor are problems of these types unique to Latin American bureaucracies.

Centralized national planning was seen in part as an answer to these problems. To at least as great an extent, its proponents considered its primary purpose to be that of assuring that the total amount of resources devoted to development, and the distribution of those resources among the various sectors, were consistent with development objectives, expressed usually in terms of growth in per capita income. The planning movement itself was inspired by external experts, especially the economists of the Economic Commission for Latin America, and by domestic economists and government officials within the Latin American countries. Far from being a response to popular demand, centralized planning met with considerable resistance from some influential private

---

[1]Planning and programming are considered in a somewhat different light in Chapter 3 (pp. 68-73). Centralized planning, as discussed below, is largely of the macro-economic variety considered there.

groups, to whom the whole idea smacked of socialism.

Nevertheless, the creation of planning mechanisms was made one of the major points in the Charter of Punta del Este, and one by one the various Latin American countries that did not already have central planning agencies created them during the next few years. By the end of 1965, seventeen of the nineteen Latin American countries (exclusive of Cuba) had produced national development plans of one sort or another, and one of the remaining two anticipated early completion of its plan. No longer associated so exclusively with the idea of a state-controlled economy, planning had become widely accepted as a useful instrument for bringing about orderly economic growth and, eventually, the sustained and balanced development of the national society.[1]

By this time, however, some of the early enthusiasts had come to the conclusion that preparation of national development plans was an interesting theoretical exercise which yielded little in terms of practical accomplishments. Regarded as a panacea in 1961, centralized planning, at least for most Latin American countries, was being discredited only five years later because it had not yet produced tangible results in accordance with early optimism. Much of the disappointment resulted from painstaking analysis of practical experience with national planning during the intervening years. The results are not unfavorable to centralized planning in principle, but they show that successful planning of this type requires some elements which in practice do not exist in many Latin American countries.

The most comprehensive systematic research of this type to date has been conducted by a group of technicians at the World Bank working under the leadership of Albert Waterston. The results of their

---

[1] *Social Progress Trust Fund: Fifth Annual Report, 1965* (Washington: Inter-American Development Bank, 1966), p. 103.

work, as published by Waterston at the end of 1965,[1] include the following conclusion among many others:

> "There is much to recommend comprehensive planning for a country which is ready for it. Some countries like Israel and Mexico, with considerable experience in preparing and executing projects and sector programs, a reasonably good statistical basis for planning and a trained and experienced cadre of technicians and administrators, have reached a stage of development in which they could profit by replacing partial with comprehensive planning. But where reliable statistics and trained economists and technicians are in short supply, where experience with planning is lacking, where administrative organization and procedure are inefficient or where the importance of getting development started soon is essential, attempts to move from the project-by-project approach directly into comprehensive planning have usually been self-defeating. Experience shows that the more complex the kind of planning, the more difficult it is to carry out. Without having first learned how to prepare and execute an integrated public investment plan and the projects which compose it, and to build up the institutional arrangements required to do these things, it has generally proved impossible for less developed countries to take on simultaneously the more difficult task of planning comprehensively for both public and private sectors."

In Latin America, the national planning agencies created in response to the recommendations of the Charter of Punta del Este as a rule began their work with a "diagnosis" which amounted to collecting and ordering

---

[1] *Development Planning: Lessons of Experience* (Baltimore: The Johns Hopkins Press, 1965), p. 68.

available data on a wide variety of subjects, and
thereafter proceeded with the preparation of short-term
public investment programs of one or a few years dura-
tion. Some improvement of coordination both among
and within sectors has no doubt been associated with
the work of the planning agencies in Latin America;
however, the most significant contribution of planning to
Latin American development to date probably has been
to call attention to the need for increasing the capacity
for preparing, evaluating, and executing development
projects. The greater part of these functions—the exception lies in part of the evaluative responsibility—must be
carried out by subject-matter specialists of the type found
in sectoral agencies. Centralized planning, as it has been
approached in Latin America, at any rate, depends upon
effective planning within the specialized sectoral agencies, and the required capacity in this respect still is
inadequately developed in many Latin American countries.

THE INTERNATIONAL LEVEL

Development is a world-wide phenomenon. The
many types of spontaneous and sponsored change which
make up the process are going on to a greater or a lesser
degree, in one form or another, in every country of the
world. Even the present trends in the most advanced
parts of the industrialized countries can be regarded as
a continuation of the general process, and the more
backward regions of those same countries have much in
common with the underdeveloped lands. Some points
closely related to the development of a given country—
particularly those of a broader economic nature—are, in
fact, more a matter of relationships *among* than of relationships *within* countries. Even though most attention
is focused on the local, regional, and national levels in
development action, some features of the process are of
such a nature that they can be effectively dealt with only
within a broader geographical framework.
One group of these features has to do with the

dissemination of technical and financial resources from the parts of the world in which they are most abundant, to those in which they are scarcest: this is the broad area of international assistance for development. It embraces the foreign aid programs of individual countries, as well as multi-national programs dealing with the entire world, or all or most of the countries in some major part of it. A broad and complex subject, international development assistance will not be considered here except to point out that, in general, its orientation is to reinforce efforts within the individual developing countries by making available resources they lack for carrying out their own programs.

Another group of features is more strictly international in character. This is the subject matter of international economics, for its central focus is the exchange of goods and services between national markets and matters related to financing this exchange; development is related to this field principally through the impact of foreign trade and finance on domestic economic systems. Cooperation among countries of the same part of the world to maximize future development for the benefit of all participating nations has become an especially important component of the subject in recent years and, except for Europe, Latin America is the part of the world in which this orientation has been of the greatest significance.

Economic studies have repeatedly shown that the restricted size of most national markets in Latin America is a major impediment to the development of additional modern factory industries. This element is clearly one of the primary considerations behind the present enthusiasm for inter-American economic integration. The domestic market in most Latin American countries is so small that many types of industry can produce for it only at extremely high cost; this, in turn, requires that the products be sold at so high a price that only a small fraction of the population can afford to buy them. One need not limit his attention to such spectacular products as, say, electric refrigerators, which are a luxury available only to a very small fraction of the total population of Latin America, in this respect. The same principle applies to all products of factory industry. If through agreements among several countries, each accepts certain specific industries in which it will specialize to produce for all members of the group, and in turn agrees to admit without import duty the products of similar industries allocated to the other members, the larger market served by each industry in this fashion would make possible sufficient economy of scale to substantially lower the price of the products. The lower price, in turn, would make it possible for a larger percentage of the people to buy, this in turn would increase industrial employment and incomes, and so on.

The Latin American integration movement is not limited to this type of cooperation to promote industrialization, and in practice attainment of such a degree of cooperation between countries may be expected to be very slow in coming. Other features include cooperation on infrastructure projects involving more than a single nation: the "Marginal Highway of the Jungle," along the eastern flank of the Andes, is the most important example of this type of project already in the execution stage. The movement toward a common market is, however, the most important feature of the integration movement itself, and it is reflected in two existing trade associations in Latin America.

LAFTA, the Latin American Free Trade Area, made up of countries in South America plus Mexico, is the largest of these two associations. Established in 1960, it has been a major factor in the growth of trade among its members from $659 million in 1961 to $1.4 billon in 1965. Because of the similarity of their export products, the Latin American countries in the past have traded much more with the United States and Europe than with one another. The growing trade among them in part is a reflection of taking advantage of opportunities for trade among the members which have long existed; but much more, it is a result of reducing tariff restrictions, up to now at the scheduled rate of eight per cent per year, and simplifying procedures.

The Central American Common Market is the second of these associations. There is a much stronger historical basis for Central American integration than for that of all of Latin America, for the five independent countries briefly were one shortly after achieving independence from Spain. Even though the forces of separatism proved too strong for the survival of this as a single national political unit, the historical antecedent combines with economic and strictly geographical considerations to produce the most favorable situation for this type of cooperation within the Hemisphere. Here progress has not been limited to reducing trade barriers, as it has to all intents and purposes in LAFTA, but it has been more spectacular in this respect than in others: internal free trade has been achieved among the five countries on products accounting for eighty per cent of all transactions among them, and remaining tariff restrictions are expected to be lifted on all but petroleum products by 1968. Special banking and clearing-house institutions already are operating for the region as a unit, and it is hoped that a common currency will one day be adopted.

While the provision of international technical and financial assistance to particular countries is beyond the scope of this section, even so brief a treatment of the international level in Latin American development operations would be incomplete if no mention were made of the integrative functions of international activities. Inter-American and world-wide technical conferences and training programs bring together key technicians working on the same type of development activities in the various countries, and thereby foster an exchange of thought and experience among the various national programs; periodic reassignment of internationally-financed technical advisors and substantive review of national projects by subject-matter specialists in the international agencies have similar results. Through these mechanisms, word of successful innovations—and of attempts that were completely abortive, as well—spreads rap-

idly among the specialists in the particular subject
in all countries of the Hemisphere. This type of informal "inter-American integration" already has been
mentioned in connection with both rural and urban community development: to a greater or lesser degree, it occurs in connection with all kinds of development activities.

DEVELOPMENT OPERATIONS AND
THE DEVELOPMENT PROCESS

Development was treated in the opening chapter of
this book as a complex process of change, change which
is occurring throughout the world and which is largely
inevitable and irreversible. It is fitting now to consider
development again as a process which is spontaneous,
at least as to its general direction and its most fundamental characteristics, at the same time that its rate
and some of its details may be influenced by conscious
intervention. If this is so, what are the purposes of
development operations of the various types which have
just been considered?

When it is assumed that some development will
occur with or without sponsorship, and that development
is desirable, then one purpose of sponsoring it is merely
to *accelerate* the rate of change. Given the key position
of technological change within the total process, the
obvious benefits of many technological improvements,
and the "hidden" nature of social costs of technological
change, a wide variety of development operations can
be designed to this end without apparent threat to the
existing social order.

However, the social costs of technological change
which are "hidden" as far as the general public is
concerned are in many cases quite apparent to social
scientists. Development involves not only adding the
new, but giving up some old and familiar ways as well.
The other of the major purposes of sponsored development, then, is to *guide* the total process, attempting
to maximize those changes which are considered desir-

able and to minimize those which are not. To do this of course calls for policy decisions based on value judgements, and the matters on which there is widespread agreement are rather few in number. Even the values concerning human dignity and the perfection of democratic institutions which form the basis for many statements of development policy emanating from the political level in Latin America pose threats to strong vested interests in those countries—where political pronouncements are one thing, and action may be quite another.

In practice, therefore, sponsored development in Latin America is strongly oriented toward the first of these two purposes. To the extent that it seeks to guide the process at all, its efforts are concentrated upon removal of absolute barriers to change and correction or avoidance of features that are widely considered to be pathological conditions: urban slums, heavy reliance on a small number of export products for which the terms of trade have degenerated in recent years, widespread disease and illiteracy, etc. But throughout Latin America, the vast bulk of all expenditures for purposes clearly labelled "development" is devoted to projects which in one way or another are intended to bring about substitution of capital for labor in the production system, and thereby to increase per capita productivity.

Even within a policy framework which so strongly emphasizes technological advance, there is a great deal of room for differences of opinion concerning the most effective ways to implement the policies. There are two major schools of thought on this subject.[1] One, the economic-technological school, is dominant in the international, national, and regional approaches to development operations. It stresses capital formation and investment

[1]Melvin M. Tumin discusses these two schools of thought at somewhat greater length in his "Social Statification and Social Mobility in the Development Process," in Richard I. Ward (ed.), *The Challenge of Development* (Chicago: Aldine Publishing Company, 1967), pp. 464-470.

in *large increments*—entire factories, major dams, etc.—
and is inclined to regard the savings potential of middle
and lower income groups as too small to be worthy of
much attention.   Fairly consistently, it selects capital-
intensive methods for carrying out investment projects—
even though in some cases it might be possible to accomplish the same work at the same or even a lower
cost by making lavish use of relatively unskilled labor
while spending much less on imported mechanized equipment.   To do otherwise would violate the economic-
technological school's principle of promoting the substitution of capital for labor in the productive process.

The other major school of thought, which is dominant in the grass-roots approach, often places great emphasis on humanitarian values in its statements of purpose.   In practice, however, it too gives high priority to
economic improvements—if only to mobilize the economic resources required to attain its other goals.   It is
quite disposed to accept improvements—capital or otherwise—in extremely small increments, and in fact stresses
the potential of the poor to bring about improvements
on their own behalf.   Many of the large-scale investments given high priority by the economic-technological
school do not appear so important to the proponents of
this one, who are likely to feel that the benefits will be
slow to spread out through the population, and will be
of such a strictly material nature that they will do little
to stimulate the sorts of human change that the humanitarian school believes should be among the major goals
of sponsored development.

Past concentration of economists on the first of
these sets of views, and of anthropologists and sociologists on the second, has impeded effective utilization
of much theoretical knowledge that already exists in the
social sciences to improve the practical results of expenditures for development.   Awareness of the potential
benefits of closer collaboration among the fields of study
concerned with development is now growing rapidly,
however.   It is quite likely that, if present trends continue, major advances on both the theoretical and prac-

tical planes will be forthcoming within a few years. While the exact nature of these advances cannot be forseen, some possibilities for more effective utilization of existing theoretical knowledge in practical development operations are readily apparent. Behavioral scientists, for example, are seldom asked to appraise the influence of sectoral projects on the people of the areas in which they are to be carried out; yet without any major improvements in their theory, they should be able to foresee possible difficulties which would not be readily apparent to economists or engineers, and also to identify potential secondary benefits which might be attained in connection with a particular project through only minor modifications in its operating plans.

At the same time that development operations can be made more effective by means of better utilization of theoretical knowledge which already exists in the social sciences, theory itself can be improved, and can grow more rapidly, by being subjected to such tests. The assertion that the social sciences are denied the benefits of the experimental method is no longer true. Almost every development project represents a potential experimental situation for these fields. Whether it is used as such, simultaneously making maximum application of existing theory to avoid embarrassing mistakes, or is conducted strictly on a trial-and-error basis, depends upon the administrators responsible for its planning and execution. It also depends upon the willingness of social scientists to learn to live with decisions over which they have no control, and within the framework of those decisions to adapt and apply their theoretical knowledge for the solution of practical development problems.

SELECTED REFERENCES

The literature both on development and on Latin America has become so large, and so many new items appear each year, that any short list of references must necessarily involve some arbitrary selection. Here, an effort has been made to present a broad panorama of recent contributions, with a decided preference for compendia made up of carefully selected articles.

The reader who already is familiar with the subject will observe that many very important, but slightly older, publications do not appear. This omission is intentional. The excellent bibliographic aids which have become available during the last few years make it an easy matter to locate references to them, and little would be served by arbitrarily choosing a few from the now-lengthy list for mention here.

Social Science Research on Latin America, edited by Charles Wagley (New York: Columbia University Press, 1964) is especially valuable in this respect for its appraisals of existing knowledge in the various academic disciplines, which as a rule are closely tied to the lengthy bibliographies for each field. Topically, Martin H. Sable's *A Guide to Latin American Studies* (Los Angeles: UCLA Latin American Center, 2 vols., 1967) is more comprehensive; it provides annotated references to an extremely large number of items in both technical and theoretical fields, and is designed more for use by the expert than by the beginner in Latin American studies. *A Selected List of U.S. Readings on Development* by Saul M. Katz and Frank McGowan (Washington: Agency for International Development, 1963), like Sable's *Guide,* is an annotated bibliography organized on subject-matter lines, but covering development on a world-wide basis instead of a broader range of subjects for Latin America alone. It is much shorter than Sable's, and is limited to references published in the United States.

The extensive bibliography in Heath and Adams (cited below) is quite comprehensive as far as the literature of sociology and anthropology is concerned, and also includes some of the major items from geography and political science. Organized geographically, it is an excellent point of departure for the beginner and the seasoned scholar alike. John R. Wish's *Economic Development in Latin America: An Annotated Bibliography* includes a few items from other fields, but basically is a guide to the literature of economics. The *Bibliography: Cases and Other Materials For the Teaching of Business Administration in Developing Countries— Latin America* (Boston: Harvard University Graduate School of Business Administration, 1966) similarly concentrates on the field of economics, but is unique as a guide to case materials which may be obtained for classroom use from the publisher.

Taken together, these bibliographic tools provide a satisfactory guide to the existing literature on Latin American development up to a short time before they were published. Articles and reviews of new books related to the subject appear from time to time in the professional journals of the various academic disciplines concerned with development, which are too numerous to be listed here. Periodical publications more specialized either on Latin America or on development include, among others, *Economic Development and Cultural Change,* the *Journal of Inter-American Studies,* the *International Development Review,* and the *Latin American Research Review.*

Two separate sets of references are given below. The first lists three readily available collections of case studies of particular development projects, the second a selection of recent books. Items dealing with the subject matter of only one or two sections of this book, and referred to in those sections, have not been repeated in the second of these lists. Again, it must be emphasized that this brief selection makes no pretense of being a comprehensive bibliography on Latin American Development. It merely suggests a few items which would be suitable for further reading on the subject.

Case Studies

Niehoff, Arthur H. *A Casebook of Social Change.* Chicago: Aldine Publishing Company, 1966.

Paul, Benjamin D. *Health, Culture, and Community: Case Studies of Public Reactions to Health Programs.* New York: Russell Sage Foundation, 1955.

Spicer, Edward H. *Human Problems in Technological Change: A Casebook.* New York: John Wiley & Sons, Science Editions, 1965.

Other Books

Arensberg, Conrad M., and Arthur H. Niehoff. *Introducing Social Change: A Manual for Americans Overseas.* Chicago: Aldine Publishing Company, 1964.

Belshaw, Cyril S. *Traditional Exchange and Modern Markets.* Englewood Cliffs: Prentice-Hall, Modernization of Traditional Societies Series, 1965.

Charlesworth, James C. (ed.). *Latin America Tomorrow.* Special Issue, *The Annals of the American Academy of Political and Social Science,* Vol. 360. Philadelphia, July 1965.

Council on Foreign Relations. *Social Change in Latin America Today: Its Implications for United States Policy.* New York: Random House, Vintage Books, 1961.

De Vries, Egbert, and José Medina Echevarría (eds.). *Social Aspects of Economic Development in Latin America.* 2 vols. Paris: UNESCO, 1963.

Erasmus, Charles J. *Man Takes Control: Cultural Development and American Aid.* Minneapolis: University of Minnesota Press, 1961.

Feinstein, Otto (ed.). *Two Worlds of Change: Readings in Economic Development.* New York: Doubleday & Company, Anchor Books, 1964.

Firth, Raymond, and B. S. Yamey. *Capital, Saving and Credit in Peasant Societies.* Chicago: Aldine Publishing Company, 1964.

Foster, George M. *Traditional Cultures: and the Impact of Technological Change.* New York: Harper & Row, 1962.

Heath, Dwight B., and Richard N. Adams (eds.). *Contemporary Cultures and Societies of Latin America: A Reader in the Social Anthropology of Middle and South America and the Caribbean.* New York: Random House, 1965.

Hirschman, Albert O. (ed.). *Latin American Issues: Essays and Comments.* New York: The Twentieth Century Fund, 1961.

Johnson, John J. (ed.). *Continuity and Change in Latin America.* Stanford: Stanford University Press, 1964.

Nystrom, J. Warren, and Nathan A. Haverstock. *The Alliance for Progress: Key to Latin America's Development.* Princeton: D. Van Nostrand Company, 1966.

Rogers, Everett M. *Diffusion of Innovations.* New York: The Free Press, 1962.

Schramm, Wilbur. *Mass Media and National Development: The Role of Information in the Developing Countries.* Stanford: Stanford University Press, 1964.

Smith, T. Lynn. *Sociological Studies of Rural Development in Latin America.* Gainesville: University of Florida Press, forthcoming.

Technology and Economic Development. Special Issue, *Scientific American,* Vol. 209, No. 3 (September 1963).

Urquidi, Victor L. *The Challenge of Development in Latin America.* New York: Frederick A. Praeger, 1964.

Veliz, Claudio (ed.). *Obstacles to Change in Latin America.* London: Oxford University Press, 1965.

Ward, Richard J. (ed.). *The Challenge of Development: Theory and Practice.* Chicago: Aldine Publishing Company, 1967.

Whiteford, Andrew H. *Two Cities of Latin America: A Comparative Description of Social Classes.* New York: Doubleday & Company, Anchor Books, 1964.

INDEX

Açude: 222
Agrarian reform: 17, 130, 131, 145, 146-147, 170, 179-180
Agricultural extension: 121-122, 124, 137, 145-148, 196, 215
Agriculture: *see* rural development
Alliance for Progress: 15-17
Andean hoe farming: 142, 176
Andean Indian Program: 175-195

Barriada: 163, 199-200
Birth Control: 112-113
Bolivia: Pillapi Project, 179-184
Brazil: Northeast, 217-234

Cargos (civiles y religiosos): 36-37, 47
Change: economic, 6-7, 19; external agents of, 28; processes, 57-60; rate of, 9-11, 66-68; self-generating, 12-14, 60; social, 6-9, 67-68, 198, 204; technological, 5-6, 65-68
Colonization and settlement: 128, 146, 147, 149, 212, 213, 215-216, 228
Colono system: 133-134, 136 176, 179, 187
Commercialization: 7, 10, 57-60, 88, 123-125, 149, 168-170, 179-181, 189, 213
Community: defined, 52-53; rural, 136, 138
Community development: 53, 146, 148-149, 172-206
Compadrazgo: 35-37, 45, 47

Death: causes of, 98; rates, 94, 96-97
Development: nature and objectives of, 1-9, 11-12, 14-18, 63-65, 238, 242-245; international, 172, 238-241; national, 172, 204-205, 234-238; regional, 54, 153, 166, 172, 204-234; local, see community development; rural, *see* rural development
Development assistance: 1-4, 76-77, 238-239, 241
DNOCS (Brazil): 222

Education: 8, 15-17, 63, 64, 66-67, 73, 78-92, 170, 176, 182, 192-193, 212, 213; and agricultural extension, 148; and family, 41, 47-49; and settlement pattern, 127; and urbanization, 150; and value orientations, 28-29
Ejidatario: 131

253

CENTER UCLA